CRITIQUE ON THE COUCH

New Directions in Critical Theory

New Directions in Critical Theory

Amy Allen, General Editor

New Directions in Critical Theory presents outstanding classic and contemporary texts in the tradition of critical social theory, broadly construed. The series aims to renew and advance the program of critical social theory, with a particular focus on theorizing contemporary struggles around gender, race, sexuality, class, and globalization and their complex interconnections.

For a complete list of titles, see page 267.

CRITIQUE ON THE COUCH

Why Critical Theory Needs Psychoanalysis

Amy Allen

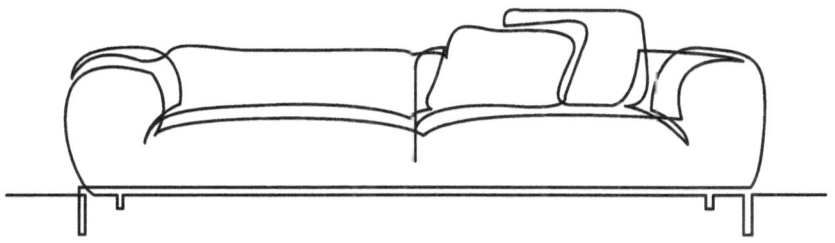

Columbia University Press

New York

Columbia University Press
Publishers Since 1893
New York   Chichester, West Sussex
cup.columbia.edu
Copyright © 2021 Columbia University Press
All rights reserved

Library of Congress Cataloging-in-Publication Data
Names: Allen, Amy, author.
Title: Critique on the couch : why critical theory needs psychoanalysis / Amy Allen.
Description: New York : Columbia University Press, 2020. | Series: New directions in critical theory | Includes bibliographical references and index.
Identifiers: LCCN 2020020823 (print) | LCCN 2020020824 (ebook) | ISBN 9780231198608 (hardback) | ISBN 9780231198615 (trade paperback) | ISBN 9780231552714 (ebook)
Subjects: LCSH: Psychoanalysis—Political aspects. | Critical theory.
Classification: LCC BF175.4.S65 A55 2020 (print) | LCC BF175.4.S65 (ebook) | DDC 150.19/5—dc23
LC record available at https://lccn.loc.gov/2020020823
LC ebook record available at https://lccn.loc.gov/2020020824

Cover design: Lisa Hamm
Cover image: Digital composite

Contents

Acknowledgments vii

Introduction: Why Critical Theory Needs Psychoanalysis (Now More Than Ever) 1

1. Kleinian Realism: Between the Intrapsychic and the Intersubjective 27

2. A System of Scars: The Problem of Ego Integration 57

3. Beyond Developmentalism: Psychoanalysis and the Critique of Progress 89

4. The Cure Is That There Is No Cure: Psychoanalysis and the Idea of Progress 121

5. Transference: Psychoanalysis and the Methodology of Critique 151

Conclusion: From Theory to Praxis 185

Notes 201

Bibliography 243

Index 255

Acknowledgments

I began the research that would eventually become this book during the 2009–2010 academic year, which I had the good fortune to spend as a Silberger Scholar at the Boston Psychoanalytic Society and Institute. Many thanks to the entire BPSI community for their warm welcome, and especially to Bonnie Smolen and Dawn Skorczewski for generous support and encouragement; Jack Beinashowitz, Martha Fisch, Cary Freidman, Richard Gomberg, Dan Mollod, Harry Penn, and Sharon Roberts for allowing me to attend their classes for analytic candidates; Joel Whitebook for insightful and challenging comments on my 2010 Silberger Lecture; and Crystal Feimster for her friendship and camaraderie.

Originally, I planned to write a very different book, one that would argue that the future of critical theory depended on a return to the insights of the early Frankfurt School, in particular the interrelated Freudian and Nietzschean critiques of the rational ego and of historical progress found in Adorno and Horkheimer's *Dialectic of Enlightenment*. After several years of work, I realized that the scope and ambition of such a project might well defeat me, and that even if I were to succeed in finishing such a book, it would be much longer than anyone might be willing to publish, let alone read. So, I decided to split the project into two books, one focusing on questions of history and progress, and the second concentrating on the reception of psychoanalysis in critical theory. Thanks to the Humboldt Foundation for the research grant that funded my initial work on this project in

2010 and 2012 and to the Forschungskolleg Humanwissenschaften in Bad Homburg for hosting me during my research stays in Frankfurt. Above all, thanks to my editor at Columbia University Press, Wendy Lochner, for her ongoing faith in this project and its author.

This book began to take its current shape as a series of three lectures delivered to the School of Philosophy and Art History at the University of Essex in 2015 as one of their summer minicourses. Many thanks to Fabian Freyenhagen, Jörg Schaub, Timo Jütten, and all of the Essex philosophers for the kind invitation, the warm hospitality, and the generous yet rigorous discussion of my work in its nascent form.

In addition, I am grateful to audiences and organizers of a variety of conferences, lectures, and other venues where material for this book was presented over the last decade, including the following: the Colloquium on Philosophy and the Social Sciences in Prague, the Goethe University in Frankfurt, the Psychoanalysis Study Group at Dartmouth College, the Psychoanalysis and Critical Theory Workshop at the New School for Social Research, the Australasian Society for Continental Philosophy, the Princeton Political Theory Graduate Student Conference, the Villanova Philosophy Graduate Student Conference, the Department of Philosophy at Concordia University, the Society for Phenomenology and Existential Philosophy, the Oakley Center for the Humanities at Williams College, the Institute for Philosophy at the Universidad Autónoma Metropolitana in Mexico City, the Center for Contemporary Critical Thought at Columbia University, the Foley Institute for Public Affairs at Washington State University, the Critical Theory Roundtable, and the Centre Marc Bloch in Berlin.

Martin Saar and Kristina Lepold did me the tremendous honor of organizing a workshop discussing the penultimate version of the manuscript at the storied Institute for Social Research in Frankfurt in November 2019. Heartfelt thanks to them and to all of the workshop participants for the constructive and illuminating discussion, which helped me to refine and clarify the final draft.

In addition to those mentioned above, thank you to the following friends and colleagues for fruitful and inspiring discussions of the ideas contained herein: Robin Celikates, Benjamin Fong, Rainer Forst, Katia Genel, Federica Gregoratto, Bernard Harcourt, Bonnie Honig, Axel Honneth, Claudia Leeb, Robyn Marasco, Inara Luisa Marin, David McIvor, Johanna

Meehan, Brian O'Connor, Isaac Arial Reed, Eva von Redecker, Duarte Rolo, Irena Rosenthal, Jana Sawicki, Yannik Thiem, and Jamieson Webster.

I owe a special debt to those generous souls who read and gave me feedback on the entire manuscript (a true labor of love if there ever was one): María Pía Lara, Noelle McAfee, and Mari Ruti. To Mari, who has forgotten more about Lacan than I will ever know, I fear my debt is unpayable. Still, I must express my undying gratitude for her generous reading of my work, for hours and hours of mind-opening intellectual discussions, for inspiring me to rethink my approach to writing, and much, much more.

Thanks to the following Penn State graduate students for valuable research assistance and insightful discussions: Jerome Clarke, Benjamin Randolph, Wayne Wapeemukwa, and Nicole Yokum.

As ever, I'm grateful to my family: Chris, Clark, Oliver, Isabelle, and Eloise.

Earlier versions (in some cases *much* earlier versions) of parts of the following chapters have appeared in print before: "Are We Driven? Critical Theory and Psychoanalysis Reconsidered," *Critical Horizons* 16, no. 4 (November 2015): 311–28 (parts of chapter 1); "Psychoanalysis and the Critique of Progress," in *Debating Critical Theory*, ed. Julia Christ, Kristina Lepold, Daniel Loick, and Titus Stahl (London: Rowman & Littlefield International, 2020) (parts of chapter 3); "Progress and the Death Drive," *Parrhesia* 26 (December 2016): 1–19 (parts of chapter 4); and "Psychoanalysis and the Methodology of Critique," *Constellations* 23, no. 2 (June 2016): 244–54 (parts of chapter 5). All of this material has been substantially revised and expanded for inclusion here.

CRITIQUE ON THE COUCH

Introduction

Why Critical Theory Needs Psychoanalysis (Now More Than Ever)

Theodor Adorno's famous claim that "in psycho-analysis nothing is true except the exaggerations" is, to be sure, itself an exaggeration.[1] And yet it captures something important about the first generation of the Frankfurt School's approach to psychoanalysis, an approach that has been decisively rejected by at least the most prominent members of the second and third generations. Indeed, perhaps more than anything else the early Frankfurt School was defined both theoretically and institutionally by its attempt to bring Marxism and Freudian psychoanalysis together in the service of a critical theory of advanced capitalist societies.[2] Such a theoretical fusion was deemed necessary to enable critical theory to come to terms with the failure of communist revolutions in Europe, the rise of fascism, and the horrors of the Holocaust—in short, the descent of the culture of enlightenment into barbarism.

Perhaps the greatest exaggeration of Freudian psychoanalysis—the height of its speculative excess—is the theory of the drives, particularly Freud's late conception of the fundamental antagonism between life and death drives, Eros and Thanatos. For early critical theorists, including Adorno, Max Horkheimer, and Herbert Marcuse, even this exaggeration contained an important grain of truth. As Martin Jay argues in his classic study of the early Frankfurt School, *The Dialectical Imagination*, these thinkers understood the death drive as an articulation of the depth of modern humanity's destructiveness and turned to libidinal drives to identify a potential source of resistance to a totally reified and administered society.[3] Their emphasis on the drives was central to their trenchant critique of what they called revisionist psychoanalysis: the interpersonal psychoanalysis of Henry Stack Sullivan, Karen Horney, and even their one-time collaborator Erich Fromm. By rejecting drive theory, the revisionists sociologized psychoanalysis, positing the seamless integration of individual and society as the goal of analytic work. In the view of the early Frankfurt School, this turned psychoanalysis into a mechanism of conformism and social normalization rather than resistance to the social order.[4] For abandoning Freudian drive theory, Fromm paid the high price of being driven out of the Institute for Social Research altogether.[5] As Marcuse put it in a 1978 interview, "The crucial point" in the debate between the first generation of the Frankfurt school and revisionist psychoanalysis "was and is the explosive content of Freudian instinct theory."[6]

Subsequent generations of critical theorists working in the Frankfurt School tradition have, by contrast, either left psychoanalysis behind altogether or domesticated it by jettisoning its explosive drive theory. Jürgen Habermas, for example, famously dropped psychoanalysis from his research program in the early 1970s, in the wake of the critical reception of his 1968 book *Knowledge and Human Interests*, substituting the cognitive developmental psychology of Jean Piaget and Lawrence Kohlberg for Freud's more complex and ambivalent philosophical anthropology.[7] But, even before making this decisive move, Habermas embraced a highly rationalist and intersubjectivist version of psychoanalysis, much more an ego psychology than an id psychology, to borrow a distinction from Fromm.[8] That is to say, even prior to his turn to cognitive psychology, Habermas's reading of psychoanalysis tended to flatten out the foreignness and absolute alterity of the unconscious, defusing its explosive content and defanging its exaggerations.[9] Ultimately, however, even this domesticated and linguistified conception of psychoanalysis proved too speculative and disruptive for Habermas: his turn toward cognitive psychology signaled his preference for a psychological framework that could be empirically confirmed and that fit more neatly with his rationalism and progressivism.[10]

Even as he has laudably attempted to renew the relationship between psychoanalysis and critical theory in the wake of Habermas's devaluation, Axel Honneth also seems uncomfortable with drive theory's speculative exaggerations. Despite Honneth's important attempt to do justice to the

"Other of reason," his interpretation of psychoanalysis focuses on the object-relations theory of D. W. Winnicott, tempered with some insights from the empirical infant research of Daniel Stern.[11] As I will discuss further on, this interpretation specifically rejects the death drive, arguing instead that aggression is the result of the pain, confusion, and anxiety that are generated by the breakup of primary fusion. At issue for Honneth is not only the speculative, exaggerated nature of drive theory in general, but also the presumed asocial and even antisocial implications of the death drive in particular.[12] Honneth's worry seems to be that a drive-theoretical interpretation of psychoanalysis presupposes an asocial or antisocial core of the human personality that is incompatible with the basic methodological assumptions of critical social theory.

While acknowledging the important historical connections between psychoanalysis and critical theory, Honneth contends that the mere fact of a historical relationship between critical social theory and psychoanalysis is not sufficient to justify an ongoing theoretical alliance between the two intellectual projects. Especially in light of what he calls the "internal historicity" of critical theory's distinctive methodology, each generation of critical theorists must pose the question of the potential relevance of psychoanalysis—or any other theoretical paradigm, for that matter—anew.[13] Taking up Honneth's challenge, this introduction addresses the following questions: What (if anything) does contemporary critical theory that seeks to take up the legacy of the Frankfurt School anew need psychoanalysis for? In other words, what work do we, as critical social theorists, need psychoanalysis to do for us now?

Psychoanalytic Realism

In his own response to the question of why contemporary critical theory needs psychoanalysis, Honneth contends, first and foremost, that the latter supplies the former with a "realistic" conception of the person or philosophical anthropology.[14] Honneth doesn't expand on what he means here by "realistic," but, given his deployment of that term, I think that it is safe to say that it does not refer to scientific naturalism or metaphysical realism. Rather, it seems to imply what we might call a kind of Geussian political realism—that is, a clear-eyed, sanguine conception of what actually motivates persons to act in the ways that they do. Honneth contrasts realism with a "moralistic idealism" that presumes that individuals are capable of having and acting upon excessively high degrees of rational reflection or insight.[15] By highlighting the irrational and unconscious forces that motivate us to act in ways that we do not fully understand and that remain stubbornly resistant to rational reflection, psychoanalysis serves as a realistic check on the tendencies toward excessive rationalism and idealism that might tempt the critical theorist qua normative theorist.

However, Honneth's own psychoanalytically informed philosophical anthropology, derived from his reading of Winnicott, remains, or so it seems to me, not quite realistic enough. It is worth noting at the outset that Honneth's original turn to Winnicott's object-relations theory, in his important early work *The Struggle for Recognition*, was motivated by his suspicion of psychoanalytic drive theory. Drive theory, in Honneth's view, entails a problematic philosophical anthropology in which intersubjectivity takes a back seat to the "intrapsychic conflict between unconscious instinctual demands and gradually emerging ego-controls."[16] Honneth turns to Winnicott to develop a thoroughly intersubjective philosophical anthropology, one that foregrounds the infant's affective relationship with their primary caregiver as an enabling condition for developing the sense of self-confidence that is the precondition for more complex and differentiated relations of recognition. Central to this account is the psychoanalytic concept of symbiosis or symbiotic fusion, which Honneth initially characterized as a prolonged state of mutual dependence and undifferentiated unity between "mother" and infant.[17] On Honneth's early reading of Winnicott, the job of the "good-enough mother" is to frustrate the infant's desires just enough so that they will gradually come to realize that the caregiver is a separate person with their own needs and desires while at the same time offering the continuous emotional support that the infant needs to develop a secure and stable practical self-relation. Through this ongoing process of reality testing and mutual attunement, the early stage of "mother"-infant fusion gradually gives way to a relationship between a caregiver and a child who experience each other as distinct entities while remaining dependent on one another's love and recognition for their basic self-confidence.

Starting in the mid-1980s, the infant research of Daniel Stern and his colleagues called into question the hypothesis of symbiosis or primary fusion.

Stern contends that even very young infants have a primary sense of self-awareness—that is, an awareness of themselves as distinct from their caregivers—and that the relationship between infant and caregiver is best understood not as one of fusion but rather as one of reciprocal interaction.[18] In his more recent work, Honneth acknowledges the challenge that Stern's research poses for his interpretation of symbiotic fusion, and he reformulates his theory of recognition accordingly.[19] Giving up the idea that the infant exists in a *state* of fusion with its caregiver, Honneth retains as a hypothesis a belief in the existence of "momentous *episodes* of fusion with primary objects."[20] Such a hypothesis is not, as Honneth sees it, incompatible with the findings of infant research since it concedes Stern's contention that infants are able to experience themselves as distinct from their environment. Episodes of merger and fusion may be irregular and episodic (experienced, for example, in moments when the infant is being fed or held), but we can nevertheless posit them as occurring. In such episodes, infants experience themselves as fused with their caregiver, such that the caregiver's actions seem to the infant to be direct extensions of their own needs and desires. Moreover, Honneth argues that these episodes are characterized by a sense of "pleasurable expansion/fusion" on the part of the infant, such that the infant's gradual realization that their caregiver exists as an independent entity is experienced as a painful loss: as "a negative phase of separation/non-fusion."[21]

However, even this modified conception of primary fusion has been sharply criticized, perhaps most trenchantly by Joel Whitebook.[22] At issue here is not so much the claim about fusion per se but, rather, the interpretation of that phenomenon. As Whitebook sees it, Honneth fails to take seriously enough the infantile omnipotence that goes hand in hand with primary fusion.[23] Insofar as infants perceive themselves to be fused with their caregiver, they do not perceive there to be any distinction between their own needs and desires and the actions of the caregiver. Whatever the caregiver does is experienced as the unmediated extension of the infant's own desires and strivings. In other words, primary fusion and infantile omnipotence are two sides of the same coin. Not only is infantile omnipotence incompatible with a relationship of recognition—ex hypothesi, the infant in a state of omnipotence does not experience the caregiver as distinct entity; hence, they are not experienced as a person capable of giving or deserving of receiving recognition—but by attempting to have fusion without omnipotence, Honneth expunges all of the ambivalence and power differentials from this state.[24]

While Honneth has granted the former point in his subsequent exchanges with Whitebook—effectively taking back his earlier equation of "symbiosis" with "undifferentiated intersubjectivity"—he remains steadfast in his attempt to have fusion without omnipotence.[25] For Honneth, the infant's process of individuation begins not from a state of phantasied omnipotence but from a relationship with "beloved objects occasionally experienced as fused with their own experience."[26] Accordingly, Honneth characterizes the fusion experience in positive terms, as a blissful feeling of physical and mental security on the part of the infant. Although he now concedes that it is misleading to characterize the state of primary fusion as itself a *relation* of recognition, Honneth nonetheless describes the "sporadic experiences of fusion as the 'zero point' [Nullpunkt] of all experiences of recognition."[27] I take this to mean that fusion gives us a completely unmediated experience of being together with another person. In such an experience, a relation of recognition may be impossible, given that recognition presupposes two differentiated subjects who recognize each other, but it is also unnecessary, for it is precisely the *blissfulness* of this unmediated being together with another person that relations of recognition strive (necessarily unsuccessfully and incompletely) to recapture. This seemingly minor terminological disagreement is actually quite significant, however, for it allows Honneth to obscure the fundamentally ambivalent character of the primary object relation and thus to purify the fusion experience that serves as the paradigm case for his notion of recognition of all entanglements with power and the desire for omnipotent control.[28]

Honneth's conception of symbiotic fusion also undergirds his distinctive account of the sources and roots of human aggression and destructiveness, which attempts to explain the pervasiveness of these phenomena without resorting to the speculative excesses of the death drive.[29] Responding to the charge that his philosophical anthropology is overly optimistic, incapable of doing justice to the "'sting' of negativity,"[30] Honneth insists that we understand negativity not as "an elementary component of our being equipped with drives," but as the "unavoidable result of the unfolding of our socialization process as internalization."[31] The sting of negativity thus resides, for Honneth, in the inevitable inadequacy of the primary relationship between infant and caregiver and in the feelings of "fear and pain, anger and sorrow" that attend the necessary rupture of primary fusion.[32] The requirement that the child recognize the caregiver's independence—and, through that independence, the demands of an independently existing reality—generates a profound anxiety that is, according to Honneth, the source of aggression. Thus, Honneth understands aggression in dynamic and relational terms, as the unavoidable result of an interactive socialization process, rather than as "the dowry of our nature as beings with drives."[33]

However, the reference to drives in the plural here is a bit misleading. Honneth claims to reject drive theory on account of its excessive focus on the intrapsychic and thus its asocial implications, but in point of fact all of his arguments against drive theory are directed against the death drive or primary aggression. Moreover, Honneth seems to presuppose something like a primary erotic drive, in precisely the sense that Freud uses that term in his later work, as a drive for building up greater and greater unities.[34] What else is the notion of symbiotic fusion that stands at the center of his theory of recognition if not the perfect embodiment of this erotic drive? It is, after all, not only the zero point of all relations of recognition but also the paradigm case of love. Thus, the target of Honneth's critique is less drive theory per se than the duality or ambivalence of the drives, and the positing of aggression or destructiveness as a fundamental drive of equal force and similar provenance to Eros.

In sum, Honneth makes two key moves in his interpretation of psychoanalysis, both of which lead him away from a fully realistic conception of the person: first, he transforms the fundamentally ambivalent psychoanalytic conception of primary fusion—with narcissism and omnipotence as its other face—into a state of blissful, unmediated being together with another person that serves as the paradigm case of his conception of recognition; second, he conflates the aggressive or death drive with drive theory per se, then rejects "drive theory" while tacitly presupposing the existence of a prosocial, erotic drive for unification through symbiosis. Taken together, these moves have the effect of displacing human drives for destruction, mastery, aggression, and omnipotence (in short, for power, at least in some of its most recognizable forms) from the centerpiece of his philosophical anthropology and thus from his conception of social life. The result is an account of the person that is unrealistic in a specifically Geussian sense, insofar as it obscures the fundamental role that power plays in human psychic and social life.

Nevertheless, Honneth is undoubtedly correct to suggest that we need a philosophical anthropology that is compatible with critical theory's distinctive methodology. In light of critical theory's commitments to the sociality of the self and to the historicity of theories and concepts, any interpretation of psychoanalysis that understands the drives in reductively biologistic terms, posits a fundamentally asocial or antisocial core to the self, or makes ahistorical claims about human nature seem problematic. However, we need not reject drive theory in order to avoid these problems.[35] As I shall argue in further detail in chapter 1, Melanie Klein's conception of the drives emphasizes the fundamental antagonism between life and death drives while understanding the death drive in psychological (rather than reductively biologistic) and social (rather than a- or antisocial) terms. Unlike Freud, Klein equates the death drive with primary aggression; as a result, her account does not depend on the appeal to speculative biology that underpins the Freudian version. Given her distinctive understanding of the relationship between drive and object, the Kleinian death drive is a distinctive mode of social relatedness, one that entails relating to others aggressively and destructively. Klein's work thus offers critical theory the possibility of a realistic psychoanalytic account of the person that is at the same time thoroughly psychological and social.

To be sure, Klein, like Freud, tended to present her findings in universal and ahistorical terms—or at least she tended not to explicitly historicize her theories of psychic subjectivity—and the notion of the drives in particular seems to stake a universal, ahistorical claim about fundamental features of human nature. After all, Freud once described the death drive, memorably, as an "indestructible feature of human nature."[36] However, as Benjamin Fong has recently argued, the insights of psychoanalytic drive theory can be defended without making strong claims about indestructible features or innate constituents of human nature and instead on the basis of more modest claims about the implications of certain (for all we know or perhaps even for the time being) inescapable preconditions for human existence. From the psychoanalytic point of view, perhaps the most important of these preconditions is the fact that human beings, unlike many other animals, are born into a protracted state of helpless dependence upon their caregivers.[37] As Fong elaborates, "What care *is* can be radically different in different societies, but *that* human beings enter life completely dependent on the responses of other human beings (and for a fairly lengthy amount of time in comparison to other animals) is invariable."[38] To say this is not necessarily to commit oneself to strong claims about a timeless and immutable human nature; it is to make a more modest claim about what we might call, following Hannah Arendt, the human condition, a condition that places constraints on what kinds of creatures we can become and what that process of becoming is like. Fong argues that in light of these constraints "there will be certain drives that all human beings share; but *how* these particular drives are formed—and, in turn, how they impact our lives and thus what they mean to us—as well as the *vicissitudes* available for their expression vary markedly in different societies and at different times."[39]

If the drives are understood as rooted in certain (for all we know or at least for the time being) inescapable facts about the human condition, and if their structure and content is taken to be historically and socially constituted and therefore malleable and plastic, then drive theory need not be incompatible with critical theory's commitment to historicization.[40] Moreover, even this rather modest conception of drives has important and far-reaching consequences. Whitebook argues that the fact that we are born helpless and dependent on the care of others means that socialization is necessary for us to become subjects. As he explains, this starting situation has profound implications for our relationship to power: "As helpless children, we confronted the seemingly omnipotent Otherness of our physical and socio-familial environments, an Otherness that was beyond our control, and this drove us—and to one degree or another continues to drive us—to pursue omnipotent solutions that seek to deny that helplessness."[41] On this view, the fact that our initial human condition is one of helpless dependence on our caregivers gives rise not only to drives for love and connection with others, but also to drives for aggression, destructiveness, and domination. Once formed, these drives become a permanent part of all of our relationships with others, including (perhaps especially) our love relationships. As we will see further in chapter 1, this is precisely where Klein's conception of drive theory starts: with the infant in a relationship of love and attachment to their primary caregiver that is at the same time a relationship of complete helplessness and dependence, with all of the frustration and aggression such a relationship elicits. In other words: a relationship structured around a fundamental and intractable ambivalence.[42]

Rethinking Developmentalism

A return to psychoanalysis not only provides critical theory with a realistic conception of the person; it can also help critical theory to rethink its commitment to developmentalist, evolutionary, stage models of self and society. As I mentioned earlier, Habermas turned away from Freudian psychoanalysis and toward cognitive psychology at least in part because of his preference for a psychological framework that fit more neatly with his rationalism and progressivism. As I will argue in more detail in chapter 3, although there remains a strong rationalist, developmentalist, and progressive strand in Freud's thinking that rests on Eurocentric models of social evolution, psychoanalysis also offers powerful resources for rethinking developmental schemas.

To see why such a rethinking is needed, let's briefly review Habermas's intertwined accounts of individual moral-cognitive development and social evolution. Building on work in cognitive and moral psychology, Habermas constructs a developmental account of individuation through socialization that marks the self's progression from preconventional to conventional to postconventional modes of ego identity. From the point of view of cognitive development, this progression is marked by greater and greater degrees of abstraction, generalization, and reflexivity. Through the process of individuation through socialization, individuals develop a progressively decentered understanding of the world, a development that rests on the linguistic ability to take up and differentiate between an interrelated set of speaker perspectives (first-, second-, and third-person perspectives) and world relations (objective, intersubjective, and subjective worlds). This linguistic achievement is necessary for the development of communicative competence, which requires the further ability to differentiate between three distinct types of validity claims—to truth, normative rightness/appropriateness, and sincerity—that map on to the three world-relations. According to Habermas's pragmatic theory of language, every utterance raises at least one of the three validity claims (in fact, most utterances will raise all three claims simultaneously) and communicative competence consists in the ability to thematize the specific validity claims raised in a particular utterance, and, when necessary, to defend those claims with reasons. From the point of view of moral development, ontogenesis consists in a transformation from an initial dependence on an external (usually parental) authority for judgments of right and wrong (the preconventional stage) through an internalization of that authority relation that results in feelings of guilt and shame (the conventional stage) to an ability to reflect autonomously on social norms and consider whether such norms are genuinely valid (postconventional autonomy). Taken together, these cognitive and moral developmental processes generate postconventional subjects who are able to reflect critically on the conditions of their own genesis.[43]

Habermas's theory of social evolution as the development from premodern and traditional to modern and posttraditional societies closely mirrors his developmental model of the self. Although he rejects strong philosophies of history that assert the necessity, unilinearity, or uninterruptibility of historical progress, Habermas nevertheless maintains that we can rationally reconstruct a universal and invariant evolutionary logic of developmental stages through which societies evolve and develop. Social evolution is, for Habermas, a cumulative, progressive, directed process of increasing rationalization in both technological and moral practical domains. The latter consists in a progressive decentration of worldviews; differentiation of objective, intersubjective, and subjective worlds and corresponding validity claims; and a heightening of reflexivity. This conception of social evolution is central to Habermas's distinction between mythical and modern worldviews.[44] According to Habermas, modern worldviews represent an advance over mythical worldviews in that, first, they enable the differentiation between objective, intersubjective, and subjective worlds and their corresponding validity claims and, second, they understand themselves *as worldviews*. Their openness to critical assessment supports their claim to superior rationality and reflexivity.

These two strands of Habermas's work are deeply intertwined. His theory of communicative rationality rests on a reconstruction of the implicit or intuitive knowhow of a specific group of people: communicatively competent members of modern societies, where both "competence" and "modernity" refer to the mastery of the three-world structure of communication, the ability to differentiate between three world-relations and their corresponding validity claims, and the resulting enhanced capacities for reflexivity. I have argued elsewhere that the intertwining of these two dimensions leads to a deep puzzle about the structure and status of Habermas's strategy for grounding normativity. Put briefly, does the theory of modernity justify his account of discursive rationality or vice versa, or do the two theories mutually reinforce each other?[45] However one answers this question, a different problem looms. As Sanjay Seth explains, "Habermas is aware of, but nonetheless boldly undeterred by, the problems of drawing analogies between the development of an individual from childhood to adulthood and the development of worldviews or knowledges. He is similarly undeterred by the knowledge that such analogies have a long and unpleasant history, as justifications for the colonization of irrational, childlike 'races' by mature and rational ones."[46] In other words, Seth suggests that Habermas at least implicitly accepts a version of the recapitulationist thesis according to which ontogeny, or the development of the individual, recapitulates phylogeny, the development of the species. As I discuss further in chapter 3, this thesis has a long and ignominious history, including in the development of evolutionary anthropology, where it was used to justify a series of Eurocentric and racist claims about so-called primitives and savages. This suggests that, if critical theory is to confront its Eurocentrism, it needs to rethink not only its commitment to pernicious theories of social evolution, but also its (mostly deeply implicit) embrace of recapitulationist themes.

However, this argument by itself doesn't indict developmentalist or stage models of the self. After all, we might still think that those models offer a compelling account of individual development even if we reject the theory of social evolution with which they are linked and the (implicit) recapitulationism that links them.[47] Why, then, should critical theorists reject the developmental stage model of ontogenesis defended by Habermas, and in what sense does psychoanalysis provide an important corrective?

In a nutshell, the problem with the Habermasian model—like the broadly speaking Kantian model of autonomy on which it is based—is its rationalism, and its accompanying understanding of the self as founded upon the mastery or suppression of the drives. In stark contrast with Habermas, the early Frankfurt School was sharply critical of the Kantian rational ego. Horkheimer and Adorno famously drew on psychoanalytic and Nietzschean insights to develop a critique of the domination of inner (and outer) nature under bourgeois capitalism.[48] Building on their reading of Freud, Horkheimer and Adorno contended that bourgeois society rests on the introversion of sacrifice: the internalized renunciation of instinctual drives in the service of pursuing economic gain. For them, the rational ego itself is a structure of domination whose function is to gain mastery over the unruly forces of the id. If the Kantian theory of autonomy provided the theoretical account of this ego structure, Freudian psychoanalysis laid bare its empirical genesis. On this view, the bourgeois self is held together by a structure of internalized domination that mirrors the ego's dominating relationship to external nature and to other subjects.

As Whitebook has argued, this critique dovetails in interesting ways with Lacan's psychoanalytic critique of the ego.[49] For Lacan, the ego is an imaginary, alienated, narcissistic, defensive structure, formed through a process of misrecognition in which the infant substitutes their unified image in the mirror for their incoherent, fragmented experience of themselves. The ego thus presents an obstacle to psychoanalysis, which targets the discourse and subject of the unconscious. As Lacan puts it in one of this early seminars, "The essence of the Freudian discovery" consists in the "decentring of the subject in relation to the ego."[50] Indeed, he goes so far as to say that "one trains analysts so that there are subjects in whom the ego is absent. That is the ideal of analysis, which, of course, remains virtual. There is never a subject without an ego, a fully realized subject, but that in fact is what one must aim to obtain from the subject of analysis."[51] Lacanian analysis thus aims to break down the conscious, rational ego that is propped up by Kantian notions of autonomy.

To be sure, the Adornian and Lacanian critique of the ego leaves us with some difficult questions. For one thing, it arguably presupposes as normal a form of the ego that is actually deeply pathological. As Whitebook notes, "Critics of the ego, like Adorno and Lacan, prompted by a philosophical suspicion of synthesis, tend to hypostasize pathological, rigidified forms of ego formation into the ego as such. As a result, they are left only with a choice between two poisons, namely: violent unification or no unification at all."[52] This either/or choice leaves aside the possibility that there might be nonviolent, nondominating conceptions of ego integration that could correspond, for example, to Adorno's image of genuine reconciliation as the noncoercive togetherness of the manifold.[53] Adorno (if not Lacan) faces a further problem in that he trenchantly criticizes the bourgeois, rational ego for its coercive, dominating tendencies and, at the same time, identifies ego *weakness* as a prime causal factor in the rise of authoritarian personalities. This leaves him in the uncomfortable position of simultaneously criticizing and defending the authoritarian ego.

I'll discuss these issues further in chapter 2, but for now it is worth noting that Habermas's account of individuation through socialization can be understood as an attempt to find a way out of the problem of the ego—and thus should also be assessed from this perspective.[54] Unlike Marcuse, who accepted the basic Adornian premise that the rational ego is repressive and violent and argued for the generation of an alternative, utopian sensibility via a regression to embodied, polymorphous, narcissistic pleasure,[55] Habermas attempts to resolve the problem of the ego via his turn to communicative intersubjectivity. According to Habermas and several of his most prominent defenders, the turn away from the philosophy of consciousness and to linguistic intersubjectivity allows him to offer a nonrepressive account of rationality and ego identity that overcomes the reifying logic of identity thinking.[56] As such, communicative intersubjectivity claims to offer a way out of the impasse generated by Adorno's critique of the ego.

However, it is far from clear that the turn to communicative intersubjectivity, as important and groundbreaking as it is, actually addresses the problem of the repressive coerciveness implicit in the Kantian model of rationality and autonomy.[57] However much the theory of communicative action may improve our understanding of intersubjective relations, it does not thereby resolve the problems that arise in the relationship between subject and object. The latter was Adorno's main focus insofar as his critique of the ego as a structure of internalized domination concerns the relationship between rational ego (subject) and material nature (object), including the bodily drives and impulses that must be brought to heel through the process of individuation.

Habermas initially attempted to resolve this problem through his thoroughly linguistified understanding of the unconscious. Even in his early engagement with psychoanalysis, Habermas rejected Freud's distinction between thing-presentations and word-presentations and insisted on the linguistic, and thus communicable, nature of primary process. This, in turn, allowed him to understand repression as a linguistic process through which certain experiences are excommunicated from consciousness and come to form a distorted, privatized unconscious.[58] As Habermas says, "The ego's flight from itself is an operation that is carried out in and with language."[59] However, as Whitebook contends, inasmuch as this interpretation does away with the very notion of nonlinguistic (bodily, material, objective) inner nature, it does not so much resolve the problem of the ego's domination of inner nature as sidestep it altogether. This Habermasian move could even be understood as a peculiar kind of performative contradiction: it is a clear case of identity thinking, of the subsumption of not only concrete materiality and embodied nature but also of the utter foreignness of the unconscious within the paradigm of linguistic intersubjectivity, carried out in the name of doing justice to the other.[60]

Later, after his turn toward cognitive and developmental psychology, Habermas implicitly addresses the problem of the ego in the context of his sympathetic critique of Kohlberg's account of moral development. Acknowledging that Kohlberg's account rests on the Kantian opposition between duty and inclination, Habermas briefly flirts with the idea of supplementing Kohlberg's six-stage model of the progression from preconventional to conventional to postconventional modes of moral psychology with a seventh stage that would, as Whitebook puts it, "involve the unfettered communication ... between the ego and the other regions of the personality."[61] Although this move might have provided him with the resources needed to resolve the problem of the coercive, rigidly integrated, bourgeois Kantian ego through a model of "free intercourse" between rational and inner nature,[62] Habermas quickly retreated from this position, leaving the problem of the ego unresolved.[63]

Confronting the problem of the ego without remaining, as Adorno arguably does, mired in paradox requires developing a nonviolent, nonrepressive model of ego or psychic integration, one that associates maturity not with the coercive mastery of inner nature but rather with the ego's expansion and enrichment through the ongoing incorporation of more and more unconscious content. At the same time, confronting the problem of the ego without explaining it away, as Habermas could be said to do, requires retaining a robust conception of the unconscious, one that takes seriously precisely its foreignness—that is, its inability to be translated into rational, communicative thought without remainder. In chapter 2, I shall argue that Klein's conception of the ego offers a promising model for addressing these problems. For Klein, ego integration is not a process of dominating inner nature but an ongoing, open-ended process of enrichment and expansion. Thus, her account is responsive to the Adornian and Lacanian critique of the ego while providing the basis for a meaningful conception of rationality and autonomy. Moreover, like Habermas's, Klein's account of the subject is intersubjective from the ground up, though hers is a rich and ambivalent conception of intersubjectivity that emphasizes the affective, phantasmatic aspects of our relations with others. In this way, Klein's account combines an intersubjective perspective with a robust account of unconscious, intrapsychic experience.

As I will argue in more detail in chapter 3, Klein also breaks in important ways with classical developmental Freudian schemas. The key innovation here is Klein's positional model of the psyche, which emerges in her late metapsychology. This model distinguishes between the paranoid-schizoid and depressive positions, where these are understood not as stages of development but as configurations of object relations or ways of organizing psychic experience. Although the depressive position is understood as an achievement of sorts, Klein also maintains that individuals oscillate between both positions throughout their lives, and some Kleinians even insist on the virtues of the paranoid-schizoid position. Moreover, although Klein often speaks, particularly in her early work, about overcoming the depressive position, she is equally clear that the depressive position can never be *fully* overcome, but instead must be continually and ongoingly worked through. Therefore, Klein's positional model is not a developmental stage model in any straightforward sense.

This has two crucially important implications for Klein's work as a resource for contemporary critical theory. First, because her positional model of the self is based on an account of pre-Oedipal infantile experience and concerns the psychic processes and transformations undergone during the first year of life, it does not depend on Freudian models of psychosexual development. This is not to say that Klein herself did not accept or endorse such models—undoubtedly she did, and she drew on those models frequently in her own clinical work and writings. It *is* to say that one can accept her metapsychology without also being committed to those models and thus without becoming entangled in complex and thorny debates about the normalizing conceptions of gender and sexuality that such models may imply. Second, Klein's positional model does not in any way map on to social evolutionary theories about the transition from "primitive" through religious to modern, secular societies. Again, this is not to deny that Klein herself endorsed some version of recapitulation theory; it is just to claim that the Kleinian model of the psychic self does not *depend on* recapitulationist views. Emphasizing this point provides a response to critics, such as David Eng, who have rightly taken Klein to task for her deeply troubling remarks about colonialism. As I discuss in chapter 3, notwithstanding this trenchant critique, Klein's metapsychology offers powerful resources for working through the residual Eurocentric racism that pervades Freudian developmental schemas, evident in the deeply problematic psychoanalytic conception of "the primitive." This is important because if critical theory is to draw productively on psychoanalysis for a critique of the ongoing legacies of colonialism and racism, then we'll need a version of psychoanalysis that has confronted and begun to work through its own Eurocentrism.[64]

Psychoanalysis as Critique

In addition to offering critical theory a more realistic conception of the person and helping it to think through its commitment to developmental schemas at the individual and social levels, psychoanalysis also provides a compelling model for the aims and methods of critique. An engagement with psychoanalysis can prompt critical theory to rethink its understandings of emancipation and progress beyond abstract utopianism and transformative praxis beyond narrow rationalism.

Starting with utopianism, recall that the early Frankfurt School turned to psychoanalysis not only for a compelling diagnosis of the problems of bourgeois capitalist societies but also for an account of the unconscious as a stratum of human experience that is stubbornly resistant to existing social norms. As Whitebook has argued, the Frankfurt School thereby connected the psychoanalytic unconscious to the problem of utopia. For at least some members of the early Frankfurt School, the unconscious marks out a space of radical alterity from which critique can be launched, or what Whitebook calls "the good Other" of the "repressive ego and the logic of domination."[65] Relatedly, Whitebook reads the move away from psychoanalysis in contemporary Frankfurt School critical theory as a retreat from this utopian horizon that goes hand in hand with the liberal-reformist character of much of that work.

Nowhere is the utopian reading of psychoanalysis more evident within the Frankfurt School tradition than in the work of Marcuse. Unlike Adorno, who adhered to a strict *Bilderverbot*, a prohibition on concrete images of utopia,[66] Marcuse drew on psychoanalysis to construct a robust picture of what Inara Marin has called a "libidinal utopia."[67] As I discuss in more detail in chapter 4, Marcuse endorses the basic premises of Adorno's Freudian critique of the ego, according to which the bourgeois, rational ego is held together through the domination of inner nature. But the key to Marcuse's escape from the paradox of the ego lies in his distinction between socially necessary and surplus repression. Although Marcuse acknowledges that some degree of repression of instinctual nature is necessary for the formation of society, much of the repression that we experience as members of late industrial capitalist societies is no longer necessary and in fact serves only to uphold capitalist domination. Thus, true progress for Marcuse consists in undoing the work of surplus repression, ending the reign of the repressive rational ego, and unleashing the forces of Eros so that they may infuse society with a new sensibility emphasizing imagination, artistic creativity, and embodied pleasure.

Whitebook traces the retreat from utopia in contemporary critical theory to Habermas's early linguistification and later rejection of psychoanalysis. By linguistifying the unconscious in his early work, Habermas implicitly denies himself access to the stratum of human experience that is not wholly reducible to linguistic intersubjectivity and therefore has the potential to resist social control. This leaves him stuck with reformism, unable to assimilate the utopian impulses of earlier Frankfurt School critical theory. As Whitebook puts the point:

> Psychoanalysis . . . can be of service in avoiding "a joyless reformism" that is insensitive to the question of "a fulfilled life" only insofar as a robust notion of the unconscious is maintained. One essential source for visions of a better society—visions that could be debated in a just public sphere—is the psychic imaginary and its refashioning of the contents of cultural tradition. Without the input of the imaginary, any such debate, while possibly being just, is in danger of being empty.[68]

In other words, only by retaining a robust notion of the unconscious can critical theory provide itself with the resources needed to nourish its utopian imaginary. Obviously, a critical theory that leaves psychoanalysis behind altogether is cut off from these resources, but so too is a critical theory that interprets psychoanalysis without the ambivalence of the drives that gives the theory of the unconscious its vitality.

And yet the problem of utopia as it arises at the intersection of psychoanalysis and critical theory is still more complex. After all, as I have argued elsewhere, there is a curious way in which post-Habermasian critical theory is simultaneously too utopian and not nearly utopian enough.[69] It is too utopian on account of its tendency to make strict conceptual distinctions between norms and power relations (communicative versus strategic action; genuine versus ideological forms of recognition). It is not nearly utopian enough on account of its reformism (whether liberal or socialist), its reconstructive methodology (whether focused on deliberative political institutions in relation to the public sphere, on the one hand, and legal and administrative structures, on the other; or on the relationship between family, civil society/markets, and democratic rights), and its related willingness to defend something that bears more than a passing resemblance to the status quo.

Psychoanalysis, too, stands in a complicated relationship to utopia. While it may be true that the psychoanalytic unconscious marks out a stratum or mode of human experience that lies stubbornly outside of social control—and so can inspire utopian imaginaries—it is also the case, as Whitebook has claimed elsewhere, that psychoanalysis is opposed to the idea of utopia in principle.[70] The thought here is that positive images of utopian societies rest on a denial of human aggression and destructiveness and a disavowal of the inevitability of human finitude, loss, and lack. As such, utopianism represents an expression of infantile omnipotence and grandiosity.

The fundamental ambivalence of these different meanings and valences of utopianism is perhaps best expressed in Adorno's work. Clearly, Adorno was no reformist, at least not in his theoretical work. However much he may have contributed practically to the project of reforming the German university system upon his postwar return to Frankfurt, in his written work he remained committed to the claim that bourgeois capitalism is a wrong form of life and that only on the basis of radical change would something resembling progress in the future be possible.[71] Moreover, Adorno aimed to identify those fragments of experience that resist complete incorporation or integration into existing bourgeois capitalist society: the moment of nonidentity, the somatic impulse, the drives. In that sense, Adorno could be read as preserving something of the utopian impulse that early critical theory found in the psychoanalytic unconscious.

Still, Adorno is equally suspicious of the seductions of utopian speculation that rest on false promises of reconciliation. Indeed, the refusal of such false promises is the very core of dialectical thinking for Adorno. Dialectical thinking is, as he puts it, "the refusal to accept the denial or elimination of contradictions.... Instead it makes contradiction into an object or theme of philosophical reflection itself."[72] Hence, although Adorno occasionally offers glimpses of what would constitute genuine reconciliation (linked to his image of a noncoercive "togetherness of diversity"), his utopianism is best understood as negativistic—indeed, counterfactual.[73] He writes:

> The only philosophy which can be responsibly practiced in face of despair is the attempt to contemplate all things as they would present themselves from the standpoint of redemption. Knowledge has no light but that shed on the world by redemption: all else is reconstruction, mere technique. Perspectives must be fashioned that displace and estrange the world, reveal it to be, with its rifts and crevices, as indigent and distorted as it will appear one day in the messianic light.[74]

Taking up this standpoint is both "the simplest of things" and at the same time "the utterly impossible thing," insofar as it requires a subtle yet profound shift in perspective, "a standpoint removed, even though by a hair's breadth, from the scope of existence," and, as such, a standpoint that is indelibly marked by the "distortion and indigence which it seeks to escape."[75]

This ambivalent relationship to utopian themes can also be found in Lacan—which may help to explain why, in many ways, Adorno's work seems closer to that of Lacan than it does to that of Habermas or Honneth, despite the fact that the latter are so often grouped together with Adorno as members of the Frankfurt School.[76] On the one hand, Lacan's account of the ethics of psychoanalysis places great importance on the subject's unwillingness to give ground relative to their desire, regardless of the social consequences of such an act.[77] Mari Ruti captures this aspect of Lacan's work under the heading of subjective defiance: a resistance to the social order made possible by fidelity to the distinctive construction of one's authentic desire. As Ruti explains, "For Lacan, the unruly, chaotic drive energies of the real represent a kernel of rebelliousness that reveals the intrinsic instability of the Other, including the fact that there is no Other of the Other, no ultimate guarantee of symbolic power."[78] The real thus refers us to that aspect of human experience that resists the normalization and domestication that accompany complete incorporation into the social order. The subject who steps into the real and commits the Lacanian ethical act "follows the pulse of its own desire rather than acquiescing to the normative expectations of the big Other."[79] On Ruti's reading, Lacan, like the early Frankfurt School, offers a psychoanalytic conceptualization of a realm of human experience that lies outside of social control and thus can serve as a source of resistance to a totally reified society.

But, whereas the early Frankfurt School tended to correlate this stratum of experience with libidinal drives, the Lacanian account suggests something different, and perhaps more surprising—namely, that the force underlying the ethical act and enabling acts of defiant resistance to the social order is the death drive.[80] Why the death drive? Because defying the social order with its attendant norms and forms of recognition by means of which the subject is constituted and recognized as a symbolic being means being willing to risk a kind of subjective destitution. Even as Ruti cautions against those readings of Lacan that characterize complete self-shattering as the aim of Lacanian ethics, she also notes that "a kernel of antihegemonic negativity (a trace of the death drive, of identity-dissolving jouissance) can . . . be found in more or less any act of defiance."[81]

And yet Lacan, like Adorno, remained skeptical of utopian thinking insofar as this mode of thought holds out the promise of a future of plenitude and wholeness in which the subject's symbolic castration is fully healed and its lack completely filled in. As Ruti explains, "One cannot, in the Lacanian context, speak about an analytic 'cure,' about an ultimate solution (what Lacan mockingly calls 'the Sovereign Good') that would, once and for all, release the subject from its suffering."[82] However, one can speak of better and worse ways of navigating the peculiar track of one's idiosyncratic desires. We may never be able to fully break free of our repetition compulsion, but we can hope "to enter into the cycle of the repetition compulsion in less injurious ways."[83] Therefore, even if, from the Lacanian perspective, "our every attempt to fill our lack unavoidably falls short of its goal. . . . the intrinsic impossibility of complete satisfaction is what sustains us as creatures of becoming and what allows us, over and again, to take up the inexhaustible process of creating meaning."[84] For Ruti, this process of creating meaning involves harnessing the potentially destructive drive energies of the real for the purpose of revitalizing our symbolic existence; "creativity," as she puts it, "presupposes an encounter with negativity."[85] But this means that negativity—even the negativity of the death drive—is not incompatible with and in fact may even serve as the occasion for the initiation of creative processes of becoming. As such, Ruti contends (contra influential readers of Lacan such as Lee Edelman and Slavoj Žižek) that Lacan's articulation of the death drive is compatible with a hopeful orientation to the possibility of a better future: "Far from foreclosing the future..., Lacanian negativity holds open the future as a space of ever-renewed possibility."[86]

These considerations suggest that critical theory needs psychoanalysis in order to articulate a meaningful conception of resistance to social norms and the prospects for emancipation without falling into problematic forms of utopian thinking or false models of reconciliation. Psychoanalysis thereby offers critical theory a way of rethinking the *aims* of critique. Relatedly, psychoanalysis prompts critical theorists to reconsider our understanding of critical *method*. Indeed, commentators on Habermas's work on Freud have noted that his engagement with psychoanalysis focuses almost exclusively with the problem of method. In his seminal study of Habermas's early work, Thomas McCarthy notes that "Freudian psychoanalysis plays a more limited role in Habermas's treatment of the 'links' between individual psychology and institutional framework than it did for earlier critical theorists," and "his orientation to Freud's own work is more strongly methodological than was theirs."[87] Habermas turns to psychoanalysis not so much for its ambivalent philosophical anthropology or the ways in which it questions or undermines developmental trajectories but rather for its methodological insights into, as McCarthy puts it, "a more precise conception of the logic of a reflective science" that "provides us with guidelines for the construction of a critical social theory."[88] Even though he himself abandoned this project in the early 1970s, Habermas's methodological interpretation of psychoanalysis set the stage for a certain reading of critical method that continues to resonate in contemporary Frankfurt School critical theory.

This idea that psychoanalysis serves as a model for the methodology of critical theory is developed most systematically in Habermas's early work *Knowledge and Human Interests*. There, Habermas interprets psychoanalysis as a form of knowledge and practice that incorporates methodical self-reflection. Although his reading of Freud pays close attention to the papers on analytic technique, where transference plays a crucial role, Habermas nevertheless puts rational reflection, insight, and interpretation at the center of his understanding of psychoanalysis. On his view, psychoanalysis enables individual transformation through the power of critical insight; analogously, critical theory enables social transformation through the power of critical insight (though this process must be mediated through social and political movements and institutions). Although Habermas later gave up this model in the wake of the critical reception of his early work, I shall argue in chapter 5 that it has been quietly resuscitated in Axel Honneth's work and more explicitly defended by Robin Celikates.

Although each of these accounts attempts to do justice to the role of the affective, the motivational, and the practical—in short, the nonrational—aspects of psychoanalysis, none of them takes seriously enough the role of the transference. Habermas, Honneth, and Celikates tend to favor a rationalistic understanding of psychoanalysis, such that their account of how analysis works rests primarily on the role of rational insight and reflexivity. This is, however, a highly selective and partial understanding of psychoanalytic method. Even for Freud, and certainly for Klein and Lacan, analysis does not work primarily through the mode of rational insight; indeed, the latter is quite often understood to be a mode of defense that all too easily becomes an impediment to genuine transformation.

Because none of these thinkers pay sufficient attention to the role of the transference in psychoanalytic method, they also fail to pose the question of what this might mean for the analogy to critical method. Can we reimagine the analogy between psychoanalysis and critique on the basis of a more complex, dynamic, and not merely rationalistic account of psychoanalytic technique? What could a conception of critique modeled on the working through of a transference relation possibly look like? Perhaps surprisingly, I argue that we can find some clues to how to address these questions by turning (once again) to Michel Foucault and Adorno.

❊ ❊ ❊

Contemporary critical theory needs psychoanalysis for (at least) three reasons: to temper its tendencies toward normative idealism, to rethink its developmental models of self and society, and to theorize the aims and methods of critique beyond utopianism and rationalism.[89] Thus, critical theorists have much to gain from a renewed engagement with psychoanalysis. But not just any interpretation of psychoanalysis will do. Although it will take the remainder of this book to fully make my case, my primary thesis is that psychoanalytic drive theory, particularly the version developed by Melanie Klein, offers critical theory a realistic conception of the person that tempers its tendencies toward normative idealization and disrupts its developmental schemas. Far from leaving critical theory mired in pessimistic despair, however, this realistic conception of the person also serves as the foundation for creativity, reparation, and productive individual and social transformation.

Chapter 1 focuses on Klein's realistic conception of the person. The core argument is that Klein's commitment to primary aggression renders her conception of the person thoroughly realistic while her relational conception of the drives makes that conception compatible with the methodological commitments of critical theory. The key to this argument is teasing out Klein's understanding of the relationship between the intersubjective and intrapsychic aspects of experience. Because she views subjects as object-related from the start, Klein understands the self in fundamentally intersubjective or relational terms, but, because of her commitment to drive theory and her related emphasis on unconscious phantasy, the intrapsychic dimensions of experience play a prominent role in her account as well. As a result, her philosophical anthropology is richer, more complicated, and more ambivalent than accounts such as Honneth's. At the same time, her relational conception of the drives is compatible with and uniquely productive for critical theory.

Chapter 2 takes up the problem of the ego. The overall claim is that Klein's account of ego integration corresponds with and productively extends Adorno's relatively undeveloped remarks about nonreified cognition. In this way, Klein helps to show a way out of the paradox of the ego that emerges in Adorno's work as a result of the conjunction of his critique of the ego as a structure of internalized domination and his (seemingly contradictory) claim that ego weakness leads to authoritarian personalities. For Klein, ego strength and integration are not about the mastery of inner nature but about enriching the ego through the incorporation of unconscious content and through closing the gap (as much as is possible) between one's phantasied representations of one's primary objects (what Klein calls "internal objects") and the actual other human beings on whom those representations are based.

Chapter 3 turns to the problem of progress in relation to psychoanalysis. Focusing on progress in a backward-looking sense, as a judgment about historical development, I argue that, although Freud's official position on the psyche is bound up with problematically Eurocentric notions of civilizational development and progress, his unofficial position not only breaks free of but also subverts this type of developmental thinking. With her positional model of the self, Klein moves even further in this direction and does so in ways that avoid some of the problematic claims about primary narcissism that Freud's unofficial position endorses. This strand of psychoanalytic thinking thus relies neither on developmental-historical social evolutionary models nor on potentially self-congratulatory (not to mention Eurocentric) backward-looking claims about historical progress as a "fact" in order to explicate its conception of psychic integration.

Chapter 4 explores further the question of progress this time understood in a forward-looking sense, as change for the better. Beginning with a critical discussion of Marcuse's attempt to reconcile the possibility of progress with the postulate of the death drive in *Eros and Civilization*, I argue that his insights can be productively developed by turning to Klein's conception of reparation and creativity as expressions of the work of mourning. Drawing on this discussion and putting Klein into conversation with Freud, Lacan, and Adorno, I sketch a less speculative, more negativistic conception of progress as an ethical-political imperative, one that is, I argue, compatible with the assumption of the death drive.

Chapter 5 takes up the question of method. Whereas Habermas understands psychoanalysis—and, by analogy, critique—to work primarily through the force of rational insight, I ask what this analogy implies if we take seriously the role of transference in analytic technique. Drawing on Jonathan Lear's structural account of transference, I argue that the best analogue for this account of analytic method is critique understood as problematizing genealogy. Emphasizing transference does not, however, mean leaving rational insight behind altogether. I turn to Adorno's account of philosophy as interpretation to rethink the role of rational insight in relation to this structural account of transference.

The bulk of this book is devoted to the abstract philosophical and even metatheoretical argument that only by engaging with psychoanalysis can critical theory address some of its problematic tendencies and blind spots. Throughout this discussion, questions of politics occasionally emerge and hover in the background. The conclusion draws the political implications and relevance of Kleinian psychoanalysis into sharper focus. In it, I argue that Klein's framework offers critical theorists a rich and resonant vocabulary for diagnosing the dysfunctions of our politics, including the contemporary resurgence of right-wing authoritarian movements, without falling into the temptation to pathologize our political opponents.

1

Kleinian Realism

Between the Intrapsychic and the Intersubjective

I argued in the introduction, following Axel Honneth, that critical theory needs psychoanalysis first and foremost for its realistic philosophical anthropology or theory of subjectivity, in order to correct for the tendency—relatively common in at least certain strands of contemporary Frankfurt School critical theory—toward normative idealism. However, Honneth's interpretation of psychoanalysis does not, in my view, provide the realistic conception of the person that he argues is needed. Engaging psychoanalysis through a thoroughly intersubjectivist reading of D. W. Winnicott, Honneth dispenses with the death drive and interprets fusion experiences as the *Nullpunkt* of relations of recognition. In so doing, he screens power, ambivalence, and omnipotence out of his philosophical anthropology.[1] The result is a conception of subjectivity that is more compatible with his normative theory of recognition, but also (and perhaps for that very reason) decidedly less realistic.

In this chapter, I propose that critical theorists can find a realistic philosophical anthropology that also coheres with our core methodological commitments in the work of Melanie Klein. To be sure, for anyone who is familiar with Klein's work, it might seem outrageous to describe her account of subjectivity as realistic. After all, she is often criticized for the wildly speculative nature of her work, the overly sophisticated mental states she attributes to very young children and even infants, and her deeply pessimistic conception of human nature. And yet I will contend that Klein offers a realistic conception of the person in the sense specified in the introduction. Moreover, because of her unique relational conception of Freudian drive theory, her metapsychology is consistent with the core methodological commitments of critical theory, particularly its understanding of the self as socially or intersubjectively constituted. The key to Klein's contribution, I argue, is the way that her account of subjectivity weaves together what Jessica Benjamin has termed the "intrapsychic and intersubjective aspects" of the self.[2] While it will take the remainder of this chapter to lay out the details of this account, the main point is rather simple: because she views subjects as object-related from the start, Klein understands the self in fundamentally relational terms; but, because she emphasizes the duality of the drives and the role of unconscious phantasy, her account of subjectivity is richer, more complicated, and more ambivalent—in short, more realistic—than Honneth's.[3]

In what follows, I begin by laying out the basic features of Klein's mature metapsychology, the centerpiece of which is her distinction between the paranoid-schizoid and depressive positions. Next, I turn to Klein's unique conception of the drives. I argue that Klein departs from Freudian drive theory in two key ways—by reconceiving the relationship between drive and object, and by rearticulating the death drive as primary aggression—which, taken together, make her conception of the drives compatible with the core methodological commitments of critical theory without sacrificing its realism. This leads me to Klein's notion of phantasy, which is deeply bound up with her account of the drives. Klein's emphasis on the ways in which all of our relations with others are filtered through, and all too often distorted by, phantasy considerably complicates her object-relational conception of the psyche. However, against those who accuse Klein of downplaying or even ignoring intersubjective relations or environmental factors entirely, I argue that such relations play at least two crucial roles in her account: first, a certain kind of relation to one's primary caregiver is needed to enable the transition to and working through of the depressive position; and, second, a primary goal of Kleinian analysis is to narrow the gap between phantasy and reality, between internal and external objects, between one's phantasmatic perception of external others and who they actually are, even as we must acknowledge that this gap can never fully be closed. Appreciating both of these points is crucial to understanding the complex interplay of the intrapsychic and intersubjective dimensions of experience in Klein's work and thus to assessing the fruitfulness of her theory of subjectivity for critical theory.

Kleinian Metapsychology

Klein's work underwent significant development and transformation over the course of her life.[4] As a result, the distinction between the paranoid-schizoid and depressive positions that most readers take to be central to her work becomes explicit only relatively late in her career and her life. This distinction represents both the culmination and the clearest expression of Klein's original metapsychology. Klein was an early pioneer of analytic work with very young children, and because her metapsychology emerged out of—indeed was her way of systematizing and making sense of—her clinical experience, it differs from the classical Freudian model insofar as it centers on the pre-Oedipal phases of psychic development. Thus, although one can find, particularly in Klein's early work and in her discussions of case material, numerous references to classical Freudian theories of psychosexual development, her mature metapsychology neither recapitulates nor in any way depends on such theories. Rather, her account focuses attention on what she regarded as the deeper, more archaic layers of the psyche, and their associated fundamental anxieties. As R. D. Hinshelwood explains, such anxieties "are about survival or annihilation, about the formation or disintegration of the ego and of its objects."[5]

At the core of Klein's metapsychology, and crucial for understanding her distinction between paranoid-schizoid and depressive positions, is her claim that object relations are in place from the very beginning of life. The first object—or, more precisely, part-object—is the breast, and the infant relates to this object from birth.[6] As Klein puts it in an important passage: "There is no instinctual urge, no anxiety situation, no mental process which does not involve objects, external or internal; in other words, object-relations are at the *centre* of emotional life. Furthermore, love and hatred, phantasies, anxieties, and defences are also operative from the beginning and are *ab initio* indivisibly linked with object-relations."[7] For Klein, the infant is object-related from birth, meaning that they are related both to external objects (actual other people, first and foremost the primary caregiver) and to the psychic representatives of those other people, which Klein calls "internal objects." As a result of the complex relationship between external and internal objects, object relations are from the beginning filtered through and thus potentially distorted by psychic phantasy in ways that I will explore further in what follows.

The claim that object relations are present from the beginning of life goes hand in hand with Klein's claim that there exists a rudimentary, not fully coherent, and relatively unintegrated ego—but an ego all the same—in place from the beginning of life. As Hanna Segal explains, for Klein, "sufficient ego exists at birth to experience anxiety, use defense mechanisms and form primitive object-relations in phantasy and reality."[8] With this idea, Klein implicitly rejects a core commitment of Freud's mature metapsychology: the notion of primary narcissism.[9] In his mature work, Freud contended that infants begin life in a state of undifferentiated merger or fusion not only with the primary caregiver but with the external world as a whole. Perhaps the most famous discussion of primary narcissism occurs in the opening chapter of *Civilization and Its Discontents*, where Freud explains the oceanic feeling—a feeling of being at one with the universe that his interlocutor had identified as the source of religious belief—as a residue of this early experience of undifferentiation. As he puts it, "Originally the ego includes everything; later it separates off an external world from itself."[10] On this view, the infant's sense of themselves as an entity separate from others and the rest of the world is developed over time through a painful process of reality testing that undermines the feeling of infantile omnipotence that goes hand in hand with primary narcissism. Klein's rejection of primary narcissism has profound implications for her metapsychology, inasmuch as it renders her account relational to the core.[11] To be sure, as I will discuss in more detail in the following, intrapsychic phantasy plays a crucially important role in Klein's account, and when the infant (or the adult!) is overwhelmed by phantasy, their experience has an omnipotent character.[12] Still, Klein rejects the idea that the early infant is merged or fused either with their environment or with their caregiver (and thus the related idea that the aim of psychic development is that of establishing a boundary between self and other) in favor of a conception of the infant as having a rudimentary, not fully coherent ego that relates to fragmented part-objects.

Perhaps the most striking feature of Klein's distinction between the paranoid-schizoid and depressive positions is the language of position itself.

The term "position" is distinct from notions of developmental stages, and, although in some sense the transition from the paranoid-schizoid to the depressive position is an achievement, the positions are not stages that one passes through and leaves behind. Rather, as Hanna Segal describes it, the term "position" refers to "a specific configuration of object relations, anxieties and defenses which persist throughout life."[13] With this conception of the position in mind, we can offer a preliminary characterization of the distinction between the two positions. In the paranoid-schizoid position, the subject relates to part-objects; experiences a high degree of persecutory anxiety; relies on splitting, idealization, and demonization as defenses against such anxiety; and is easily overwhelmed by phantasy. In the depressive position, by contrast, the subject experiences depressive anxiety and guilt, but also develops the capacity for integration that enables it to relate to objects as whole objects; to withstand the ambivalence that inevitably results from the realization that the loved (idealized) and hated (demonized) part-objects are one and the same; and to narrow without ever fully closing the gap between phantasy and reality.

The paranoid-schizoid position is the starting point for Klein's metapsychology. As we have already seen, Klein holds that object relations are in place from the very beginning of life, with the first object being the mother's breast. Because the early ego is relatively incoherent and unintegrated, the infant starts out in a state of extreme anxiety that Klein relates to psychosis.[14] This is not to say that all infants are psychotic (a view that was occasionally mistakenly attributed to Klein),[15] but rather that she believes that the psyche has a psychotic core.[16] For Klein, this means that primordial psychic experience consists of a rudimentary ego terrified by the relative lack of coherence or integration of itself and its objects. The hallmark of the paranoid-schizoid position is, for Klein, the ego's experience of itself as "in bits."[17] Thus, the infant in the paranoid-schizoid position experiences their primary object as a part-object (as the breast, rather than as the mother or primary caregiver) and, as a defense against anxiety, they split that part-object into a good, gratifying breast that nourishes, loves, and protects them, and a bad, frustrating, persecutory breast that withholds nourishment and care. This splitting of the breast, according to Klein, "results in a severance of love and hate."[18] The infant loves and is attached to the good breast—after all, without such an attachment the breast wouldn't be an object at all, in the psychoanalytic sense of that term—and hates and feels persecuted by the bad breast, which is experienced as persecutory and destructive.

But the story is still more complicated than this, because, even in the early stages of infancy, the psyche's relation to its primary object is shaped not only by splitting but also by complex dynamics of projection and introjection involving both the good and the bad breast. Indeed, the infant's phantasy of the good breast in some sense is the result of the projection of their love and libidinal impulses outward, into the breast, and the parallel phantasy of the bad breast results from the projection of their hatred, aggression, and destructiveness. At the same time, the infant introjects both the bad breast and the good breast, taking them back into the rudimentary ego, transforming them into internal objects. Although the infant introjects the bad breast in order to attempt to control it, this move also heightens the experience of danger and anxiety, because now the persecutory object is both outside and inside the ego. By contrast, the introjection of the good breast creates an internal protector that enables the infant to defend against anxiety and comes to form the core of the developing ego.[19] As Klein writes, "This first internal good object acts as a focal point for the ego. It counteracts the processes of splitting and dispersal, makes for cohesiveness and integration, and is instrumental in building up the ego."[20] Successful navigation of the paranoid-schizoid position consists in achieving an optimal balance between projection and introjection—splitting off and projecting the bad parts of the self and introjecting the good parts of the object.[21]

This brings us to the depressive position, which, for Klein, represents a developmental achievement marked by greater integration of both the ego and its objects. However, we have to be careful here, because, as I will discuss further in subsequent chapters, Klein has a very specific understanding of ego integration, and the sense in which her account can be understood as a developmental one is complicated. The key moment in the transition to the depressive position occurs when the infant first recognizes the mother or primary caregiver as a whole object, which Klein thinks happens early in the first year of life. This transition is facilitated by repeated experiences of "gratification by the external good object"—that is, "the mother's love and understanding of the infant"—which enable the infant "to break through" the "schizoid states" of the paranoid-schizoid position.[22] When this transition takes place, the infant realizes that the object that they have been attacking and destroying in their phantasies (the bad breast) is the very same object that they also love and depend on (the good breast)—a realization that gives rise to depressive anxiety. Whereas persecutory anxiety results from the fear of the ego's annihilation and complete disintegration, depressive anxiety is caused by the fear of the loss and destruction of the loved object.[23] As Klein explains, when the infant enters the depressive position, "the loved and hated aspects of the mother are no longer felt to be so widely separated, and the result is an increased fear of loss, states akin to mourning and a strong feeling of guilt, because the aggressive impulses are felt to be directed against the loved object."[24] In this way, Klein's depressive position is closely bound up with the drive for reparation, which is the urge to repair the damage that was done, whether in phantasy or in reality, to the object.

Interestingly, many contemporary readers of Klein stop here, taking her account of the depressive position to be the hallmark of psychological maturity. As a result, there is something of a tendency in contemporary appropriations of Klein to valorize the depressive position and related concepts such as depressive agency.[25] Although this use of Kleinian concepts has much to recommend it, it is worth pointing out that, particularly in her early work, Klein presents the depressive position as something to be *worked through* or *overcome*.[26] Klein never describes what might lie *beyond* the depressive position very precisely, nor does she ever characterize it as a new, third position, but she does frequently suggest that working through or overcoming the depressive position is a precondition for normal psychological development. I will discuss this issue more fully in chapter 3, but for now will simply note that, for Klein, "overcoming" consists not in achieving some radically distinct position, but rather in continually working through the initially overwhelming and destabilizing experience of depressive anxiety, thereby enhancing one's ability to manage ambivalence without resorting to splitting, bring one's internal and external objects into closer alignment, and engage in acts of reparation.

The depressive position not only entails a relation to the object as a whole object, with both good and bad, loved and hated aspects; it also gives rise to a corresponding integration of the ego. This aspect of Klein's work will be the primary focus of the next chapter, but for now we can understand integration to mean both that the infant in the depressive position experiences themselves as less fragmented and incoherent and that their relationship to their internal objects begins to correspond more closely with the actually existing external objects—parents or primary caregivers—that are the basis for those internalized introjections.[27] As I will discuss in more detail, Klein regards complete integration of the ego and synthesis of internal and external situations to be impossible in principle, and yet she takes increased integration to be an important developmental and analytic goal. At the core of the depressive position is the infant's acknowledgement and acceptance of the fundamentally ambivalent nature of their relationship to their primary object. As the infant moves into the depressive position, they are "made to realize that the loved object is at the same time the hated one; and, in addition to this, that the real objects and the imaginary figures, both external and internal, are bound up with each other."[28] The infant enters the depressive position when they are able to know the mother or primary caregiver as a whole person (as both good and bad breast, loved and hated object) and to experience this figure as a real, external object who is at the same time also the object of their persecutory and idealizing phantasies. Thus, the acceptance of ambivalence goes together with a better understanding of the relationship between one's internal and external objects, between psychic reality and external reality. I'll come back to this point when I consider Klein's understanding of the relationship between the intrapsychic and intersubjective aspects of experience in more detail.

Drives as Relational Passions[29]

Klein regarded Freud's late account of the death drive as a monumental discovery, "a tremendous advance in the understanding of the mind."[30] This made Klein somewhat unique among Freud's contemporaries and immediate followers, most of whom refused to accept and were even somewhat embarrassed by the notion of the death drive.[31] Klein, by contrast, found that Freud's late account of the duality of life and death drives resonated powerfully with her pioneering analytic work with children. As she put it: "I recognized, in watching the constant struggle in the young infant's mental processes between an irrepressible urge to destroy as well as to save himself, to attack his objects and to preserve them, that primordial forces struggling with one another were at work."[32] However, in Klein's view, neither Freud himself nor his followers fully appreciated the significance of this discovery; hence, psychoanalysis tended to underestimate the role of aggression in human psychic and emotional life. Klein therefore understood herself to be working out to their logical conclusions the implications of Freudian drive theory by developing a perspective from which "the interaction of the life and death instincts will be seen to govern the whole of mental life."[33]

At the same time, Klein's drive theory diverges significantly from Freud's. Like Freud's, Klein's account of the drives developed and changed over time; in what follows, I will not attempt to do justice to all of the complexities, shifting perspectives, and internal inconsistencies in these two accounts. Instead, I focus on reconstructing the two key features that distinguish Klein's conception of drive from Freud's: first, the relation between drive and object; and, second, the relationship between the theory of the drives and the speculative biology that underpins the Freudian account. On the basis of this reconstruction, I argue that Kleinian drive theory offers a compelling alternative to the Freudian account, one that constitutes a uniquely productive resource for a critical theory inasmuch as it preserves the emphasis on primary aggression without running afoul of the basic methodological commitments of critical theory.

Let me begin with the relationship between drive and object. Freud's drive theory is notoriously contested, with critics accusing him of a crude biological reductionism and defenders insisting in response on the distinction between *Instinkt* and *Trieb*.[34] Moreover, his theory undergoes considerable transformation over time, most notably in that his early distinction between libidinal and ego or self-preservative drives eventually gives way to the duality of Eros versus Thanatos. Nevertheless, a fundamental assumption that runs throughout these quite different versions is that drives have priority over objects both temporally and functionally.

Freud famously defines drive in "Instincts and Their Vicissitudes" as "a concept on the frontier between the mental and the somatic, as the psychical representative of the stimuli originating from within the organism and reaching the mind, as a measure of the demand made upon the mind for work in consequence of its connection with the body."[35] This definition reveals drive as a border concept in that it refers to the mental or psychological representations of stimuli that have their sources in somatic processes. The implication is that drives are rooted in stimuli that arise internally, from within the organism, that exert a force or pressure to which the organism must respond. Although Freud is quite clear that psychology concerns itself only with the aims and effects of the drives, leaving the study of their somatic sources to the biologists, he is equally clear that drives have bodily or somatic roots.[36]

In "Instincts and Their Vicissitudes," Freud defines the object as "the thing in regard to which or through which the instinct is able to achieve its aim."[37] For Freud, the objects to which drives become attached are in an important sense highly contingent. He writes: "[The object] is what is most variable about an instinct and is not originally connected with it, but becomes assigned to it only in consequence of being peculiarly fitted to make satisfaction possible. . . . It may be changed any number of times in the course of the vicissitudes which the instinct undergoes during its existence."[38] This basic conception of the relationship between drive and object is reiterated later in *Beyond the Pleasure Principle*, where drives are defined as "the representatives of all the forces originating in the interior of the body and transmitted to the mental apparatus" and presented as giving rise to impulses that are "freely mobile processes which press towards discharge."[39]

To be sure, Freud's conception of the drives has undergone radical transformation by the time he writes *Beyond the Pleasure Principle*, a transformation with massive implications for Freudian metapsychology. In his recent work, Benjamin Fong has masterfully reconstructed the shift from what he calls Freud's early mechanism model to his later organism model of the psyche.[40] On the mechanism model, drives are somatic in origin, internally rooted stimuli that impinge on the psyche from within. According to this model, the psyche is a stimulus processing machine, and the drives represent an internal disturbance, upsetting the psyche's attempts to maintain stability and achieve quietude. Fong maintains that this early conception of the drives completely falls apart in Freud's papers on metapsychology. On his reading, "Instincts and Their Vicissitudes" attempts to outline the mechanism model, but quickly runs aground on the distinction between psyche and soma; as a result, Freud ends up contradictorily characterizing drives both as the stimuli that produce psychical representations and as the psychical representations themselves.[41] As Fong puts it, "The definition of drive here seems to undo the psyche-soma relation it is meant to explain" leading to a "collapse of the distinctions between psyche, soma, and world" that throws Freud into a full-fledged theoretical crisis.[42]

According to Fong, this crisis leads Freud to formulate a radically new version of drive theory and, relatedly, a new model of the psyche as organism. On this view, drives are no longer understood as internally emerging forces that disrupt the psyche's efforts to maintain stability and quietude; rather, "the drives themselves seek the quietude that was previously the aim of the psyche."[43] This leads Freud to claim that the drives are fundamentally conservative in that they seek quiescence, understood as a return to an earlier state of inanimacy. I'll come back to the details of Freud's conception of the death drive; for now, the important point is that on the organism model of the psyche, drives are not bodily or somatic forces that are in conflict with the psyche—they are the internal, organizing forces of the psyche itself. As such, drives can be shaped in relation to the environment. Fong writes:

> Drive, in the late model, is indeterminate at first and comes only to acquire aim and force in the complex interchanges of early life, i.e., in relation to the environment. We are held, caressed, cooed at, coddled, fed at the breast, or in close bodily contact and we can also be neglected or cared for in an impersonal way. Later we are encouraged, corralled, admonished, disciplined, screamed at, etc. It is in these experiences that drives are not elicited but formed—we learn what it is to love, to master, to aggress—and their formation coincides with the development of psychic life itself.[44]

Fong's reading of Freud's late organism model of the drives provides the basis for a compelling response to a standard objection to psychoanalytic drive theory—namely, that it is guilty of a crude biological reductionism at odds with the broadly social constructivist commitments of much contemporary social theory (including, but not limited to, critical theory in the Frankfurt School vein). However, although he reads drives as formed in a social context, Fong maintains that there are certain basic preconditions of human life that set limits within which drives take shape. Acknowledging this does not, he insists, commit us to "some timeless bedrock of human *nature* that culture merely surrounds," but it does entail the idea that "there are a few important things about how we come to exist that pose particular problems for us and constrain the range of our possibilities."[45] In other words, there are certain (for all we know) universal and transhistorical preconditions that delimit the character of the drives—for example, the fact that we are born helplessly dependent on caregivers, without whom we cannot survive.

Despite the radical and far-reaching implications of Fong's reinterpretation of Freud's late drive theory, it is not clear to me that this reinterpretation impacts Freud's conception of the relationship between drive and object. Reconceptualizing drives as the internal organizing forces of the psyche—as opposed to somatically rooted internal stimuli—does not necessitate giving up Freud's claim that drives are primary and the objects to which they attach secondary and contingent. Indeed, something like this view seems to be presupposed in the passage quoted earlier, when Fong maintains that the drive is "indeterminate at first and comes only to acquire aim and force in the complex interchanges of early life, i.e., in relation to the environment." Fong's reading of the organism model may well open the drives up to being shaped by external, social forces, allowing for a much less reductionistic reading of the drives, but it does not quite get us all the way to a relational conception of the drives themselves.

By contrast, Klein radically reconceptualizes the drives as fundamentally oriented or directed toward objects.[46] For her, the drives are not just interior, psychic forces that can be shaped by the social environment through the medium of one's relations to others; they are relational passions. Although, to be sure, like Freud she views the drives as constitutionally given or innate motivational forces, she fundamentally reimagines the nature of these forces.[47] She makes her departure from Freud on this point clear in her late paper "The Origins of Transference." For Klein, the term "object" refers not just to the object of an instinctual aim, but also to "an object-relation involving the infant's emotions, phantasies, anxieties, and defences."[48] Conversely, as I have discussed earlier, all emotions, phantasies, anxieties and defenses involve internal or external objects; thus, object relations are at the center of our psychic life.[49] As a result, Kleinian drives are, as Jay R. Greenberg and Stephen Mitchell note, "antithetical, object-related passions" and "complex, multitextured, passions involving others."[50]

In other words, for Klein, because libidinal and aggressive drives are inherently directed toward objects, they are relational through and through; indeed, they are best understood as competing modes of relationality.[51] Although Fong mounts an impressive challenge to the traditional, biologically reductive reading of Freudian drive theory, he retains the presumption that drives are forces within the individual (whether those forces are conceived in biological or psychic terms) that stand over and against the social—hence, that must be shaped or formed by social relations. Therefore, even on this much more socially malleable conception of drives, the drives themselves represent a residue of antisociality within human beings. In making this assumption, Fong is arguably being faithful to Freud, who retains an antisocial conception of the drives long after he has abandoned the mechanism model of the psyche. Indeed, this assumption lies at the core of his argument in *Civilization and Its Discontents*, where the central human struggle is between the push to gratify libidinal and aggressive drives, on the one hand, and the need to keep those drives in check in order to make social order possible, on the other.[52] On both the mechanism and the organism models of the psyche, the conflict between the demand for drive gratification—however this is understood—and the competing demands of social reality is central to human experience.[53] For Klein, by contrast, as Greenberg and Mitchell explain, "the central conflict in human experience . . . is between love and hate, between the caring preservation and the malicious destruction of others. Love and hate are already object-related and therefore have an unmediated connection to social reality."[54] That is to say, for Klein the central human conflict that finds its roots in the duality and ambivalence of the drives is between *two competing modes of social relatedness*.[55]

This brings us to the second major difference between Kleinian and Freudian drive theory. Unlike Freud, who arrived at the notion of the death drive late in his life and struggled to incorporate this insight into this model of the psyche, Klein spent much of her career grappling with the duality of libidinal and aggressive drives.[56] In fact, as I will discuss further, this opposition forms the basis for her distinction between the paranoid-schizoid and depressive positions. Moreover, unlike Freud, Klein articulates her understanding of the drives in thoroughly psychological terms that dispense with the speculative biological underpinnings of Freud's account in *Beyond the Pleasure Principle*.

Freud's late version of drive theory starts from the presumption that drives are fundamentally conservative. As he describes, "*An instinct is an urge inherent in organic life to restore an earlier state of things* which the living entity has been obliged to abandon under the pressure of external disturbing forces."[57] It is precisely because drives "impel towards repetition" or "the restoration of an earlier state of things"[58] that they give rise to the compulsion to repeat, which Freud sees at work in a range of phenomena, from the child's famous fort/da game to the war neuroses.[59] Since the ultimate earlier state of things is that of inanimacy (that is, of death), Freud reasons that *"the aim of all life is death,"* and that the instinct to return to an inanimate state—the death drive—is primary.[60] This conclusion obviously causes something of a problem for Freud's earlier postulation of an instinct for self-preservation. As a result, he downgrades the ego or self-preservative instinct into a component of the death drive, "whose function is to assure that the organism shall follow its own path to death" and shall be able "to die only in its own fashion."[61] The sexual or libidinal drives are accordingly reconceptualized as the opposing drive to seek immortality through the perpetuation of the germ cells; they are folded into the broader conception of Eros or the life instincts, which seek to preserve the life of the species, and represent the binding force that "holds all living things together" and joins them together into ever greater unities.[62] On this view, the sexual or libidinal instincts become the specific form that Eros or the life instinct takes when directed toward objects.

"The dominating tendency of mental life," Freud writes, "and perhaps of nervous life in general, is the effort to reduce, to keep constant or to remove internal tension due to stimuli (the 'Nirvana principle'...)—a tendency which finds expression in the pleasure principle, and our recognition of that fact is one of our strongest reasons for believing in the existence of the death instincts."[63] However, this way of understanding the death drive introduces a further complication into Freud's metapsychology. Insofar as the aim of the pleasure principle is "to free the mental apparatus entirely from excitation or to keep the amount of excitation in it constant or to keep it as low as possible," it too serves the function of "the most universal endeavor of all living substance—namely to return to the quiescence of the inorganic world."[64] This leads to the somewhat confusing implication that "the pleasure principle seems actually to serve the death instincts."[65] In other words, it turns out that, in this text at least, the pleasure principle has no beyond because it is actually in the service of the death drive, not in opposition to it.[66]

Although many readers of Freud understandably shy away from the speculative biology encapsulated in references to the Nirvana principle, Fong's reconstruction of the organism model of the psyche offers a compelling reinterpretation of this aspect of Freud's thought. Fong contends that Freud's aim is not, as is commonly assumed, to *derive* his account of the psyche from his speculative biology, nor is it to *apply* the latter to the former. Instead, his aim is to use the insights of biology to construct a *model* that elucidates the structure of the psyche. This way of reading Freud allows Fong to offer a novel interpretation of Freudian drive theory that distinguishes the death drive—the drive to return to the quiescence of the inorganic state, a drive that pushes for the dissolution of the boundary between self and other—from the drive to mastery, a self-subversion or internal transformation of the death drive that aims to protect the self by creating and preserving a barrier between self and other.[67] Moreover, and more important for our purposes, it has the implication that the usefulness of Freud's model does not stand or fall with the accuracy of the biological claims articulated in connection with it, precisely because the biological account serves neither to *justify* nor to *ground* but simply to *illustrate* his understanding of the drives.

Fong does a remarkable job of rendering Freud's recourse to speculative biology not only respectable but even plausible. Nevertheless, it seems to me that there are reasons to favor the Kleinian account. Regardless of how one reads the relationship between Freudian drive theory and the speculative biology in terms of which it is articulated, as I have argued, Freud maintains a view of internally generated drives that are only secondarily and derivatively turned outward toward objects—libido being the displacement of Eros, and aggression the displacement of the death drive. On this view, the death drive is an internal tendency toward disintegration, and aggression its outward deflection. As Jonathan Lear makes the point: "Aggression is thus understood as a secondary, defensive phenomenon. On this account people are aggressive towards others because they deflect outwards an internal tendency to decompose."[68] Lear further argues that this way of thinking of the relationship between the death drive and aggression ends up paradoxically getting in the way of the development of a satisfactory psychodynamic conception of aggression. Freud's account of the death drive "lulls one into thinking one has a theory of aggression when that is what is missing. . . . Freud never succeeded in giving aggression its due place in the psychoanalytic interpretation of life; and it is the death drive that got in the way."[69] In keeping with her distinctive understanding of the relationship between drive and object, Klein, by contrast, reinterprets the death drive *as* primary aggression, understood not as a principle governing the psychic organism that can subsequently be deflected outwards onto objects but rather a destructive mode of relation between psyche and primary object.[70] Her departure from both the mechanism and organism models of the psyche in the direction of a fully psychological and relational account led Klein to enthusiastically embrace the death drive while simultaneously identifying it with what Freud regarded as only one of its particular manifestations. While Fong expresses concerns about this aspect of Klein's approach,[71] I contend that this is a distinctive advantage of her view, for two reasons: first, because it decouples her account from the speculative biological story on which Freud's model in some sense still relies, even if only for purposes of elucidation, and thus frees her from the subsequent challenge of deriving love and aggression from the life and death drives; and, second, because it enables her to provide a more fully developed account of the fundamental role played by aggression in human psychological and social life.[72]

The duality of life and death drives and Klein's commitment to the primacy of aggression inform her basic metapsychological distinction between the paranoid-schizoid and depressive positions. As I've already indicated, the infant in the paranoid-schizoid position relates to the primary object—the breast—both lovingly and destructively. By splitting the breast into an idealized good breast that is the source of all that is good and nourishing and a demonized, persecutory bad breast that withholds care and nourishment, the infant splits love from hate, while continuing to relate to the primary object in both ways. As Klein puts it: "The baby's first object of love and hate—his mother—is both desired and hated with all the intensity and strength that is characteristic of the early urges of the baby. . . . Love and hate are struggling together in the baby's mind; and this struggle to a certain extent persists throughout life and is liable to become a source of danger in human relationships."[73] However, considered from a more abstract point of view, the paranoid-schizoid position as a whole is structured by the death drive. For Klein, the "predominance of destructive impulses . . . goes with the excessive weakness of the ego" that is characteristic of the paranoid-schizoid position.[74] In this way, Klein links the predominance of aggression or destructive impulses with the disintegration and fragmentation of objects (experienced as part-objects) and ego (experienced as in bits) in the paranoid-schizoid position.

This implies that even though the infant in the paranoid-schizoid position loves or is libidinally attached to their primary object, their starting point is one in which the death drive or aggression is ascendant.

By contrast, in the depressive position, love or the erotic drive is primary, in at least two senses. First, as I already indicated, it is the primary caregiver's love that enables the infant to move out of the paranoid-schizoid position and attain some measure of coherence and integration. Second, the ability to relate to the object as a whole object that has both good and bad, loved and hated parts, and to hold these features of the object together without resorting to splitting or other manic defenses is itself a manifestation of Eros. Klein explains the link between love and the capacity for ego integration that is the hallmark of the depressive position as follows: "If . . . the life instinct predominates, which implies an ascendancy of the capacity for love, the ego is relatively strong, and is more able to bear the anxiety arising from the death instinct and to counteract it."[75] In the Kleinian paradigm, ego integration is a hard-won and fragile achievement facilitated by Eros, understood as the drive to bind things together into ever greater unities.[76] However, as will become clearer in the next chapter, ego strength for Klein refers not to the capacity to master instinctual drives but to the ability to expand and enrich the ego by incorporating more and more unconscious content; as a result, ego integration is, for her, a necessarily incomplete and open-ended process.

Phantasy, or, Internal Objects

The concept of phantasy is central to Klein's conception of object relations and also to her unique conception of the interplay between intrapsychic and intersubjective dimensions of experience. Building upon the Freudian notion of psychic reality, Klein's account of phantasy—spelled with a "ph" in order to indicate that it is unconscious and thus distinct from our everyday conception of fantasy as daydreaming—presupposes that all of our relations with others, going all the way back to our early relationship with our primary objects, are necessarily and inescapably mediated and filtered through our internal object world in ways that are unconscious.

The most comprehensive discussion of Klein's conception of phantasy is found not in Klein's own work but in a paper written by her close collaborator Susan Isaacs.[77] Isaacs defines phantasy as "the mental corollary, the psychic representative, of instinct."[78] Careful readers will note that this definition mirrors Freud's early definition of a drive, from "Instincts and Their Vicissitudes," viz: "The psychical representative of the stimuli originating from within the organism and reaching the mind."[79] This might give the impression, contrary to my argument in the previous section, that Klein endorses an orthodox Freudian conception of drives after all. Focusing exclusively on this aspect of Isaacs's definition also gives the impression that phantasy is the psychical representative of a psychical representative of a bodily instinct—in which case the concept doesn't seem to be particularly helpful. However, as Isaacs develops her account of phantasy, it becomes clear that phantasy is distinct from drive and, at the same time, like the drives, phantasies are related to objects from the start.

A phantasy is a psychical representative of a drive, according to Isaacs, in the sense that it "represents the particular content of the urges or feelings (for example, wishes, fears, anxieties, triumphs, love or sorrow) dominating the mind at the moment."[80] In other words, phantasy refers to the specific shape, structure, and content taken by the drives in our unconscious experience. Isaacs offers several examples, drawn from Klein's account of psychic development. A child who is libidinally attached to his mother's breast—who is driven by love, we might say—"*experiences* this desire as a specific phantasy—'I want to suck the nipple.' If desire is very intense (perhaps on account of anxiety), he is likely to feel: 'I want to eat her all up.'"[81] By contrast, a child who is driven by aggression, perhaps as a result of frustration, might experience those aggressive impulses as a phantasy of biting the breast or tearing it into bits.[82] To be sure, the young infant isn't capable of expressing this phantasy verbally; phantasy, like Freud's notion of primary process, is distinct from the language of conscious thought. As Isaacs makes this point: "The primary phantasies, the representatives of the earliest impulses of desire and aggressiveness, are expressed in and dealt with by mental processes far removed from words and conscious relational thinking, and determined by the logic of emotion."[83] Indeed, on the Kleinian picture, "by the time a child can use words—even primitive words such as 'Baby o-o-oh'—he has already gone through a long and complicated history of psychic experience."[84] Under certain conditions (for example, in the context of an analysis), these phantasies may later become capable of being expressed verbally. And yet, in another sense, phantasy is "the 'language' of... primary instinctual impulses."⁸⁵ That is to say, phantasy gives the drives—understood as general and inchoate dispositions or modes of relating to objects lovingly or destructively—specific meaning, structure, shape, and texture.

If, as Klein assumes, there are drives operating from the beginning of life, then phantasies must also take shape from the beginning of life. Isaacs writes: "Phantasy enters into the earliest development of the ego in its relation to reality, and supports the testing of reality and the development of knowledge of the external world."⁸⁶ This means that Klein's account of the infantile experience should be understood as an account of the shape, structure, and content of our most basic phantasies. For example, Klein's good breast doesn't refer simply or straightforwardly to the body part that the infant encounters while feeding but to the crude phantasy of a part-object that arises out of the experience of having one's hunger satisfied. Of course, these phantasies are connected to embodied experience—the experience of having bodily hunger satiated (or not) and the breast or bottle as the physical source of that experience. As Isaacs puts it, "The earliest phantasies... spring from bodily impulses and are interwoven with bodily sensations and affects. They express primarily an internal and subjective reality, yet from the beginning they are bound up with an actual, however limited and narrow, experience of objective reality."⁸⁷ Yet phantasy is in no way reducible to bodily sensations. As Isaacs explains, bodily experiences and sensations are not so much the source of phantasies as their "material of expression."⁸⁸ Moreover, through the operation of phantasy, the infant imbues the breast, as Klein says, "with qualities going far beyond the actual nourishment it affords."⁸⁹

Phantasy stands in a complicated relationship to drives, as well as to the dynamics of introjection and projection that are so crucial to Klein's account of psychic development. Isaacs calls these dynamics "mental mechanisms," and she characterizes phantasy as "the operative link" between such mechanisms and the drives.⁹⁰ On the one hand, phantasies represent the meaningful content of drives that are understood as fundamentally directed toward objects; as such, phantasies are also necessarily "directed to objects of some kind."⁹¹ On the other hand, phantasies are bound up with the mechanisms of introjection and projection, which are psychic processes through which objects are either "taken into the self and become part of it" or "disowned and attributed to some person or group of persons, or some part of the external world."[92] The mechanism of introjection is closely related to—yet distinct from—the phantasy of incorporation; similarly, projection is bound up with phantasies of spitting out. Both are connected to drives. The phantasy of incorporation represents the erotic or libidinal drive and is correlated to the mechanism of introjection, by means of which external objects or part-objects are brought into and made part of the self; the phantasy of spitting out represents or gives content to the aggressive drive and is correlated to the mechanism of projection, by means of which parts of the self are split off or disowned and projected into some other person or persons. "Thus," Isaacs concludes, "*phantasy is the link between the id impulse and the ego mechanism*, the means by which the one is transmuted into the other. 'I want to eat that and therefore I have eaten it' is a phantasy which represents the id impulse in the psychic life; it is at the same time the subjective experiencing of the mechanism or function of introjection."[93]

The phrase "I want to eat that and therefore I have eaten it" reveals the omnipotent character of early phantasies. An early phantasy is omnipotent in the sense that it "tends to be felt as actually fulfilling itself, whether with an external or an internal object."[94] However, unlike the Freudian account, where infantile omnipotence is the flipside of primary narcissism, Isaacs's Kleinian account is somewhat more nuanced. Initially, infants are easily overwhelmed by the force of their own desires and impulses, to the extent that they seem to "fill the whole world at the time when they are felt. It is only slowly that he learns to distinguish between the wish and the deed, between external facts and his feelings about them."[95] In other words, although the young infant does not exist in a state of complete undifferentiation, they are easily overwhelmed by phantasy and must slowly and painfully learn to bring their phantasied, internal objects into closer alignment with the actual, external others on whom they are based.

With her account of the dynamics of projection and introjection, Klein can be seen as both expanding upon and at the same time transforming Freud's account of these processes. For Freud, projection and introjection are situated within his theory of primary narcissism. As he explains in "Instincts and Their Vicissitudes:"

> In so far as it is auto-erotic, the ego has no need of the external world, but.... it cannot avoid feeling internal instinctual stimuli for a time as

unpleasurable. Under the dominance of the pleasure principle a further development now takes place in the ego. In so far as the objects which are presented to it are sources of pleasure, it takes them into itself, 'introjects' them. . . . ; and, on the other hand, it expels whatever within itself becomes a cause of unpleasure (. . . the mechanism of projection).[96]

Klein's notion of the internal object is rooted in Freud's account. The internal object, for Klein, refers to a phantasied image of an object (or part-object) taken to be part of one's internal psychic world.[97] In this sense, Klein's phantasied internal object has a functional similarity to the Freudian notion of primary narcissism: it refers to the inner psychic reality that must slowly, over time, and through difficult and painful experiences, be brought more closely into alignment with the demands of external reality.[98] However, although Klein acknowledges that this gap can never fully be closed, as this would mean the elimination of unconscious phantasy, the Kleinian subject is nonetheless related to others and to external reality from the very start, inasmuch as Klein's internal objects are themselves phantasmatic representations of actually existing external objects.[99] Thus, the task of psychic development is not, as it is for Freud, that of establishing boundaries between self and other that will make genuine relations with other subjects and with external reality possible in the first place; it is the difficult work of sorting out to what extent one's internal phantasied representations coincide with the external objects on which they are based.[100]

On Klein's account, phantasy inevitably shapes and potentially distorts our perception of reality, and thus of the flesh and blood others with whom we interact, in fundamental and ultimately unsurpassable ways. That is to say, it is not possible to interact with others in a way that isn't filtered through our own phantasy life. However, as I've indicated, Klein believes that we can and should strive to bring our unconscious phantasy life, or our relation to our internal objects, more in line with the actual others on whom those internal objects are based—even as we must acknowledge that these two poles can never completely converge. Hanna Segal puts this point well: "From the moment of birth the infant has to deal with the impact of reality, starting with the experience of birth itself and proceeding to endless experiences of gratification and frustration of his desires. These reality experiences immediately influence and are influenced by unconscious phantasy. Phantasy is not merely an escape from reality, but a constant and unavoidable accompaniment of real experiences, constantly interacting with them."[101] Similarly, Hinshelwood aptly describes the attempt to "sort out the reality of external objects from their distortion by primitive unconscious phantasies" as "the task of a lifetime."[102]

The Intrapsychic and the Intersubjective, or, Klein and Critical Theory

We are now in a position to see how Klein brings together the intrapsychic and intersubjective aspects of experience in a fascinating and original (and perhaps for that very reason, often misunderstood) way. Although Klein was often faulted for ignoring or downplaying environmental factors in child development and for a related overemphasis on unconscious phantasy, internal objects, and psychic reality, as I read her, the intrapsychic and intersubjective dimensions of experience are in a constant and complicated interaction.[103] Moreover, it is her attention to the interplay between these two dimensions of experience that gives her understanding of intersubjectivity its richness, complexity, and ambivalence.

Precisely her originality on this point has led not only to frequent misunderstandings of Klein but also to criticisms from both the intersubjective and intrapsychic camps. More intersubjectively oriented critics such as Greenberg and Mitchell have characterized Klein as occupying a "transitional position within the history of psychoanalytic ideas" and have criticized her unique "position midway between the drive/structure tradition and her growing use of relational/structure assumptions and formulations" as untenable, even "ill-fated."[104] On their view, Klein's continued adherence to drive theory stands in the way of her developing a full-fledged object-relational view, rendering her theory internally inconsistent. By contrast, Lacanians tend to regard Klein's work as overly concerned with the actual environment, specifically with the type of mothering or parenting one receives as an infant, in ways that not only disregard intrapsychic forces but also seem to suggest that there's no hope for those who have been inadequately parented as young children.[105] This may result from reading Klein through the lens of other members of the object relations tradition—thinkers like D. W. Winnicott, Ronald Fairbairn, and Michael Balint—in ways that fail to appreciate that tradition's departures from her work. In contrast to both of these readings, I'm inclined to agree with Meira Likierman, who understands Klein's work "not as a transitional and incomplete version of an object relations model, but rather, as a genuine theoretical alternative that, while drawing on Freudian drive theory on the one hand, and object relations thinking on the other, fashions a unique view of the psyche."[106]

My previous discussions of Klein's conception of the drives, her commitment to the primacy of the death drive, and the importance of phantasy and internal objects to her account should be sufficient to dispel the Lacanian worry that Klein is overly concerned with environmental factors. But they may do so at the risk of heightening the criticism launched from the relational side, that she disregards such factors altogether. This criticism has been raised powerfully by Jessica Benjamin. Although she finds Klein's account of intrapsychic experience—specifically her discussion of splitting in the paranoid-schizoid position—tremendously productive, Benjamin nevertheless contends that Kleinian theory does not "fully confront the subject with the outside other, with anything external to its own projections and identifications."[107] On Benjamin's reading of Kleinian theory, "if the self can contain the tension between the positions of being good and bad, between envy and reparation, the relation to the 'whole object' will follow. Alterity is not in itself formulated as a problem."[108] In other words, Klein overemphasizes the intrapsychic and ignores the intersubjective dimension.

As astute readers of Klein such as Hinshelwood, Likierman, Michael Rustin, and Hanna Segal have pointed out, however, the claim that Klein views the subject as trapped in its own projections and identifications and ignores external, environmental factors is a distortion of her actual view.[109] That this is the case can be seen by returning to Klein's understanding of the term "object." For Klein, "object" refers not only to the object of the drive, but also to a specific object relation—namely, the relation between infant and primary caregiver. As she puts it, "My use of the term 'object-relations' is based on my contention that the infant has from the beginning of post-natal life a relation to the mother (though focusing primarily on her breast) which is imbued with the fundamental elements of an object-relation, i.e., love, hatred, phantasies, anxieties, and defences."[110] Moreover,

Klein emphasizes that this primary object relation is not *merely* a phantasied or hallucinatory relationship to an internal object, and, moreover, that this is precisely what constitutes her break with Freud's hypothesis of primary narcissism. She writes: "from birth onwards, a relation to objects, primarily the mother (her breast) is present. This hypothesis contradicts Freud's concept of auto-erotic and narcissistic stages which preclude an object relation."[111] Thus, although our relationship to external objects (including, perhaps most especially, the primary object) is necessarily structured by and filtered through our intrapsychic phantasies and projections, it remains a relationship (however mediated) to an external object. At the risk of pointing out the obvious, without an *actual* "breast"—that is to say, without a person who provides or withholds milk, nourishment, love, and gratification—there could be no infantile phantasy of a good or bad breast.

Given the centrality of her conception of the relation between drive and object, then, Klein at least implicitly recognizes the importance of environmental factors throughout her work. Moreover, as I discussed previously, certain kinds of environmental experiences also play key roles in her account of psychic development. Foremost among these is her claim that the move to the depressive position is enabled by the infant's receiving consistent love and care from their primary caregiver. Klein acknowledges repeatedly that the love and responsiveness of the primary caregiver enables the infant to internalize the good object and begin the transition to the depressive position. For example, in one important discussion of the transition to the depressive position, Klein maintains that, "among other factors, gratification by the external good object again and again helps to break through these schizoid states," and she further clarifies in a footnote that "the mother's love and understanding of the infant" constitutes such gratification.[112]

Similarly, Klein famously maintained that the superego (the quintessential internal object) is often much crueler and more aggressive than the external objects (the parental figures) on which it is based. Although this keen insight into the superego—one of the few features of Klein's work to have been taken up explicitly by Freud—emphasizes the disconnect between external and internal objects in a way that once again gives primacy to the internal, it also goes hand in hand with Klein's claim that overcoming this disconnect, to the extent that this is possible, is a primary aim of working through the depressive position.[113] For Klein, the integration of the ego enhances perception of both internal and external objects and thus facilitates the synthesis of internal psychic reality with external reality.[114] That is, an important aim of working through the depressive position is to bring one's internal and external objects into closer alignment. This is not to say, however, that the gap between internal and external objects can ever fully be closed. To believe that it could be closed would be to claim (utterly implausibly, from the Kleinian psychoanalytic point of view) that unconscious phantasy can be wholly eliminated from psychic life.

The lingering perception that Klein neglects environmental factors and relationships to external others may stem in part from her analytic technique, which focused almost exclusively on analyzing the transference and paid correspondingly little heed to environmental factors. But note that adopting a technique that concentrates on analyzing the transference and thus on the patient's psychic reality is not in any way incompatible with the belief that external or environmental factors can have an important, sometimes devastating, impact on psychic development. It reflects, rather, the belief that those environmental factors are inevitably filtered through the lens of unconscious phantasy, and that the aim of psychoanalysis is to transform this inner world as a means of transforming the analysand's relationships with others and with external reality. Something like this picture is implicit in Phyllis Grosskurth's description of Klein's analytic technique:

> The analyst represents not only actual people, past and present, but internalized objects which from infancy have contributed to the foundation of his superego. The analyst must be on guard to ensure that there is a constant interaction between reality and phantasy so that the distinction does not become blurred. Moreover, in the transference situation, the figures always belong to *specific* situations, and only by perceiving these situations can the analysand understand the nature and content of the transferred feelings.[115]

In other words, in the transference, the analyst represents *both* the external objects on which the analysand's internal objects are based and their role in specific situations that mark the analysand's psychic development *and* the internalized objects that populate the analysand's psychic reality. And the aim of the analysis is to allow for constant interaction between reality and phantasy while ultimately preserving the distinction between the two.

Segal captures this interplay between phantasy and reality quite well when she insists that, for Klein, while unconscious phantasy constantly and inevitably filters and even distorts our perception of reality, reality in turn "is experienced, incorporated, and exerts a very strong influence" on unconscious phantasy.[116] Therefore, it seems too strong to say that Klein denies the role of environment and the relation to external others in psychic development. What she does deny—and this may be the nub of the issue—is that aggression and persecutory anxiety are caused by a bad environment. In fact, this is perhaps her most substantial disagreement with Winnicott, for whom, as Jan Abram explains, "the failure of the environment is absolutely at the root of all psychopathology."[117] On this point, Klein and the rest of the object relations tradition may well diverge.[118] Once again, however, I maintain that this is not a bug but a feature of Klein's view, not only because it enables her to give a fuller and deeper account of the pervasiveness and intractability of aggression in human psychological and social life, but also because it actually rescues her from the problematic tendency to suggest that all psychopathology is the result of bad parenting (typically, mothering). Undoubtedly, failures in primary caregiving can and very often do have impacts on individual psychological and emotional development—and the more significant the failures, the more devastating those impacts may be. From this it does not follow that all psychopathology is the result of parental failures. To insist that it does is not only to make a rather basic logical error but also to (unfortunately and perhaps unwittingly) court the stereotype that the whole point of psychoanalytic treatment is to blame your mother for all of your problems. To the extent that Klein breaks with the Winnicottian view that all psychopathology is rooted in failures of the environment, then, I would say: it's a good thing, too.

Thus, for Klein, although the infant is object-related from the start and although the drives themselves are understood relationally, as dispositions or tendencies to interact with others lovingly or destructively, we can never experience an external other except through the lens of our own phantasies, anxieties, and projections. This is how I understand her claim that "love and hatred, phantasies, anxieties, and defences" are "*ab initio* indivisibly linked with object-relations."[119] This is true for the infant, for whom "every external experience is interwoven with his phantasies and on the other hand every phantasy contains elements of actual experience,"[120] but it is equally true for the adult.[121] On the Kleinian view, intersubjectivity is basic to subjectivity, but it is also always entangled with intrapsychic phantasy and projection. In this way, Klein allows us to view subjectivity as socially and intersubjectively constituted while emphasizing that these dimensions of experience are inevitably mediated through (intrapsychic) unconscious phantasy and therefore, ultimately, through the drives (because phantasy is what gives content, structure, and meaning to inchoate drives). This makes Klein's account of intersubjectivity much more complex and ambivalent than other social and intersubjective accounts of the self that reject the notion of the drives and view the self as intersubjectively constituted all the way down. Although Klein believes that we can and should strive to bring our internal objects more closely in line with the external objects (that is, the actual other people) on which they are based, her account of phantasy entails that this gap can never fully be closed.

We are now in a position to see how Klein's distinctive relational conception of drives and her related account of the interplay between intersubjective and intrapsychic forces offers a distinctive contribution to critical theory. For those who may be inclined to think that critical theory was right to leave psychoanalytic drive theory behind, the basic worry is that drive theory commits us to the assumption of an innate, biologically determined, and deterministic antisociality at the core of human nature. Such an assumption is thought to be incompatible with one of the core methodological commitments of critical social theory: that human beings are socially, culturally, and linguistically constituted in specific historical contexts. However, as I see it, the distinct advantage of Kleinian drive theory is that it does not commit us to a problematic assumption of a biologically determined antisociality. Rather, on the Kleinian account as I have reconstructed it, aggression and destructiveness are relational passions—constitutive tendencies to relate to others in certain ways, modes of sociality itself rather than innate antisocial tendencies. Moreover, as I have argued, Klein's account of the drives is not biologically reductionist. Kleinian drives are psychological and relational forces that express themselves through the body. Given the fundamentally relational nature of drives for Klein, her account can be connected to a more historicized understanding of how inherently inchoate, amorphous, and unstructured drives can be shaped in very different ways by different social and cultural circumstances, even though Klein herself admittedly does not develop her work in this direction. Hence, accepting a Kleinian conception of drives need not commit one to the ahistorical view that drives express themselves in the same ways in all societies, that aggression and destructiveness are somehow culturally or socially invariant, or even that they are always bad.

Thus, Kleinian drive theory is compatible with critical theory's basic methodological commitment to understanding subjectivity in social or intersubjective terms. Not only that, Klein's emphasis on both the complex interplay between reality and phantasy, between the intersubjective and the intrapsychic dimensions of human experience, offers critical theorists a realistic conception that understands persons as fundamentally social beings who are torn between two different and conflicting modes of sociality, between our drive to connect with others and our urge to destroy those connections (and perhaps to destroy those others, even if only in phantasy). Klein avoids the temptation to offer an overly optimistic, prosocial conception of the person that flattens out the ambivalence inherent in human sociality while at the same time avoiding the opposite temptation to interpret the intrapsychic operation of the drives in a way that undermines the very possibility of intersubjectivity. By theorizing the balance between intersubjective and intrapsychic elements in which neither aspect is reducible to the other, Klein represents a midpoint between two extremes. At the same time, her work beautifully highlights what Jessica Benjamin calls the "double-sidedness of the relation to the other"—that is, the fact that we are always at the same time relating to both the outside other and the other within.[122]

❊ ❊ ❊

By retaining the primacy of aggression or the death drive, Klein gives full weight to the persistence and intractability of aggression in human social life. As such, her account of the person is realistic in the relevant sense. However, by reconceptualizing the drives as fundamentally and necessarily directed towards objects, and thus as predispositions to relate to others lovingly or destructively, Klein articulates her realistic conception of the person in relational terms. Moreover, she understands object relations as necessarily mediated and filtered through the lens of unconscious phantasy, thus preserving the richness, complexity, and ambivalence that is often missing from intersubjectivist accounts that dispense with the language of drives. In this way, her model allows critical theorists to preserve the explosive content of drive theory within the methodological constraints of critical theory.

As I've noted throughout this chapter, psychological maturity for Klein consists in the ability to relate to whole objects. This requires the subject to integrate its good and bad experiences of the object, to overcome the tendency to split the object into idealized and demonized parts, and to withstand that ambivalence that results from the realization that the loved and hated object are one and the same. This, in turn, corresponds to what Klein refers to as both the strengthening and the integration of the ego: the transformation from an inchoate, disorganized ego that experiences itself as in bits to an ego that is in some sense whole.

Klein's emphasis on ego integration and ego strength as the goals of psychic development and of analysis might give rise to the worry that her theory serves to prop up the ego's narcissism and thereby feeds into problematic fantasies of psychic wholeness to which psychoanalysis should be opposed. Lacan gives voice to this type of worry when he contends that the goal of analysis for the object relations school is "to make it well-rounded, this ego, to give it the spherical shape in which it will have definitively integrated all its disjointed fragmentary states, its scattered limbs, its pregenital phases, its partial drives, the pandemonium of its egos, countless and broken up as they are. A race to the triumphant ego."[123] The triumph of the ego, for Lacan, means strengthening the defenses against the discourse of the unconscious—precisely the opposite of what psychoanalysis should aim to achieve. But what precisely does Klein mean by "ego integration," and does her understanding of this term have the problematic implications of narcissism, defense against the unconscious, and fantasies of wholeness that Lacan attributes to the object relations position? This will be the focus of the next chapter, where I will also situate Klein's account of ego integration in relationship to the work of the early Frankfurt School.

2

A System of Scars

The Problem of Ego Integration

In his 1995 book, *Perversion and Utopia*, Joel Whitebook outlines what he calls "the problem of the ego" in Freud, a problem that stems from a deep tension, if not outright contradiction, in Freud's work.[1] This tension is captured in the stark contrast between two of Freud's best-known claims. On the one hand, there is Freud's dictum "Where id was, there ego shall be"; on the other hand, his oft-cited contention that "*the ego is not the master in its own house.*"[2] The first statement supports a reading of Freud as a staunch defender of classical Enlightenment values such as rationality, autonomy, secular science, and progress. On this reading, which dovetails with the ego psychology school of psychoanalysis that rose to prominence in the mid-twentieth century in the United States, the goal of psychoanalysis is to strengthen the ego in its ongoing battle to master the instinctual impulses of the id. The second statement, by contrast, supports a mirror image reading of Freud as trenchant critic of the Enlightenment, whose theory of the unconscious undermines our faith in reason and autonomy by revealing the ego to be a narcissistic, imaginary construction that rests on fantasies of wholeness and mastery. On this broadly speaking Lacanian view, the aim of psychoanalysis is to engage in the discourse of the unconscious, and for this the ego must be dismantled rather than strengthened.

(How) can these two Freudian conceptions of the ego be reconciled? Whitebook maintains that if we are to do justice to the complexity of Freud's vision, we cannot simply jettison one strand while championing the other.[3]

The challenge is to figure out how they might fit together. For Whitebook, the answer lies in the fact that the realization that the ego is not the master of its own house prompts a decentration and humbling of the ego that is crucial for the curbing of infantile omnipotence—and thus for the ego's own process of enlightenment.[4] Hence, the choice between strengthening or dismantling the dominating ego is a false one; the task, instead, is to envision a decentered, humbled, and finite yet still coherent ego capable of rationality and autonomy.

Whitebook finds the outlines of such a conception of the ego in Freud's late work *Inhibitions, Symptoms, and Anxiety*. There, Freud writes:

> To return to the problem of the ego. The apparent contradiction is due to our having taken abstractions too rigidly and attended exclusively now to the one side and now to the other of what is in fact a complicated state of affairs. We were justified, I think, in dividing the ego from the id, for there are certain considerations which necessitate that step. On the other hand the ego is identical with the id, and is merely a specially differentiated part of it. If we think of this part by itself in contradistinction to the whole, or if a real split has occurred between the two, the weakness of the ego becomes apparent. But if the ego remains bound up with the id and indistinguishable from it, then it displays its strength.[5]

In this passage, Freud suggests a potential solution to the problem of the ego: the apparent contradiction between his claims about the ego's weakness relative to the id and his aspirations for its strength and mastery can be resolved when we understand ego weakness as a function of a dissociation or split between ego and id and ego strength, correspondingly, as a function of the merger or association between the two.[6] Along these lines, Freud understands repression here as the ego's refusal to associate itself with certain instinctual impulses; this refusal requires a great deal of the ego's energy to maintain and generates symptoms that emerge at the site of the split-off impulses.[7] On this revised picture, Whitebook contends, the aim of psychoanalysis is not ego's domination of id impulses but rather the achievement of an "expanded unity" of the ego through a process of "undoing repressions" that enables "'free intercourse' with the split-off foreign material."[8] As Whitebook explains, "The ego does not most effectively establish 'mastery' over the id, as is often assumed, by dissociating itself from and suppressing the id's instinctual material. On the contrary, it achieves this end and enriches itself at the same time and to the same extent by establishing 'free intercourse' with that material."[9] According to this reading, Freud offers here a new conception of ego strength that provides a way out of the problem of the ego, though this is a relatively underdeveloped aspect of his work that many of his readers have failed to appreciate.[10]

In this chapter, I contend that Klein's account of ego strength and integration should be understood not in terms of the triumph of the narcissistic ego against the discourse of the unconscious, but along the lines that Whitebook has traced: as a function of its expansion and enrichment through the ongoing incorporation of previously split-off unconscious content. To the extent that this is the case, Klein's account of ego strength can escape the sharp critique of the ego articulated not only by Lacan but also by Adorno. Moreover, Klein's account provides important resources for critical theorists looking to move beyond the distinctively Adornian version of the problem of the ego. Although Lacan and Adorno both criticize the ego for its rigidity, its narcissistic and paranoid structure, and its implication in what Adorno calls the domination of inner nature, Adorno, unlike Lacan, clings steadfastly to the standpoint of the ego on the grounds that it is necessary for the formation of autonomy and thus for critical resistance to fascism and authoritarianism.[11] This generates a perhaps intentionally unresolved paradox at the heart of Adorno's conception of the ego, one that seems to leave us stuck embracing an authoritarian, narcissistic ego (and the nuclear family structures that are allegedly necessary for its development) in order to preserve the possibility of critique.

Klein helps us to envision a way out of this paradox, by providing a model of psychic integration that corresponds with Adorno's fleeting and suggestive but underdeveloped remarks on the possibility of genuine reconciliation and the structure of nonreified cognition.[12] As Peter Dews has emphasized, Adorno's critique of the ego was deeply historically indexed; he viewed the compulsive, coercive mode of ego integration to have been necessary at a certain stage of history, as part of human being's attempt to liberate themselves from the fearsome power of nature. "Accordingly," Dews continues, "the 'spell of selfhood' cannot be seen simply as an extension of natural coercion; rather, it is an illusion which could, in principle, be reflectively broken through by the subject which it generates—although the full realization of this process would be inseparable from a transformation of social relations."[13] Klein's conception of ego integration, I contend, provides a model of what subjectivity might look like once it has broken through the spell of the coercive, compulsive, dominating mode of ego identity. Hers is a model not of the dissolution of the ego, but rather of what Dews calls a "true identity" that "would be permeable to its own non-identical moment."[14] The Kleinian integrated ego is, to borrow Adorno's evocative description, "a system of scars which are integrated only under suffering, and never completely."[15]

In order to make this case, I will begin by reviewing the paradoxes that emerge as a function of Adorno's critique of the ego. Although I defend Adorno against what I call the paradox of self-defeat, I argue that there is a residual paradox of authoritarianism in his work. Following Jessica Benjamin, I contend that the way out of this paradox is through intersubjectivity; however, in order to avoid the challenges raised in Adorno's critique of revisionist psychoanalysis, intersubjectivity must be understood in Kleinian terms. Klein combines her complex and ambivalent conception of intersubjectivity with a noncoercive, nondominating, and open-ended conception of ego integration. This conception not only avoids Adorno's critique of the ego—it also resonates powerfully with his fleeting references to the character of nonreified cognition, nonidentity thinking, and genuine reconciliation.

Paradoxes of the Ego (in Adorno)

The idea that the rational ego is a coercive, narcissistic, paranoid, and dominating structure is a prominent theme in Adorno's critical theory, closely linked to his reading of Freudian psychoanalysis. This theme emerges perhaps most clearly in the *Dialectic of Enlightenment*, where Adorno and Horkheimer mobilize Nietzschean and Freudian insights to produce a damning critique of the formation of modern, bourgeois subjectivity through the domination of inner nature.[16] Drawing on Freud's critique of civilization as founded on the renunciation of instinctual drives and his account of the ego as the psychic agency tasked with bringing the id to heel under its rational mastery, Adorno and Horkheimer transform this structural account into a historical one, generating a searing indictment of bourgeois society's entanglement with domination. Their understanding of the relationship between the formation of rational, bourgeois subjectivity and the domination of inner nature is summed up in one of the most famous and striking passages from *Dialectic of Enlightenment*: "Humanity had to inflict terrible injuries on itself before the self—the identical, purpose-directed, masculine character of human beings—was created, and something of this process is repeated in every childhood. The effort to hold itself together attends the ego at all its stages, and the temptation to be rid of the ego has always gone hand-in-hand with the blind determination to preserve it."[17] In other words, the ego is held together through violence, through an injurious relation to inner nature.

Adorno and Horkheimer's psychoanalytically inspired critique of the ego culminates in one of the central theses of the text: "The history of civilization is the history of the introversion of sacrifice—in other words, the history of renunciation."[18] Adorno and Horkheimer exemplify this thesis through their interpretation of Odysseus—whom they anachronistically describe as the "prototype of the bourgeois individual"—insofar as he must continually sacrifice parts or aspects of himself in order to save himself.[19] Although many examples from Homer's *Odyssey* are offered in support of this claim, the familiar story of Odysseus's encounter with Polyphemus illustrates this logic particularly well. As Adorno and Horkheimer tell it, the key to Odysseus's escape from Polyphemus's cave is that, when the Cyclops asks his name, Odysseus cleverly replies, "Nobody." Although his escape is also a function of his cunning, Adorno and Horkheimer read this utterance as an act of linguistic self-sacrifice on Odysseus's part. As they put it, "He declares allegiance to himself by disowning himself as Nobody; he saves his life by making himself disappear."[20] The lesson that Adorno and Horkheimer draw from this story is that Odysseus's "self-assertion, as in the entire epic, as in all civilization, is self-repudiation."[21]

Later, in *Negative Dialectics*, Adorno extends this critique of the ego into a critique of Kantian morality, which, for him, is predicated on absolutizing "the solid identically maintained authority" of the ego as "the necessary premise of morality."[22] Freudian psychoanalysis reveals what Kant did not yet realize: "The empirical genesis of what, unanalyzed, was glorified by him as timelessly intelligible."[23] This is true not only for the superego, which is empirically rooted in "blindly, unconsciously internalized social coercion,"[24] but also for the ego, which, Adorno contends, "is not something immediate. The ego itself is mediated. It has arisen from psychoanalytic termini: it has branched off from the diffuse energy of the libido."[25] Although Kant acknowledges the heteronomous and compulsive nature of conscience (the superego), arguing for its dissolution in practical reason, he does not acknowledge the extent to which the "unreflected rule of reason, the ego's rule over the id, is identical with the repressive principle."[26]

However, as Whitebook has argued, this way of taking up the Freudian account of the ego generates serious problems for Adorno's account. Specifically, Whitebook identifies two paradoxes that emerge in Adorno's critique of the ego. The first, which I will call the paradox of self-defeat, arises from the fact that Adorno and Horkheimer "equate the autocratic ego with the ego as such. For them the integration of the self is inherently violent."[27] This means, according to Whitebook, that Adorno and Horkheimer are stuck claiming that not only the process of ego formation but also, by extension, the very project of enlightenment itself is "self-defeating" in the sense that "it systematically eliminates the possibility of achieving its own goal."[28] As a result, they implicitly undermine the possibility of finding a way out of the dialectic of enlightenment and are left longing for an impossible and unimaginable utopia.[29] On Whitebook's reading, their radical critique of the ego is at least partly responsible for generating the theoretical impasse that leads Adorno and Horkheimer into political quietism and conservatism.[30]

The source of this problem, as Whitebook sees it, is that Adorno and Horkheimer understand the ego as a primarily defensive structure tasked with the maintenance of boundaries, the control of the instinctual impulses emanating from the id, and the enforcement of rationality. But to take this as an account of the ego per se is, as Whitebook notes, to equate "a pathological mode of ego formation, namely, the obsessional, with the ego as such."[31] By identifying this pathological mode of ego formation with the ego as such, Adorno and Horkheimer fail to avail themselves of the resources afforded by the alternative conception of psychic integration found in Freud's late work, according to which ego strength is a function not of repression and mastery of instinctual nature but rather of greater openness to and incorporation of unconscious content (inner nature).

Whitebook contends that Adorno's aesthetic theory offers readers some glimpses of what a nonreified form of synthesis or relation to the world might look like. In his aesthetic theory, Adorno sketches a "*logic that might* govern the integration of a nonreified society in the future, where whole and part, universal and particular, would be held together in a different way."³² This logic is based on the kind of "'nonviolent togetherness of the manifold' he [Adorno] thought he perceived in advanced works of art."³³ And yet Adorno never fully developed a corresponding model of psychic integration; had he done so, he might have been able to imagine a way out of the dialectic of enlightenment. On Whitebook's reading, however, Adorno couldn't take this step because he "*identified the obsessional ego with the ego as such.*"³⁴ This assumption prevented him "from considering less coercive forms of ego integration that could become the basis for possible forms of postconventional identity."³⁵

Moreover, the corollary of this conception of the compulsive and coercive character of the rational ego is an understanding of freedom as the dissolution of the ego. Adorno and Horkheimer seem to endorse such a conception in the *Dialectic of Enlightenment*, for example, when they claim that "the fear of losing the self and suspending with it the boundary between oneself and other life, the aversion to death and destruction, is twinned with a promise of joy that has threatened civilization at every moment."³⁶ But the dissolution of the ego is typically a transient state, one that can be experienced in moments of ecstasy or intoxication; as such, it cannot be an ongoing alternative to the coerciveness of the ego. Thus, according to Whitebook, although Adorno illuminates clearly the stark choice between rigid, coercive, yet rational unity and freedom that comes at the cost of dissolution, he is unable to move beyond this diagnosis. He leaves us stuck with a problematic choice between the "rigidly integrated ego of conventional identity and the Dionysian dissolution of the self."³⁷ Moreover, for Whitebook, it is Adorno's "assumption that the unity of the self must necessarily be coercive" that "prevents him from appropriating his own insights."³⁸

However, Whitebook's claim that Adorno and Horkheimer view ego integration as *inherently* violent and coercive is questionable. Unlike Whitebook, I read *Dialectic of Enlightenment* as telling a more historically contingent story about the development of enlightenment and related notions such as bourgeois rationality or subjectivity. Although it is true that the text posits an essential tension between enlightenment rationality in the broad sense and power relations understood as the control or domination of inner and outer nature, and it aims at illuminating this conceptual aporia, it also insists that the particular unfolding of this entanglement that has led to the barbarism and totalitarianism of the twentieth century must be understood as historically contingent. In other words, it is a mistake, I think, to read *Dialectic of Enlightenment* as offering a negative philosophy of history. Although the concept of bourgeois enlightenment subjectivity is, in a broad sense, entangled with the domination of inner nature, the particular forms that this takes in modern capitalist societies are contingent. Recognizing this point is essential for understanding the sense in which *Dialectic of Enlightenment* aims to hold up a mirror to enlightenment in order to enable it to disentangle itself from blind domination.[39] If this way of reading the text is compelling, then it follows that the target of Adorno and Horkheimer's critique is not the ego or the self per se, but the form of ego integration required under bourgeois capitalism. This, in turn, suggests that the point is not to celebrate the Dionysian dissolution of the ego but rather *to criticize the type of society in which such dissolution comes to look like freedom*. Indeed, Adorno suggests as much in the following passage from *Negative Dialectics*: "If the role, the heteronomy prescribed by autonomy, is the latest objective form of an unhappy consciousness, there is, conversely, no happiness except where the self is not itself. Historically, the subject has fought its way out of a state of dissociation and ambiguity, and if the immense pressure that weighs upon it hurls the self back into that state—into schizophrenia—the subject's dissolution presents at the same time the ephemeral and condemned picture of a possible subject."[40] In other words, a conception of autonomy predicated upon the domination of inner nature and an account of heteronomy understood as the dissolution of the self are mirror images of each other, and both are objective forms of an unhappy consciousness. The dissolution of the subject is thus not a genuine realization of freedom but rather an "ephemeral and condemned" state.

Thus, Adorno and Horkheimer's critique of the ego is not, as Whitebook fears, necessarily self-defeating. To be sure, they do not offer a fully developed alternative account of a less violent, nondominating mode of subject-formation or ego integration. As Whitebook himself notes, however, important glimpses of such an account can be found scattered throughout Adorno's work. I will return to these issues later in the chapter and argue that Adorno's account of nonreified subjectivity can be productively extended by drawing on Kleinian insights. For now, let me turn to the second paradox of the ego that emerges in Adorno's work: the paradox of authoritarianism. This paradox emerges as a result of the historical dimension of Adorno and Horkheimer's critique of the ego—that is, it is a function of the very feature of their view that rescues them from the paradox of self-defeat. To state the problem simply: even if one emphasizes the historical dimension of their critique of the ego, it is still the case that they view the autonomous, rational ego as *both* a structure of internalized domination *and* a necessary condition for resistance to fascism and authoritarianism.[41]

Jessica Benjamin articulates this paradox beautifully in her classic article, "The End of Internalization": "At the center of critical theory's analysis of modern capitalism is a paradox about the nature of resistance to domination. Those aspects of consciousness where this resistance might be located—critical reason, individuation, integrity and ultimately resistance itself—are tied to the process of internalizing authority. As a result, the rejection of authority can only take place through its prior acceptance."[42] In other words, however historically indexed their critique of the (bourgeois, rational, paranoid, narcissistic) ego may be, Adorno and Horkheimer regard this specific structure of internalized domination as necessary for both individual autonomy and genuine resistance to modern capitalism. Thus, they see great danger in the emergence of new, postliberal forms of capitalism and mass society where authority is increasingly exercised directly over individuals, rather than being mediated through processes of psychic internalization that take shape within the context of the bourgeois family. In this postliberal, mass society context, possibilities for critique and resistance are increasingly foreclosed. As Benjamin puts it: "In the face of this situation the critical theorists look backward to the form of instinctual control which was the basis for ego development and reason in the past—individual internalization—and argue that only it contained a potential for the formation of a critique of domination."[43]

Lars Rensmann has demonstrated that Adorno and Horkheimer's claim about ego weakness in mass society was crucial to their analysis of anti-Semitism and of the authoritarian personality.[44] As more direct and unmediated forms of individual domination emerge in postliberal societies, the result is a decrease in individual autonomy and a corresponding increase in social conformity. This sets the stage for their diagnosis of the authoritarian personality, a Weberian ideal type of modern subjectivity that is particularly prone to endorsing fascism, racism, and modern anti-Semitism.[45]

Rensmann contends that the "essential link" among the various elements of the authoritarian personality—conventionalism, submissiveness to authority, aggression, coldness, love of power, cynicism, tendency to stereotypical thinking and projection, and fixation on sexuality—is the weakness of the ego in postliberal subjectivity.[46] Ego weakness renders the individual incapable of mastering internal conflict, including, most notably, the demands of the superego. Under such conditions, individuals are more likely to externalize their conscience in the form of blind submission to an authoritarian leader.

A full discussion of the theoretical and methodological complexities of the authoritarian personality study is beyond the scope of this discussion.[47] Fortunately the basic conceptual outlines of the paradox of authoritarianism are visible in other Adornian texts, including his well-known essay "Freudian Theory and the Pattern of Fascist Propaganda." There, Adorno argues that ego weakness is the psychological structure that underlies and makes fascist propaganda effective. Indeed, he maintains that the distinctive problem of the current historical moment—the essay was written in 1951—is "the decline of the individual and his subsequent weakness."[48] The main question of this essay is what transforms otherwise rational individuals into a mass who will support aims that are incompatible with their own rational self-interest. On Adorno's analysis, fascism is authoritarian in its structure; therefore, individuals undergo the regression that transforms them into a mass because of their willingness to submit to authority. This means, in turn, that fascism rests on and exploits authoritarian personality structures. Fascism exploits the tendency to ego weakness by directly manipulating and controlling the unconscious: "For, while psychology always denotes some bondage of the individual, it also presupposes freedom in the sense of a certain self-sufficiency and autonomy of the individual."[49]

Adorno's engagement with psychoanalysis, then, seems to lead to a paradox after all. Although it can be rescued from the paradox of self-defeat, Adorno's critique of the ego does seem starkly at odds with his lament for the ego weakness that results from the decline of the bourgeois individual. (How) do these two aspects of Adorno's conception of the ego fit together? Is the dominating, coercive, rational ego a necessary evil, the price that must be paid for defending civilization against the regressive dangers of fascism?[50] To be sure, one could double down here and defend Adorno by pointing out that he is simply calling our attention to one of the contradictions of our own society. This, after all, is what he sees as the job of the critical theorist, given that we live in a thoroughly antagonistic society, a society that "is not a society *with* contradictions or *despite* its contradictions, but *by virtue of* its contradictions."[51] It is the deeply antagonistic, contradictory nature of our society that gives rise to the need for a negative dialectics, a dialectics not of identity but of nonidentity, a dialectics that, rather than culminating in a higher order synthesis, strives to articulate the unreconciled state of our concepts and our social reality.[52] Following this line of thinking, perhaps Adorno would say that the whole point is to articulate without resolving the contradictory, antagonistic tendencies in contemporary societies because only on this basis is genuine critique possible.

Still, this response seems to leave Adorno in the uncomfortable position of claiming that we can only be against fascism in our politics by being for what Foucault would later refer to as the fascism in our heads.[53] From a feminist perspective, it also leaves him in the regrettable position of lamenting the decline of the patriarchal bourgeois family, at least to the extent that this family structure and its concomitant Oedipal drama is thought to be necessary for the process of socialization to autonomy.[54] Moreover, as Adorno himself says in another context about a different paradox, "it would be an intellectual defeatism to leave the impasse as it is."[55]

The challenge posed by the paradox of authoritarianism is this: How can we envision an account of psychic integration that is not only noncoercive and nondominating but that also allows for the possibility of resistance, autonomy, and critique? If such a possibility could be envisioned, then we would not be stuck celebrating an authoritarian mode of ego integration—and the patriarchal family structures on which it is based—in order to salvage the possibility of autonomy. Benjamin suggests that the key is to take a route not envisioned by early critical theory (but certainly well explored by subsequent generations): intersubjectivity. She asks: Could "the possibility of resisting authority . . . not be grounded in that aspect of the subject which once accepted authority, but instead in that aspect which seeks mutuality? Could not the potential for emancipation be grounded in an intersubjective theory of personality, rather than an individual psychology of internalization?"[56] This is not to deny Adorno and Horkheimer's diagnostic claim about the dangers of the more direct forms of domination that have emerged with the rise of the culture industry; it is simply to suggest that critical theorists need not throw their lot in with bourgeois subjectivity in order to preserve the possibility of resistance to such dangers. We might instead turn to intersubjectivity as a resource for rethinking autonomy. Still, this strategy raises a further problem: if we are not to run afoul of Adorno's warning about false forms of reconciliation that obscure existing social antagonisms, we will have to avoid the facile turn to intersubjectivity that Adorno criticized so devastatingly in his discussion of revisionist psychoanalysis. In the following sections, I argue that Klein offers an intersubjective psychoanalytic perspective that avoids Adorno's critique of revisionism and provides us with a model of ego integration that is noncoercive, nondominating, and open-ended.[57]

Adorno's Critique of Revisionism

Revisionist psychoanalysis was Adorno's term for the post-Freudian school of psychoanalysis that rejected Freud's theory of the drives and emphasized the importance of social and cultural environment on individuals.[58] Given Klein's embrace of drive theory in general and the death drive in particular, it might seem obvious that her view is not vulnerable to this critique. However, it is worth recalling the main points of Adorno's critique of the revisionists, because doing so will bring some further attractive features of her view into focus.

Adorno's critique turns on his complex and dialectical understanding of the relationship between individual and society and, relatedly, between psychology and sociology. For Adorno, the methodological and intellectual split between the disciplines of psychology and sociology both reflects the real antagonism between the individual and society in contemporary capitalism and, at the same time, blocks our ability to understand it. Thus, he claims that "the separation of society and psyche is false consciousness" inasmuch as it "perpetuates conceptually the split between the living subject and the objectivity that governs the subjects and yet derives from them," but "false consciousness is also true"[59] inasmuch as—as a matter of fact under bourgeois capitalism—"inner and outer life are torn apart."[60] The split between individual and society is thus both true, insofar as it is reflective of social reality, and false, insofar as it perpetuates and justifies the social antagonism that it expresses. For Adorno, reflecting on this antagonism by bringing the insights of psychology (specifically psychoanalysis) and sociology together is crucially important, but this does not mean integrating the two perspectives into a seamless whole. For Adorno, the integration of sociology and psychology is "an expression of helplessness, not progress. There is more hope that concentration on the particular isolate will break through its monadic crust to disclose the universal mediation at its core than that the conceptual synthesis of real decomposition could actually stop the rot. The only totality the student of society can presume to know is the antagonistic whole, and if he is to attain to totality at all, then only in and through contradiction."[61] In other words, we stand to gain more by concentrating on one side of the diremption between individual and society, on what Adorno calls "the particular isolate"; such an approach is more likely to yield insight into "the universal mediation" at the core of such phenomena.

The general thesis of Adorno's critique of revisionist psychoanalysis is, then, that it represents a false and problematic way of relating psychology to sociology, one that denies and obscures rather than articulating and illuminating the fundamental antagonism between individual and society. Revisionism is thus a "sociologization of psychoanalysis" that emphasizes social, cultural, and environmental influences on the psyche "at the expense of hidden mechanisms of the unconscious."[62] As such it is too superficial to provide critical insights into society.

Adorno defends this thesis in a variety of ways. On a methodological level, he argues that the revisionists' rejection of drive theory commits them to an excessively rationalistic account of the psyche that "sever[s] the ego from its genetic relationship to the id" and that "amounts to a negation of [Freud's] theory."[63] Relatedly, revisionists downplay or overlook the role of trauma and damage in Freud's account of the psyche and, more generally, seem uninterested in the impact of the individual's past on their present character or personality. For Adorno, this approach obscures the fact that "a totality of the character, assumed by the revisionists as given, is an ideal which would be realized only in a non-traumatic society.... The totality of the so-called 'character' is fictitious: one could almost call it a system of scars, which are integrated only under suffering, and never completely."[64] Indeed, Adorno contends that the revisionists are committed to "a harmonious belief in the unity of a person, which is impossible in the existing society, perhaps is not even desirable at all."[65] By eliminating castration—the primordial traumatic experience, for Freud, and one that, according to Lacan, splits the subject in a way that permanently undoes the possibility of psychic unity, totality, or harmony—from psychoanalysis, the revisionists have in fact castrated psychoanalysis, rendering it unable to illuminate contemporary social reality.[66]

Furthermore, by failing to acknowledge the diremption between society and individual, the revisionists are led—perhaps unintentionally—to a position of naïve optimism, social conformism, and conventional morality.[67] Unlike Freud, whose thinking about morality was fundamentally antagonistic—marked by "on the one side, psychological-genetic dissolution of the moralistic ideas, through reduction to the origin of the superego and the neurotic guilt feelings; on the other side, the abstract proclamation of moral values untouched by the psychological insights"—the revisionists simply side uncritically with existing societal morality.[68] Misunderstanding the source of the conflict between individual and society, revisionism expresses a "sympathy for adaptation" to contemporary society.[69] In so doing, revisionism betrays the best insights of Freud, who, although he did not "proceed from sociological categories," nevertheless "understood the pressure of the society on the individual in its concrete forms."[70] Ironically, although revisionism was motivated in part by a reaction against Freudian orthodoxy and authoritarianism, revisionist psychoanalysis is, because of its conformist tendencies, friendlier to authoritarianism and repression than Freudian thought was.[71] Whereas Freud's work emphasizes the divide between individual and society and thus the painful and traumatic nature of adaptation to reality, revisionism, by contrast, "wants to overcome this negativity by treating the inhumane relationships as if they were already human."[72]

Finally, Adorno attacks the revisionists' turn to love as an antidote to Freud's authoritarian coldness. Their emphasis on love as an analytic tool overlooks the possibility that Freud "makes himself so austere in order to break the petrified conditions."[73] Adorno continues: "The possibility of change is not promoted by the falsehood that after all, we are all brothers but only by dealing with the existing antagonisms. Freud's coldness, which expels every fictitious immediacy between doctor and patient, and openly admits the professionally mediated nature of the therapy, does more honor to the idea of humanity by unrelentingly eliminating its appearance than comforting consolation and warmth of command do."[74] With their emphasis on "comforting consolation and warmth," revisionists seek to deny a more ambivalent experience of love, one that "necessarily contains the admixture of despair."[75] For Adorno, this is the only kind of love possible under current social conditions; the revisionists overlook the possibility that perhaps "Freud's misanthropy is nothing else than hopeless love and the only expression of hope which still remains."[76] However misanthropic it may be, Freud's hopeless love expresses hope by reflecting something true about the existing diremption between individual and society.

Indeed, Adorno contends that Freud's greatness as a thinker lies precisely in his willingness to leave such contradictions unresolved and to scorn "the pretended systematic harmony where things in themselves are torn asunder."[77] In so doing, Freud "makes the antagonistic character of social reality apparent" and "reveals something of objective unreason."[78] The revisionists, by contrast, smooth over the contradictions of Freudian theory: "In their hands, Freudian theory turns into another means which assimilates psychological movements to the social status quo."[79] For them "society and the individual, adaptation to the all-powerful reality and happiness coincide."[80] By replacing Freud's emphasis on the conflictual and ambivalent drives with an account of social, cultural, and environmental influences on individual psychology, the revisionists turn a blind eye to the antagonistic relation between individual and society and endorse conformity and adaptation to the status quo as the goals of analysis. Ironically, in their attempt to do justice to the relationship between social and cultural forces and individual psychology, the revisionists deprive themselves of the resources that could enable them to illuminate this relationship. By contrast, "rigorous psychoanalytic theory, alive to the clash of psychic forces, can better drive home the objective character especially of economic laws as against subjective impulses, than theories which, in order at all costs to establish a continuum between society and psyche, deny the fundamental axiom of analytic theory, the conflict between id and ego."[81] Psychoanalysis captures the historical truth of contemporary society—even if it doesn't understand this *as* a historical truth—only when it focuses on the individual psyche and its internal conflicts.

How does Kleinian psychoanalysis fare in the light of Adorno's critique of revisionism? First of all, as should be clear from my discussion in the previous chapter, although Klein is not inattentive to the impact of environmental factors on individual development, and although she recasts Freud's theory of the drives in a relational mode, she remains a drive theorist. Given her commitments to primary aggression, to the fundamental ambivalence of the drives, and to the ineliminable nature of unconscious phantasy, Klein's theory is very much an id psychology, not an ego psychology. As Fred Alford puts this point, Klein's drive theory "connects her work to that part of Freud's that the Frankfurt School found so valuable: the demanding, not readily civilized nature of the drives."[82] In this respect, Alford continues, Klein avoids the "'neo-Freudian revisionism' the Frankfurt School so carefully sought to avoid."[83]

Moreover, because of her distinctive psychological and relational conception of the drives—according to which drives are modes of relating to others either destructively or lovingly—Klein avoids the problems that Adorno diagnoses in neo-Freudian revisionism without resorting to a problematically reductionist biologistic conception of the drives. As Whitebook notes, given their worries about the facile, Whiggish progressivism of revisionist psychoanalysis, Adorno and Horkheimer favored a biologistic interpretation of classical Freudian drive theory. In light of her commitment to primary aggression, Klein preserves what Whitebook calls the "the moment of essential non-identity between individual and society," but she does so without rooting this moment in an "inassimilable biological core of the individual."[84] Klein thus provides a third alternative, beyond the biologistic articulation of drive theory and the revisionist alternative: a psychoanalytic theory that emphasizes antagonism, nonidentity, and ambivalence without relying on a reductive biologism about drives.

But what about the charge of social conformism? Does Klein's emphasis on the integration of the personality render her conception of psychoanalysis problematically conformist? To be sure, Klein emphasizes the reality principle and the importance of bringing one's internal objects into closer alignment with external reality; in that sense, Klein endorses the idea that psychoanalysis aims toward some sort of adaptation to reality. However, as I argued in the previous chapter, Klein also believes that because of the ineliminable role of unconscious phantasy in structuring and filtering our relationships with others, the gap between our internal and external objects can never be fully closed. Thus, complete integration of individual psychic reality and external social or environmental situations is, on her view, in principle impossible.

Finally, given the crucial role of love in Klein's theory, particularly in explaining the move to the depressive position, does she not fall prey to Adorno's critique of the revisionists' emphasis on love? On this point, it is worth noting that Adorno seems primarily concerned with the revisionists' focus on love in the context of analytic treatment. And it is true that analysis of the transference is central to Klein's conception of analytic technique. A primary goal of analysis, for Klein, is to enable the analysand to more securely establish her internal good object, which in turn helps to facilitate further integration.[85] In some sense, this requires the analyst to *be* the good object for the analysand. This means that for Klein, the analyst's job is to supply love, support, and nourishment so that the analysand can more securely internalize the good object and draw on it for the integration, expansion, and enrichment of the ego.

Although this might make it seem as if the Kleinian analyst offers unconditional affirmation to the analysand—the kind of "comforting consolation and warmth" that Adorno mocks as unable to coldly and austerely stand up to the contradictory and antagonistic nature of existing social relations—in fact, nothing could be further from the truth. For Klein, if the analyst occupies the role of the good object, the analogue for the milk that the analyst/good breast provides isn't affirmation, consolation, or warmth but rather *interpretations*. As Klein states: "As in infancy, repeated happy experiences of being fed and loved are instrumental in establishing securely the good object, so during an analysis repeated experiences of the effectiveness and truth of interpretations given lead to the analyst—and retrospectively the primal object—being built up as good figures."[86] In other words, the analyst's task, for Klein, is to give the analysand good, nourishing interpretations—even if (and perhaps even especially when) doing so requires telling the analysand something they do not want to hear. Moreover, Klein's account of analytic transference is, like her account of love more generally, highly ambivalent. As she explains in her account of envy, the analysand frequently not only rejects a good interpretation, but then goes further and expresses hostility toward the analyst. Klein understands this as an instance of wanting to spoil the milk from the good breast, and, by extension, of wanting to spoil the analyst as a good object precisely because it is good.[87] Both love and analytic transference are, for Klein, deeply marked by ambivalence and as such contain a significant "admixture of despair."

In sum, despite her emphasis on intersubjectivity, Klein's commitments to drive theory, primary aggression, and ambivalence render her conception fundamentally distinct from that of the revisionists. Moreover, her thoroughly relational conception of the drives provides a way of preserving the negative, antagonistic moment that Adorno found so crucial in drive theory without resorting to a reductive biologism.

Klein on Ego Integration

This brings me to Klein's account of ego integration, which, I contend, not only avoids Adorno's critique of the ego but also provides a way out of the paradox of authoritarianism in which Adorno remains mired, one that corresponds to his own fleeting sketches of a nonreified relationship between subject and object. This might seem like a strange suggestion; after all, Adorno tended to be extremely critical of any and all talk of integration.[88] On his view, integration is closely aligned with identity thinking: the subsumptive logic by means of which concrete particularity and difference are swallowed up by concepts is a logic of integration. The centrality of this theme to his critical theory and his deep-seated opposition to this logic are both evident from the fact that he frequently referred to his own philosophical method of negative dialectics as a logic of *dis*integration.[89] For him, the logic of integration is characteristic of both modern philosophy—in particular of the idealist tradition of Kant and Hegel—and of capitalist modernity. The integrative logic of modern capitalism is a central theme in Adorno and Horkheimer's critique of the culture industry, which, they claim, destroys spontaneity and difference, enforces sameness and uniformity, and absorbs consumers into the universal by positioning them as fungible, replaceable stereotypes.[90] In so doing, the culture industry directly imprints the power of bourgeois capitalism onto individuals.[91] For Adorno and Horkheimer, "the miracle of integration, the permanent benevolence of those in command, who admit the unresisting subject while he chokes down his unruliness—all this signifies fascism."[92] This logic of integration that is characteristic of modern, bourgeois capitalism culminates in the violence of the Holocaust. As Adorno puts the point with characteristic bluntness: "Genocide is the absolute integration."[93]

It therefore makes sense that Adorno was sharply critical of psychoanalytic approaches that focus on integration. For him, to say that the goal of psychoanalysis was the achievement of a well-integrated psyche was to suggest that the subject should reconcile itself to a world that is riven by internal conflict and contradiction. Such integration constitutes, for Adorno, "a false reconciliation with an unreconciled world."[94] Moreover, for Adorno, ego integration and ego strength ultimately converge, since, in the context of bourgeois capitalism, the well-integrated ego is one that has successfully mastered its internal conflicts, brought its instinctual nature to heel.

In light of this, Klein's frequent references to ego strength and ego integration as the goals of analysis might seem to rule out in advance any sort of rapprochement between Klein and Adorno. Indeed, Klein goes so far as to claim that integration is at the core of her conception of psychoanalysis when she restates Freud's famous dictum "Where id was there ego shall be" as follows: "The ultimate aim of psycho-analysis is the integration of the patient's personality."[95] Although this might at first glance suggest adherence to a problematic account of ego integration predicated upon the internalization of domination, once we understand correctly what Klein means by the integration of the self that is called for in this passage, we will see that her account actually coheres with Adorno's remarkably well. Indeed, Klein provides a productive model of the psyche that corresponds to Adorno's fragmentary and incomplete gestures toward a vision of nonreified cognition.

As I discussed in the previous chapter, Klein maintains that there is a rudimentary and relatively incoherent ego in place from the beginning of life, and that it is this ego that engages in early object relations. To review briefly: initially, object relations are organized in the paranoid-schizoid position. In this position, the ego "largely lacks cohesion, and a tendency towards integration alternates with a tendency towards disintegration, a falling into bits."[96] This corresponds to a high degree of persecutory anxiety, a fear that the rudimentary ego will be annihilated, and to a corresponding tendency to split objects into good/loving and bad/persecutory as a defense against that anxiety. The move from the paranoid-schizoid position—in which the psyche experiences both itself and its objects as split, fragmented, and partial—to the depressive position is facilitated by the introjection of the good breast, which "counteracts the processes of splitting and dispersal, makes for cohesiveness and integration, and is instrumental in building up the ego."[97] The key moment in the transition to the depressive position is when the infant recognizes the mother, who has up to now been split into good and bad part-objects (i.e., good and bad breasts), as a whole object. This move represents a more integrated mode of experience, whereby the infant realizes that the bad, persecutory breast that they have attacked and destroyed in phantasy is one and the same as the loving, nourishing good breast that they both love and depend upon, but it also gives rise to depressive anxiety, rooted in the fear of the annihilation of the loved object.

As the infant moves into the depressive position, they experience both their objects and themselves in a more integrated way—indeed, developing the capacity for integration is one of the defining features of the depressive position. As Klein puts it: "I see the formation of the ego as an entity to be largely determined by the alternation between splitting and repression on the one hand, and integration in relation to objects on the other."[98]

But what precisely does integration mean for Klein? Consider the following passage:

> With the introjection of the complete object in about the second quarter of the first year marked steps in integration are made. This implies important changes in the relation to objects. The loved and hated aspects of the mother are no longer felt to be so widely separated, and the result is an increased fear of loss, states akin to mourning and a strong feeling of guilt, because the aggressive impulses are felt to be directed against the loved object. The depressive position has come to the fore. The very experience of depressive feelings in turn has the effect of further integrating the ego, because it makes for an increased understanding of psychic reality and better perception of the external world, as well as for a greater synthesis between inner and external situations.[99]

As this passage makes clear, integration, for Klein, has nothing to do with a (false) conception of reconciliation whereby the fundamental antagonism between hate and love is overcome. Indeed, Klein maintains that ambivalence is *heightened* by the experience of integration. The processes of integration and synthesis that are hallmarks of the depressive position, according to Klein, "cause the conflict between love and hatred to come out in full force.... Ambivalence is now experienced predominantly towards a complete object. Love and hatred have come much closer together and the 'good' and 'bad' breast, 'good' and 'bad' mother, cannot be kept as widely separated as in the earlier stage."[100] Thus, integration signals, for Klein, not the reconciliation or overcoming of ambivalence but rather a mode of experience in which the psyche can withstand the fundamental ambivalence of its relationship to its primary object without resorting to the splitting and internal fragmentation that are the hallmarks of the paranoid-schizoid position.

Moreover, as I have discussed in more detail previously, the internal integration of the ego goes hand in hand with a greater synthesis or integration of the ego's internal psychic reality with its objective social reality. In other words, the integration of the ego also entails the difficult, ongoing, and never-ending process of bringing one's internal and external objects, the intrapsychic and intersubjective dimensions of experience, into closer alignment, while acknowledging that, given the fundamental and ineliminable role of phantasy is our psychic life, the gap between these two can never fully be closed.[101] Ego integration, for Klein, thus entails the twofold realization that "the loved object is at the same time the hated one," and that "the real objects and the imaginary figures, both external and internal, are bound up with each other."[102]

Accordingly, the goal of ego integration informs Klein's conception of the aims of psychoanalysis. As she puts it:

> In analysis we should make our way slowly and gradually towards the painful insight into the divisions in the patient's self. This means that the destructive sides are again and again split off and regained, until greater integration comes about. As a result, the feeling of responsibility becomes stronger, and guilt and depression are more fully experienced. When this happens, the ego is strengthened, omnipotence of destructive impulses is diminished ... and the capacity for love and gratitude, stifled in the course of splitting processes, is released.... By helping the patient to achieve a better integration of his self, [analysis] aims at a mitigation of hatred by love.[103]

From this passage, it is clear that ego strength and ego integration are more or less interchangeable terms for Klein. However, this connection reveals that ego strength for Klein has nothing to do with establishing rational mastery or the dominance of inner nature; rather, it simply refers to enhancing the ego's capacities for integration.

This passage also indicates some of the complicated and multivalent connections between ego integration and love. In some sense, love is a condition for the possibility of the capacity for integration, insofar as the experience of love and support from one's primary caregiver enables the infant's move into the depressive position. The various splitting mechanisms characteristic of the paranoid-schizoid position, Klein explains, "result in the feeling that the ego is in bits. This feeling amounts to a state of disintegration. In normal development, the states of disintegration which the infant experiences are transitory. Among other factors, gratification by the external good object again and again helps to break through these schizoid states."[104] Moreover, the transition to the depressive position represents the ascendancy of love over hate, insofar as Klein understands aggression as a destructive force that disintegrates and fragments both ego and its objects and love, by contrast, as an integrative force, as the drive to bind things together into greater unities.[105] Finally, in the depressive position and in the analytic situation, love and the drive for reparation emerge as countervailing forces that can help to mitigate the destructive effects of primary aggression.

The emphasis on love indicates that Klein's is an essentially expansive conception of the ego where integrating and strengthening the ego means augmenting or enriching the personality in a way that doesn't eliminate but rather embraces both ambivalence and difference. Because love is understood—in line with the late Freudian conception of Eros—as the capacity to bind things together in ever greater unities, this is an open-ended and incomplete process. Thus, as I discuss in more detail in the next chapter, just as the depressive position can never be fully worked through and left behind, there can be no such thing for Klein as complete integration of the ego. Whatever lies "beyond" the depressive position is just the continual working through of the initially overwhelming experience of depressive anxiety and the ongoing enhancement of one's abilities to manage ambivalence without resorting to splitting and other manic defenses. Increasing trust in one's capacity to love and in one's reparative abilities to mitigate one's own destructiveness help to further the experience of integration,[106] as does more securely establishing one's internal good object, whether through the process of emotional maturation or through the work of analysis.[107] But none of this brings the process of integration to a close.

With this picture in place, we can return to the Lacanian and Adornian critique of the ego, outlined earlier. Does Klein's conception of ego integration present a whole, well-rounded ego that definitively integrates all of its fragmented states, thus racing to the "triumphant ego," as Lacan claims in his critique of object relations theory?[108] Is she committed to a coercive and rigid conception of ego integration, predicated on the domination of inner nature? Is the Kleinian ego narcissistic and paranoid, locked in the self-enclosed identity of its own projections, unable to relate to the object on its own terms? I think the answer to all of these questions is no, for the following reasons.

First, as I have just argued, Klein views both love and integration as fundamentally open-ended processes that are by definition incomplete and ongoing. As Klein puts the point: "Complete and permanent integration is in my view never possible. For under strain from external or internal sources, even well integrated people may be driven to stronger splitting processes, even though this may be a passing phase."[109] Even for the best-integrated ego, there is always the tendency to fall back into splitting and fragmentation, especially under times of stress. Hence there is no triumph of the ego, no possibility of a complete and definitive integration of all of the ego's fragmented states, no achievement of closure or wholeness.

Second, and relatedly, as I discussed in the previous chapter, Klein regards primary aggression as ineliminable. Thus, aggression constitutes an ever-present force that perpetually threatens us with falling back into splitting and fragmentation and that must be mitigated in an ongoing way through our capacities for love and reparation. Because primary aggression is ineliminable, there can be no ultimate reconciliation of ambivalence; the best we can hope for is to develop the capacities that enable us to better manage ambivalence.

Third, Klein's account of subject formation turns not only on integration but also on *loss*. The depressive position is, after all, *depressive*, melancholic. It emerges in response to an experience of loss—specifically, the loss of the idealized good object. For Klein, the idealization of the object is a defense against persecutory anxiety.[110] Insofar as moving to the depressive position entails overcoming splitting and experiencing the object as a whole object, as both good and bad at the same time, it also entails the loss of idealization. In other words, moving to the depressive position requires giving up the phantasy of the idealized, all-powerful, and all-nourishing good breast (and its evil twin, the phantasy of the demonized, all-powerful, persecutory bad breast) and accepting the ambiguity and complexity of one's primary object and the ambivalence of one's relationship to it. Thus, the depressive position is predicated not only on the fear of having destroyed the good object with one's destructive attacks, but also on the actual loss of the idealized good object. Klein's distinction between manic and genuine forms of reparation is instructive here.[111] In manic reparation, the subject attempts to put the lost or shattered object back together and pretend that it never attacked or destroyed the object in the first place—pretends, in other words, to make the object and, by extension, itself *whole*. Genuine reparation, by contrast, involves accepting the loss of the idealized good object and the harm that one has done to the object in phantasy and in reality and *containing* all the resulting ambivalence, complexity, and ambiguity. For Klein, the illusion that the ego can triumphantly integrate all of its fragmented states is a form of manic defense against the melancholic structure of the ego.

Finally, Klein regards the integration of the ego as crucial to the move *out* of the paranoid-schizoid position, in which the psyche is caught up in its own projections and overwhelmed by phantasy and psychic reality. Although, as I argued in the previous chapter, Klein understands subjects as from the very beginning engaged in object relations, she also contends that in the paranoid-schizoid mode we are less in contact with the actual external others on whom our internal objects are based. So there is an image of a narcissistic and paranoid ego in Klein, but for her this is the relatively rudimentary and incoherent ego of the paranoid-schizoid position. The paranoid-schizoid ego mirrors Adorno's account of the ego in the grips of identity thinking, an image that Peter Dews describes evocatively as "the pathos of a self helplessly confined within the circle of its own immanence, unable to make contact with anything external which does not turn out to be simply its own reflection."[112] However, for Klein this self-enclosed, narcissistic ego is a relatively immature position that is mitigated, if never finally overcome, through the ongoing work of ego integration. Although, as I have emphasized repeatedly, Klein insists that the gap between our intrapsychic phantasied representations of our objects and the actual external others on which those representations are based can never fully be closed—because to do so would be to eliminate unconscious phantasy altogether—it can be narrowed, and to do so is precisely to come closer to relating to the object on its own terms.

Ego integration, for Klein, is an ongoing, incomplete process of incorporating more and more unconscious content into a richer, more internally differentiated, and more expansive ego that can tolerate the ambivalence that results from the duality of the drives and can mitigate the distortions of phantasy in its object relations. When Klein cites Freud's dictum "Where id was there ego shall be," for her this means not that the ego rests on the repression of the id or the domination of inner nature, but that the ego continually expands outward, enriching itself by incorporating more and more previously split-off unconscious contents and engaging less narcissistically with others. When Klein says that the ultimate aim of psychoanalysis is the integration of the analysand's personality, this is not to be achieved by strengthening the ego at the expense of the unconscious—in that way, Klein's work is diametrically opposed to the ego psychology tradition—but rather through the ego's sympathetic, open-ended, and nondominating receptivity of otherness. Given Klein's emphasis on the melancholic structure of the depressive ego and her critique of manic reparation, her account of ego integration could be described using Adorno's evocative words as "a system of scars, which are integrated only under suffering, and never completely."[113]

Kleinian Psychoanalysis and Adornian Negative Dialectics

Adorno was fond of paraphrasing a fragment from Epicharmus, which he rendered as follows: "Mortals must think mortal thoughts, not immortal ones."[114] This fragment, for Adorno, "contains within itself something like the critique of the traditional identity claim."[115] In other words, to acknowledge the mortality and finitude of the subject is tantamount to acknowledging its own limitations, including its inability to subsume all objects under its concepts. However, on the dialectical flipside, it is only by thinking mortal thoughts that immortal ones may be grasped. By recognizing its own finitude and mortality, philosophy is capable of becoming infinite in a specific sense: not in the sense that it is "wholly in possession of its objects,"[116] but rather in the sense that it is "fundamentally open."[117] In this way, philosophy is like the work of art; both are capable of crystallizing an infinite truth within a finite form. Because of this connection, the analysis of the work of art stands as prototype for cognition in general, and thus for philosophy (understood as cognition of reality).[118]

As I discussed earlier, Adorno never spells out in any detail what a non-reified form of subjectivity or psychic integration—one that would correspond to his account of the possibilities of genuine reconciliation between subject and object exemplified by the advanced work of art—might look like. However, he does occasionally offer glimpses of such an account—for example, in his essay "On Subject and Object." There, Adorno argues, in line with his earlier critique of the ego, that the relationship between subject and object is one of domination. However, he is also quick to insist that this subject-object structure is the result of historically specific processes of coercion and domination and as such should not be hypostasized. As he puts it: "The separation of subject and object is both real and semblance. True, because in the realm of cognition it lends expression to the real separation, the rivenness of the human condition, the result of a coercive historical process; untrue, because the historical separation must not be hypostatized, not magically transformed into an invariant."[119] Indeed, Adorno claims that the hypostasization of the separation between subject and object is responsible for reproducing the structure by means of which subject dominates and coerces object. When the separation between subject and object is rendered invariant rather than historically specific, he explains, "mind then arrogates to itself the status of being absolutely independent—which it is not: mind's claim to independence announces its claim to domination. Once radically separated from the object, subject reduces the object to itself; subject swallows object, forgetting how much it is object itself."[120]

In other words, the separation and opposition between subject and object is both true because it reflects an existing, historically produced structure of domination and, at the same time, false because the assumption that this separation is absolute and historically invariant reinforces the subject's claim to independence and thus to domination. Imagining itself as wholly independent, the subject subsumes the object into itself, reducing it to the structures of its own cognition or experience and conjuring away its own status as object, including its inner nature. However, the solution to this separation and hypostasization of the relationship between subject and object is not to posit a state of primordial unity or fusion between subject and object. As Adorno puts it, "The image of a temporal or extratemporal original state of blissful identity between subject and object is romantic, however: at times a wishful projection, today just a lie."[121] And it is in this context that Adorno offers a hint as to what a different form of subjectivity—one that was not predicated on the domination of objects (whether internal or external)—might look like: "Were speculation concerning the state of reconciliation allowed, then it would be impossible to conceive that state as either the undifferentiated unity of subject and object or their hostile antithesis: rather it would be the communication of what is differentiated . . . Peace is the state of differentiation without domination, with the differentiated participating in each other."[122] Here we see a brief sketch of what a nonreified logic of psychic integration might look like for Adorno, in which subject and object are distinct and differentiated but able to communicate and participate in one another in a peaceful, nondominating way.

If the problem is that the radical separation of subject from object leads to the subject's swallowing of the object, reducing the object to itself, the solution, for Adorno, lies in the infamous primacy (or priority or preponderance) of the object. This means that there is an irreducible asymmetry between subject and object; although objects can and do exist independently of subjects, subjects cannot exist independently of their status as object, which includes both their bodily nature and their rootedness in society. Hence, Adorno contends that "no matter how subject is defined, the existent being cannot be conjured away from it,"[123] and that there should be "no ego-consciousness without society, just as no society is beyond its individuals."[124] As Whitebook helpfully insists, Adorno's doctrine of the preponderance of the object is not a return to naïve realism; to say that the object possesses priority or independence vis-à-vis the subject is not to commit oneself to the claim that we can have *unmediated* access to the object. There is, for Adorno, no possibility of accessing a pure unmediated first nature.[125] But nor does this validate the idealist position, because, as Whitebook puts it, "consciousness or language which (transcendentally) constitutes the object, is itself (empirically) constituted by the object and cannot exist independently of it."[126] Unlike identity thinking, which attempts to resolve the aporias of the subject-object split by subsuming the object within the subject, "dialectical thinking," Whitebook explains, "tries to expand the circle to meet the object."[127] Or, as Adorno puts the point, "the subject's nonidentity without sacrifice would be utopian."[128]

Although this brief sketch of an alternative, nondominating model of subjectivity is suggestive, it is admittedly very underdeveloped. Moreover, as Jessica Benjamin has argued, to the extent that it remains on the terrain of the subject-object relation, this model does not offer critical theory a compelling account of intersubjectivity.[129] In light of this concern, the turn to Klein to supplement and extend Adorno's sketch of nonreified cognition is especially helpful, precisely because, as I argued in the previous chapter, Klein's account of subject-object relations is at the same time an account of intersubjectivity inasmuch as the primary object is, for her, another person.

Moreover, building on my argument in the previous section, Klein's conception of the integrated ego—the ego in the depressive position—is not only *not* implicated in Adorno's critique of identity thinking; it also corresponds in interesting ways to Adorno's scattered remarks about nonreified cognition. Whereas Klein's paranoid-schizoid position corresponds to the problematic, coercive, compulsive, narcissistic ego that is the target of Adorno's critique, the ego in Klein's depressive position is above identity, in the sense that the fundamental ambivalence of the drives is retained without any subsumption or reconciliation of one by the other, and also above contradiction, in the sense that the splitting characteristic of the paranoid-schizoid position has been, at least momentarily, overcome.[130] The depressive ego is able to contain diverse and contradictory drives in a coherent way without either subsuming these drives under the rational mastery of the ego or splitting them into clashing poles.

In this way, we might say that Klein's account of reparation corresponds to Adorno's notion of genuine reconciliation. In contrast to the false harmony or reconciliation that is achieved through the denial of the deeply antagonistic character of the drives or their subsumption under the mastery of the rational ego, Klein's vision of the depressive ego's ability to withstand the ineliminable ambivalence between hate and love corresponds to Adorno's description of negative dialectics as the *non*identity of identity and nonidentity. Her emphasis on ambivalence—indeed, I would argue that Klein is second only to Freud as the preeminent thinker of ambivalence in the psychoanalytic tradition—coheres with Adorno's focus on social antagonisms and contradictions. Like Adornian negative dialectics, Klein's model of ego integration avoids the tyranny of identity thinking, which seeks to merge identity and nonidentity into a higher order of identity (or unity). And yet she offers a distinctive and compelling vision of genuine reconciliation: an account of integration that focuses on preserving and gathering together in a nonviolent, nondominating, even loving way the nonidentity of identity and nonidentity—that is, of subject and objects (both internal *and* external).

Klein's emphasis on unconscious phantasy and her complicated account of the relationship between the intersubjective and intrapsychic aspects of experience also corresponds in interesting ways to Adorno's claim about the preponderance or priority of the object, while simultaneously extending this claim to the realm of relationships with others. For Adorno, identity thinking—the phantasy that objects can be completely subsumed under concepts with no remainder—is connected to the subject's forgetting of its own objective nature, including its drives. Klein's work, by contrast, highlights the ineliminable role of the drives and of their psychic correlate, unconscious phantasy. Her account thus does justice to what Adorno regards as the irreducibly objective, "natural" element of human experience: the drives. At the same time, Klein acknowledges that even if the gap between our internal and external objects can never fully be closed, to bring them into better alignment is tantamount to reducing the degree of paranoid projection in our relations with others and thus coming closer to doing justice to them by relating to them on their own terms. Her insistence that we can never fully close the gap between ourselves and our objects could be read as an analogue to Adorno's insistence on the priority or preponderance of the object; there is, for both Klein and Adorno, always an ineffable aspect of the object that cannot be reduced to my subjective experience of it. In Kleinian terms, we might say that all of our experiences of others are mediated and filtered through the lens of intrapsychic phantasy, but there is something of the object that exceeds this subjective dimension of our experience. Intrapsychic phantasy cannot be eliminated—there is no unmediated access to the object, no form of intersubjectivity that is not filtered through the lens of phantasy—but neither can our object relations be reduced to intrapsychic phantasy. The gap between the intrapsychic and the intersubjective can never be fully closed in either direction.

C. Fred Alford has made a similar argument relating Klein to Adorno, though with some differences that are significant and, I think, instructive. Alford connects Klein to Adorno through their aesthetics, contending that Klein, like Adorno, regards art as an expression of "the desire to restore a shattered whole."[131] For Alford, this view of art resonates with Adorno's, for whom "the wholeness and unity to be remembered in the work of art are the wholeness, unity, and integrity of the object itself. In art, and perhaps in art alone, can this wholeness be grasped, because art is less conceptual than philosophy: art lets the object be (mimesis), it reveals the object in its totality, rather than seeking to understand and control it by forcing it into fixed categories."[132] In this way, Alford claims, "Adorno's view comes closer to Kleinian aesthetics, in which art expresses concern for the integrity of the object, an object destroyed by greed and aggression."[133]

However, Alford goes on to fault Klein with stressing "the achievement of wholeness, restoration, unity, and completeness. . . . to such an extent that the idea of art telling us the truth about a broken, fragmented reality, except by complete contrast, tends to be lost."[134] This reading downplays the importance of ambivalence in Klein's view of reparation and the related central role of destructiveness and ugliness in Kleinian aesthetics. Hanna Segal gets much closer to the truth of Klein's view of art when she writes:

> A satisfactory work of art is achieved by a realization and sublimation of the depressive position. . . . But to realize and symbolically express depression the artist must acknowledge the death instinct, both in its aggressive and self-destructive aspects, and accept the reality of death for the object and the self. . . . Restated in terms of instincts, ugliness—destruction—is the expression of the death instinct; beauty—the desire to unite into rhythms and wholes—is that of the life instinct. The achievement of the artist is in giving the fullest expression to the conflict and the union between the two.[135]

In other words, the work of art for Klein may express some sort of unity or integration, but this is an internally broken, fractured, and conflictual unity: to use Adorno's language once again, it is a "system of scars, . . . integrated . . .

under suffering, and never completely." Moreover, the suggestion that Klein's vision emphasizes wholeness, unity, and completeness only makes sense if one overlooks or seriously downplays Klein's critique of manic reparation, which clearly suggests that a complete restoration of wholeness is not only impossible but also a manic illusion. Indeed, given Klein's rejection of primary narcissism, there is no preexisting wholeness to be restored; there is only ambivalence all the way down.

This interpretive disagreement aside, I find Alford's Kleinian inspired conception of what he calls "reparative reason"—a conception that he links to Adorno's aesthetic account of nonreified cognition—to be quite productive. Alford defines reparative reason as a mode of reason that "is sensitive to the complexities and nuances of objects, rather than forcing them into rigid, prefabricated categories."[136] Alford reads reparative reason as an alternative to instrumental reason, which, in Kleinian terms, appears as a paranoid-schizoid mode of relating to objects of knowledge. But, unlike Adorno and Horkheimer, who mostly rest content with their searing critique of instrumental reason, Klein envisions an alternative. As Alford puts it: "Whereas paranoid-schizoid (instrumental) reason sees its objects in terms of the categories of prediction, manipulation, and control, reparative reason experiences its objects as they are mediated by a richer, more creative set of phantasies, phantasies concerned with precisely what Adorno wished art to concern itself with: assisting the object to become itself. This, ultimately, is what reparation is about."[137] To this I would add that Klein's account of reparative reason goes together with a rich and complicated account of intersubjectivity, one that understands the subject in fundamentally relational terms while at the same time avoiding the temptation to flatten out intersubjectivity by draining our relations with others of the negativity of primary aggression and the resulting ambivalence and complexity.

※ ※ ※

Reimagining reason in a reparative mode means that we need not bite the bullet and accept the bourgeois model of rationality and its compulsive conception of ego integration on the grounds that doing so is necessary for preserving the possibility of critical resistance to fascism. For Klein, ego integration refers not to the domination of inner, instinctual nature, but instead to the expansion and enrichment of the ego through the incorporation of more unconscious content. For Klein, there is no race to the triumphant ego, as Lacan alleges, nor is the ego ever definitively integrated. Rather, ego integration is a never-ending process, founded upon loss, in which ambivalence is not overcome but rather withstood and ongoingly worked through. In this way, the Kleinian ego resembles Adorno's evocative image of a system of scars, integrated through suffering, and never completely.

At the same time, as a result of her emphasis on the death drive understood as primary aggression, Klein avoids the conformist tendency of the revisionists to smooth over the contradictions between unconscious phantasy and bourgeois society. A critic of false images of harmony and reconciliation, she preserves what Adorno identifies as a Freudian emphasis on antagonism, nonidentity, and ambivalence while at the same time offering a complex psychological and social account of the drives. Moreover, she does so without doubling down on the repressive ego, suggesting a model of ego integration that takes aggression, negativity, and ambivalence seriously without thereby justifying the internalization of domination. In this way, Klein shows a way out of the paradox of authoritarianism.

Finally, Klein's way out of this paradox resonates powerfully with Adorno's few, scattered remarks about nonreified thinking. The depressive position entails an open-ended, nonrepressive, nondominating togetherness of difference, aligned with Adorno's description of nonreified thinking as a nontotalizing and open-ended "togetherness of diversity" that is "above identity and above contradiction."[138] Klein's depressive position is above identity and also above contradiction, able to *contain* diverse and contradictory drives without either subsuming these drives under the rational mastery of the ego or splitting them into clashing poles. For Klein, unconscious phantasy represents an ineliminable moment of nonidentity—an ineffable aspect of our experience that cannot be fully assimilated into conscious, subjective experience. In this way, Klein remains mindful of nature within.[139]

3

Beyond Developmentalism

Psychoanalysis and the Critique of Progress

In his magisterial intellectual biography of Freud, Joel Whitebook expands his account of the problem of the ego by distinguishing between two strands of Freud's thinking, which he labels Freud's official and unofficial positions. On Whitebook's interpretation, Freud's entire oeuvre is structured around the tension between these two positions. Whereas Freud's official position is Kantian, rationalist, pro-Enlightenment, and oriented toward the paternal and the Oedipal, his unofficial position is romantic, skeptical, counter-Enlightenment, and oriented toward the maternal and the pre-Oedipal. Given the complex relationship between these two strands of Freud's thinking, Whitebook characterizes Freud as a thinker of the "dark enlightenment," which is understood as a "deeper, conflicted, disconsolate, and even tragic yet still emancipatory tradition within the broader movement of the Enlightenment."[1] In other words, Freud took seriously the claims of the Counter-Enlightenment and integrated them into a staunch yet humble defense of Enlightenment ideals. With respect to the Enlightenment conception of rationality, Whitebook contends that the attempt to give human irrationality its due while still defending secular science and rationality is at the core of psychoanalysis. On Whitebook's view, this attempt to elucidate a *"rational theory of irrationality"* sets Freud apart from both "the irrationalism of the Romantics and the hyper-rationalism of the one-sided Enlightenment."[2]

Given the centrality of the concept of progress to debates over the legacy of Enlightenment rationalism, the question of progress is deeply implicated in this complex tension within Freud's thinking. Freud's official position not only champions the Enlightenment virtues of rationality and autonomy; it also articulates a developmentalist story that links the ego's progressive mastery of the archaic forces of the id to the advance of civilization from "primitive" animism through religion to scientific secularism. Moreover, these two stories are tightly linked via Freud's endorsement of the recapitulationist thesis developed by late nineteenth-century biologists working in the wake of Darwin: the claim that ontogeny, the development of the individual, recapitulates phylogeny, the development of the species. As a result of Freud's endorsement of this thesis, his official position with regard to the psyche is connected to a strong conception of civilizational development and progress. His unofficial position, by contrast, famously calls into question whether the ego can be master of its own house and, relatedly, whether civilization is worth the high price that it necessarily exacts in the form of the renunciation of instinct.

However, the problem of progress cuts even deeper than this. Freud's official position is not only (arguably, at least) hyperrationalist and insufficiently tragic; it is also implicated in Eurocentric and racist modes of developmental thinking that were imported into Freudian theory through his reliance on the evolutionary anthropology and biology of his time, all of which crystallize in the problematic figure of "the primitive." Although Whitebook acknowledges and condemns the "Eurocentric Whiggishness" of Freudian social and cultural theory, he does not directly confront the developmental racism that pervades Freud's official position.[3] Instead, he insists that the core of Freud's developmental-historical claim—that Enlightenment secularism represents a civilizational advance—can be stripped of its Eurocentrism and defended, albeit in a modified form.

Although I have no intention of suggesting that we should dismiss Freud—much less psychoanalysis as a whole—on account of the Eurocentric or racist elements of his theory, I do want to argue that if psychoanalysis is to be a productive resource for critical theory, its residual developmental Eurocentric racism will have to be confronted and worked through. Furthermore, I contend that this goal can be accomplished by drawing on and developing further the implications of what Whitebook calls Freud's unofficial position. However, contra Whitebook, I argue that this minor strand of Freud's thinking actually goes much further in subverting the notion of civilizational progress than Whitebook admits. Freud's unofficial position, as I reconstruct it, not only reminds us that what we think of as progress is always ambiguous inasmuch as it always comes at a cost—and one that we might well find too high to bear;[4] ultimately it also undermines the very point of view from which judgments about civilizational progress could be made in the first place.

Whitebook maintains that the core of Freud's developmentalism—his insistence on the superiority of the scientific point of view on the grounds that it represents the overcoming of infantile omnipotence and the acceptance of human finitude—can be maintained while jettisoning its Eurocentric overtones. In contrast, I argue, first, that, given the meaning of "the primitive" and the centrality of this figure to Freudian theory, this is significantly more difficult to accomplish than Whitebook realizes; and, second, that Whitebook's approach underplays the radicality of Freud's unofficial position, which, when taken to its logical conclusion, is subversive of progressive, developmental models of the self and of civilization. Although Freud himself never fully spelled out his unofficial position or its implications for theories of development, I contend that a compelling articulation of this view can be found in the work of one of his most original, and most often misunderstood, successors: Melanie Klein.

Psyche and Civilization: Officially and Unofficially

Although what Whitebook calls the official and unofficial positions have quite broad implications for Freud's thinking about culture, history, anthropology, science, and religion, they are initially articulated as different versions—or, perhaps better, ways of reading—Freudian metapsychology. According to Freud's official position, the starting point for the development of the subject is a self-enclosed psyche governed solely by the logic of the pleasure principle. Freud's 1911 essay "Formulation on the Two Principles of Mental Functioning" offers a synoptic overview of this account.[5] Key to this text are the related distinctions between the pleasure and reality principles, on the one hand, and primary and secondary processes, on the other. Governed by the pleasure principle, primary processes are so called because they are the "residues of a phase of development in which they were the only kind of mental process."⁶ In this phase, whatever needs may arise internally are satisfied, Freud explains, "in a hallucinatory manner, just as still happens to-day with our dream-thoughts every night."⁷ In other words, the psyche governed by primary process is monadic, self-contained, and capable of self-satisfaction.

Although Freud acknowledges that this sounds like a fictitious construct, for any such creature could not survive for very long, if it could even come into being in the first place, he nevertheless maintains that the infant taken together with its primary caregiver can be understood in this way.⁸ The infant, Freud notes, "probably hallucinates the fulfillment of its internal needs; it betrays its unpleasure, when there is an increase of stimulus and an absence of satisfaction, by the motor discharge of screaming and beating about with its arms and legs, and it then experiences the satisfaction it has hallucinated."⁹ In other words, although (and on the condition that) the infant receives care and help in meeting their needs from their caregiver, they experience the satisfaction of those needs as the result of their own activity—for example, their having screamed or kicked their arms and legs. It is only when the infant's needs go unsatisfied, when they experience disappointment and thus the failure of their hallucinatory sense of omnipotence, that the psyche begins the painful turn toward reality. At this point, a new principle of mental functioning—the reality principle—is introduced. With this principle, "what was presented in the mind was no longer what was agreeable but what was real, even if it happened to be disagreeable."¹⁰

The official position is, then, a story of separation and opposition between a monadic, self-enclosed subject and the external reality whose demands the subject must learn, begrudgingly, to acknowledge and accept. On this conception, the ego's primary functions are those of defense, against the harsh demands of the reality principle, and mediation, between the demands of reality and the internal drive for pleasure. Whitebook describes the official position as oriented toward the paternal and the Oedipal because Freud takes the father to represent and enforce the reality principle. Thus, the conflict between the pleasure and reality principles is at the core of the Oedipal conflict, and the resolution of that crisis represents the child's acceptance and internalization of the demands of reality, a process that is necessarily conflictual, even violent.¹¹ Given its focus on bringing the pleasure principle to heel under the demands of the reality principle, the official position conceives of psychological maturity or development as the progressive mastery or domination of instinctual drives. On this picture, as Whitebook explains, "the ego dominates the id, consciousness dominates the unconscious, realistic thinking dominates fantasy thinking, cognition dominates affect, activity dominates passivity, and the civilized part of the personality dominates the instincts."[12] The primary aim of the ego, on this view, is what the early Frankfurt School called the domination of inner nature, or what Cornelius Castoriadis referred to as a "power grab."[13]

This way of describing the official position already indicates what is deeply problematic about it. Indeed, Whitebook delineates three criticisms of Freud's official metapsychological position, the latter two of which expand on the idea of the psyche as a structure of internalized domination. First, there is the conceptual worry that it is far from clear that Freud can explain the turn to reality—and thus also to object-relatedness—given the starting point of a self-enclosed psyche.[14] If the psyche is completely self-contained at the start, then how can it in fact experience the disappointment that motivates its turn to reality? How is disappointment able to pierce the subject's veil of monadic self-sufficiency? And, on the flipside, insofar as the infant is able to experience disappointment, can the psyche ever truly have been self-contained in the first place? Indeed, the very fact that Freud notes that the infant can be viewed as a self-enclosed psyche *only when taken together with a maternal caregiver* suggests that there is a deep conceptual problem here, from which the ongoing psychoanalytic debates about primary narcissism stem.

Second, the official position leads Freud to claim that the work of psychoanalysis (and also of civilization) can be likened to what he called the "draining of the Zuider Zee."[15] This image suggests to Whitebook a conception of maturity understood as "a state where all the 'primitive' sludge of unconscious-instinctual life has been dredged out of mental life."[16] Talk of draining or dredging suggests an unrealistic—and deeply unpsychoanalytic—picture of a psyche from which the sludge or swamp of unconscious and instinctual life has been thoroughly eliminated.

Third, the official position leads Freud to suggest that what he calls a "dictatorship of reason" represents a laudable, even if impossibly utopian, ideal.[17] Whitebook finds it remarkable that Freud would make such a claim—"as though he was totally unaware of the critique of reason to which he had made such a substantial contribution."[18] However, his official position presents an image of an ego that not only can but should achieve a position of rational dictatorship over the unconscious, affective, irrational, instinctual, and "primitive" dimensions of psychic life, and that the goal of psychoanalysis is to foster such an ego. However, as Freud himself famously argued in other parts of his work, the complete domination of inner nature—the ego's mastery of its own house—is not only impossible but perhaps even in principle undesirable.

This brings us to Freud's unofficial position, the outlines of which can already be gleaned through Whitebook's critique of the official position. This contrasting view of the psyche begins to emerge with the account of primary narcissism in Freud's metapsychological paper "On Narcissism," but it is not fully developed until after Freud's late discovery of the death drive. Even as it comes to the fore in Freud's late work, it is never as fully developed and explicitly articulated as is the official position—hence its "unofficial" status. Instead, it must be reconstructed from sometimes fragmentary sources.

According to the unofficial position, psychic life begins in a state of unity or fusion with the primary caregiver; thus, the unofficial position is more oriented toward the maternal and the pre-Oedipal aspects of experience.[19] As Whitebook explains, "Where Freud's 'official' paternal position begins with separation—that is, the self-enclosed psychic monad confronting an external object—and must explain how the infant can break out of its monad and establish a relation with the object, the maternal perspective begins with unity, and separation emerges out of it."[20] On the unofficial view, the function of the ego is not mastery and domination but, along the lines of the Kleinian model discussed in the previous chapter, synthesis and integration. From this perspective, the ego's function consists in "preserving the material of unconscious-instinctual life and holding it together, synthesizing it into larger and more differentiated unities."[21] The strength of the ego is measured not in terms of its ability to master, repress, and dominate the id, but rather as a function of its capacity for "expansion, greater integration, and differentiation of its associative web."[22] Instead of the repression, denial, or elimination of difference, integration refers to "the ability to sufficiently tolerate the discomfort of incompatible ideas."[23] In other words, integration entails the ability to manage and withstand ambivalence.

Whitebook's primary interest in sketching the outlines of the unofficial position in Freud is to address the question of the role of the maternal and pre-Oedipal in Freud's thinking—and, relatedly, to come to grips with Freud's troubled relationship with his own mother.[24] Along the way he gives some indications of how this distinction plays out in Freud's social and cultural theory, particularly with respect to the concept of progress. Although Whitebook never articulates the implications of Freud's unofficial position for his social theory in detail, he does acknowledge that the official position on psychic development finds its analogue in Freud's account of civilizational development as a process leading from "primitive" animistic cultures through religious societies to civilizations governed by secular, scientific views, a process that Freud explicitly links with the developmental trajectory from narcissism through object love to Oedipalization. Here we can see the cultural analogues of the draining of the Zuider Zee and dictatorship of reason metaphors, discussed previously. According to Freud's official position, civilizational progress consists in a teleological development in which "primitive" stages are superseded and eliminated by more advanced ones. Through this process, the "sludge" of animistic, magical, or illusory systems of thought are purged from cultures and mature, rational, secular science installed in their place.

Whitebook acknowledges that this developmentalist picture is problematic, not least for its "Eurocentric Whiggishness" and naïveté.[25] In addition, he identifies two further problems with this conception of civilizational progress. First, Freud frequently displays the (deeply ironic) tendency to declare the triumph of science over omnipotence in a triumphalist, dogmatic—indeed, omnipotent—fashion.[26] In order to be internally consistent, Freud's opposition to magical thinking and the overcoming of omnipotence would have to be articulated in a nonomnipotent manner—that is, in a way that acknowledges the fallibilism, incompleteness, and perhaps even inevitable distortions of the scientific point of view.[27] Second, Whitebook wonders whether the demand that we overcome omnipotence by resigning ourselves to the painful reality of our finitude and insignificance might not itself be too demanding and thus, in a surprising twist, too utopian. Although resignation to our finitude is presented as the ultimate antiutopian stance, as the clear-eyed rejection of the dangerous illusions of wishful thinking, perhaps admitting our own finitude and insignificance is just too difficult for creatures like us? Ironically, again, the very modesty of Freud's vision of how we should live, its emphasis on resignation and the acceptance of our finitude, is precisely what makes it so difficult for, as Whitebook puts it, *"creatures like us—with our incorrigible propensity for omnipotence, grandiosity, and magic—to realize this goal."*[28]

Nevertheless, Whitebook insists that there is a "valid kernel" to Freud's official position on civilizational progress that is worth defending and preserving. "When we strip away the Eurocentrism and the teleological philosophy of history," Whitebook writes, "this is what remains: For Freud, the goal—in science, life, and psychoanalytic treatment—is to master omnipotence and accept *Ananke* to the extent that is possible for finite creatures like us."[29] The kernel of both civilizational and psychological maturity for Freud is the overcoming of omnipotence and the acceptance of our helplessness and insignificance.[30] Indeed, maturity in this sense is closely related to Whitebook's understanding of Freud's conception of science, which he defines as *"the methodical struggle against"* the "human penchant for magical thinking."[31]

As a result of Freud's acceptance of the recapitulationist thesis, civilizational development tracks ego development in both the official and unofficial positions. Thus, although Whitebook never fully spells out the implications of Freud's unofficial position on the psyche for his conception of civilizational progress, the reader can fill in the blanks. According to the official position, ego development is, as Whitebook explains, "a more or less unilinear process in which each 'more advanced' stage supersedes and eliminates the more 'primitive' one before it, culminating in the ascendance of the supposedly rational and autonomous ego."[32] This implies, mutatis mutandis, a model of civilizational development as a unilinear process in which more advanced cultural forms supersede and replace more "primitive" forms, culminating in the achievement of the secular and enlightened, scientifically and technologically advanced modern societies such as those found in Europe. By contrast, the unofficial position views psychic development not as a progressive process of rational mastery of the primitive strata of experience, but as *"a felicitous constellation in which 'free intercourse' is established between the more advanced and the more primitive strata of the psyche."*[33] Notice that this way of understanding the unofficial position retains the distinction between "advanced" and "primitive," implying a residual developmental claim. This, in turn, fits with

Whitebook's defense of the core of Freud's civilizational argument, the part that he claims remains after the Whiggish Eurocentrism has been stripped away: the idea that a culture of scientific secularism represents an important developmental advance over cultures animated by omnipotence, religious myth, and magical thinking. But, given his critique of Freud's official position, Whitebook maintains that the distinction between "advanced" and "primitive" would have to be articulated in a way that refrains from any sort of "power grab" on the part of the more advanced structure. When read back through the lens of civilizational development, this leads to the thought that mobilizing the insights of the unofficial position requires more "advanced" societies to present their critique of "primitive" cultures in a nondominating and nonomnipotent (chastened, open-minded, nondogmatic) way, one that facilitates "free intercourse" between the two.[34]

Whitebook contends that Freud's official position makes the mistake of turning a pathological conception of the ego—that of the obsessive neurotic—into a prescriptive model.[35] Indeed, he laments the fact that too many psychoanalysts (in particular, those inspired by American ego psychology) have followed Freud's official position and thus have adopted a view that defines maturity "as the ego's domination over other dimensions of psychic life."[36] The official position glorifies a domination of inner nature that is not only impossible but also undesirable "*in the extreme.*"[37] When translated into the domain of cultural theory, the official position likewise licenses and perhaps even glorifies the domination of rational, scientific, secular, European, and modern over animistic, traditional, religious, or "premodern" cultures. Freud's unofficial position on the psyche, by contrast, entails what Whitebook calls "a less repressive organization of the psyche, a more propitious integration of its heterogeneous parts."[38] This suggests the possibility of a civilizational analogue that, without ceding the claim about the superiority of secular, scientific, rationalized cultures, at least presents that claim in a less repressive, dogmatic, and omnipotent fashion.

However, we might well wonder whether such an account of Freud's unofficial civilizational position goes far enough in challenging the "power grab" of the ego and its civilizational correlate. After all, the problem with Freud's official position on civilizational development and progress is not *only* that it articulates the demand to overcome omnipotence in an omnipotent and unrealistic way. The problem is *also* that the very conception of civilizational maturity and development that Whitebook seeks to preserve and defend rests on a problematic conception of "the primitive" that is deeply embedded in a racist developmental story. Although Whitebook condemns Freud's Eurocentric Whiggishness, he seems overly confident that a more modest and chastened model of civilizational development can, in fact, survive the attempt to strip Freud's official position of its Eurocentric racism. Contra Whitebook, I maintain, first, that attending to the Eurocentric racism that pervades Freud's official position requires a more radical critique of progressive, developmental notions of civilization and, second, that Freud's unofficial position on progress opens up precisely this possibility.

Freud and "The Primitive"

As Celia Brickman has argued convincingly, the idea of "the primitive," far from being "a long-abandoned relic of anthropology's colonial ancestry," is in fact alive and well in psychoanalysis, where it refers first and foremost to "the raw and the rudimentary, the undeveloped, the archaic"—that is, to "characteristics of infants and regressive episodes in adults."[39] Although one might be tempted to dismiss this as an idiosyncratic usage that carries no racialized subtext, Brickman's work demonstrates exhaustively and in painstaking detail that this is not the case. The notion of the primitive in Freud's writings is deeply bound up with the racist and colonialist discourses of evolutionary anthropology on which he drew for his own social and cultural theory.[40] For Freud, the term "primitive" refers *both* to the earliest and most basic stages of psychic development *and* to so-called savages taken to be, from a civilizational perspective, less mature or advanced than Europeans.[41] Indeed, Freud repeatedly ascribes the simplest, most rudimentary, and most archaic modes of psychological functioning not only to infants but also to "so-called primitive people of all ages."[42] In virtue of this dual ascription, the term "primitive" functions as much more than a neutral psychoanalytic term that assesses levels or modes of psychic development; it also encodes a judgment about the developmental superiority of modern European subjects over what it takes to be savage or primitive cultural others.[43] Even when deployed in a purely psychoanalytic register to refer to a level of the psyche, the term "primitive," Brickman contends, "carries with it the imprint of the evolutionary premises with their racial entailments on which it was originally constructed."[44] Without denying that psychoanalysis offers powerful tools for analyzing and deconstructing racist and colonialist forms of subjectivity and thought, Brickman nonetheless insists that to the extent that Freud's conception of primitivity is uncritically adopted, psychoanalysis thereby repeats—albeit perhaps unwittingly—the "covert racializing subtext" of Freudian theory.[45]

Before demonstrating the influence of social evolutionary theories on Freud, Brickman reminds us of the rootedness of such theories in colonial encounters, particularly in the Americas.[46] Drawing on and synthesizing a wide range of research in postcolonial theory, Brickman traces the notion of the primitive back to the decision, made by Europeans at the time of colonial expansion and conquest, to see indigenous peoples as earlier versions of themselves—an image that served, in turn, to defend colonialism and to justify the so-called civilizing mission. It was on this decisionistic basis that social evolutionary (and later biological) theories of race were elaborated and contemporary "primitives" came to be seen as what Dipesh Chakrabarty has called "human embodiments of the principle of anachronism."[47] As this conception of the primitive was imported into the foundational texts and methodologies of social theory, anthropology, and biology, Brickman contends, "arguments concerning savages and infidels were transformed from religious doctrine and philosophical argument into scientific fact; effect was cast as cause, and the imputed characteristics of primitive peoples themselves were understood to allow, if not require, their domination."[48]

At the core of Freud's conception of the primitive lies the aforementioned recapitulation thesis, which links individual ontogenesis to social or cultural phylogenesis. The claim that ontogeny recapitulates phylogeny was propounded by Ernst Haeckel, a nineteenth-century German zoologist best known as a popularizer of Darwin, first and foremost as a (long since discredited) evolutionary-biological claim that the embryological development of the organism repeats the evolutionary history of the species. When taken up in the register of social theory, the recapitulationist thesis became a claim about individual and civilizational development, encapsulated in the idea that "the human child would recapitulate the history of the human race."[49] According to this thesis, the development of the individual and the evolution of civilizations converge on the idea of the primitive, understood as that which stands at the beginning of both trajectories. Acceptance of this thesis produced two corollaries, both of which became fundamental premises of social-evolutionary thinking: first, the belief that contemporary "primitives" or "savages" were living in the European past; and, second, the related methodological assumption that details about the prehistory of Europe could be ascertained through the study of contemporary indigenous peoples, and vice versa.[50]

The extensive influence of the recapitulation thesis on Freud's official position in social and cultural theory is most strikingly evident in *Totem and Taboo*. This is clear in the text's opening lines, which are worth quoting in full:

> Prehistoric man, in the various stages of his development, is known to us through the inanimate monuments and implements which he has left behind, through the information about his art, his religion and his attitude towards life which has come to us either directly or by way of tradition handed down in legends, myths and fairy tales, and through the relics of his mode of thought which survive in our own manners and customs. But apart from this, in a certain sense he is still our contemporary. There are men still living who, as we believe, stand very near to primitive man, far nearer than we do, and whom we therefore regard as his direct heirs and representatives. Such is our view of those whom we describe as savages or half-savages; and their mental life must have a peculiar interest for us if we are right in seeing in it a well-preserved picture of an early stage of our own development.[51]

By claiming that contemporary "savages" are "direct heirs or representatives" of "primitive man," and that as such they provide us with an image of "our" own prehistory, Freud clearly accepts the first premise. This claim, in turn, serves as the basis for Freud's adoption of the second premise, which is a version of what was known in anthropology as the comparative method: "If that supposition is correct," he continues, "a comparison between the psychology of primitive peoples, as it is taught by social anthropology, and the psychology of neurotics, as it has been revealed by psycho-analysis, will be bound to show numerous points of agreement and will throw new light upon familiar facts in both sciences."[52]

To be sure, Freud acknowledges some limitations of the comparative method. For example, a footnote in the early pages of the first essay of *Totem and Taboo* concludes by noting that "the difficulty ... is to decide whether we should regard the present state of things as a true picture of the significant features of the past or as a secondary distortion of them."[53] This methodological caution regarding the possible distortions that might creep into our perceptions of "primitive" groups and our resulting interpretations of prehistory does not, however, prevent Freud from putting the comparative method to expansive use. For example, famously resolving to focus on "the most backward and miserable of savages, the aborigines of Australia,"[54] Freud argues in the first essay of *Totem and Taboo* that the horror of incest among "primitives," well documented in the anthropological record, "is essentially an *infantile* feature and that it reveals a striking agreement with the mental life of neurotic patients."[55] Similarly, in the second essay, he connects the operation of taboos in "primitive" cultures with the behavior of obsessional neurotics, who "have created for themselves individual taboo prohibitions of this very kind and who obey them just as strictly as savages obey the communal taboos of their tribe or society."[56] The similarities are so striking that, Freud notes, obsessional neurosis might just as easily be referred to as "taboo sickness."[57]

The comparative method is deployed still more fully in the third essay, where Freud leans heavily on the evolutionary-anthropological thesis that the human race has developed through three stages or systems of thought: from animism (or myth) through religion to science.[58] While all three of these systems can be understood as human attempts to control the natural world, they are distinguished not only by greater degrees of control and mastery but also, somewhat paradoxically, by the progressive overcoming of omnipotence. Animism is characterized by associative thinking or the predominance of ideas over reality; it is rooted in the omnipotence of thoughts, which leads animistic systems to "replace the laws of nature by psychological ones."[59] In the transition to the religious stage, omnipotence is ascribed to the gods, though human beings retain the belief that they can influence the gods through displays of faith or acts of transgression. The scientific system of thought, by contrast, "no longer affords any room for human omnipotence; men have acknowledged their smallness and submitted resignedly to death and to the other necessities of nature."[60] Freud explicitly connects these three stages of civilizational development to the psychic development of the individual. The animistic stage corresponds to infantile narcissism, in which the infant omnipotently hallucinates the internal self-satisfaction of their own needs. The religious stage corresponds to object choice in the Oedipal stage, with the parents standing in for the gods. The scientific stage corresponds to an individual maturity characterized by the renunciation of the pleasure principle, resignation to an oftentimes painful reality, and the transfer of object love from parents to parent-substitutes, all of which are made possible by the resolution of the Oedipal crisis.[61]

Perhaps the most striking example of Freud's use of the comparative method is found in his account of the origin of totemism in the fourth essay of *Totem and Taboo*.[62] Based on his earlier analysis of animal phobias, which Freud had already concluded signal a fear of the father, Freud reasons via the comparative method that the father can be substituted for the totem animal in totemic systems of thought.[63] This speculative assumption allows Freud to fill in crucial gaps in the existing social-anthropological research into the origins of totemism. If the totem animal and the father are functionally the same, then the two principal prohibitions— against killing the totem and having sexual relations with women of the same totem clan— that constitute the core of totemism must coincide with "the two crimes of Oedipus."[64] This enables Freud to understand the rootedness of totemism, the origins of which are otherwise shrouded in an inaccessibly remote past, in the Oedipal situation. It is thus the employment of the comparative method that leads Freud to his famous hypothesis of the transition from the primal horde to the band of brothers via the murder of the primal father.[65]

The basic argument of *Totem and Taboo* is repeated throughout many of Freud's contributions to social and cultural theory, suggesting the centrality of this argument to his official position on civilizational development. For example, his analysis of the primitive mind figures prominently in his major work of social psychology *Group Psychology and the Analysis of the Ego*. There, the "group mind" is likened to "the mental life of primitive people and of children" insofar as the group mind is "impulsive, changeable and irritable"; "led almost exclusively by the unconscious"; "imperious"; "incapable of perseverance"; "has a sense of omnipotence"; is "credulous and open to influence"; "has no critical faculty"; "thinks in images"; "goes directly to extremes"; "is as intolerant as it is obedient to authority"; "respects force"; and "wants to be ruled and oppressed and to fear its masters."[66] The formation of a group mind goes hand in hand with the erosion of individual inhibitions and thus the collective regression to the primitive psychic structures that underlie psychic development. Like "primitives," groups are "subject to the truly magical power of words"—they not only "demand illusions"; they "cannot do without them."[67]

To be sure, through the establishment of institutions, procedures, and settled social roles, groups can acquire characteristics that parallel that of the mature, rational individual with its integrated ego and its capacity for rational control of the instincts. Freud's primary interest, however, is in understanding more spontaneous and less organized groups—what could also be called masses—which, he maintains, are held together by the forces of love and identification. And he finds the regressive characteristics of such groups (their "weakness of intellectual ability, the lack of emotional restraint, the incapacity for moderation and delay, the inclination to exceed every limit in the expression of emotion and to work it off completely in the form of action") strikingly similar to the mental activity of "savages or children."[68] Once again drawing on the comparative method, he thus hypothesizes that the group is a reincarnation of the primal horde, and that, "just as primitive man survives potentially in every individual, so the primal horde may arise once more out of any random collection."[69]

The story of the primal horde is invoked again in *The Future of an Illusion*, which offers perhaps the clearest—and, in Whitebook's terms, most omnipotent—version of Freud's official position on civilizational development. This text opens with the question of whether "what little civilization has thus acquired [in the realm of human affairs] is indeed worth defending at all."[70] Although, as I'll discuss further in the next section, Freud will later address this question more skeptically, here he responds with a full-throated defense of the civilizational advance represented by scientific secularism. This defense leans heavily on Freud's developmental critique of "primitive" or "savage" forms of life, at key points repeating and extending the argument of *Totem and Taboo*. For example, in answering the question of the source and value of religious ideas, Freud maintains that religion is the next step after totemism. Both stem from the same historical-developmental sources: humanity's need to defend itself against the superior forces of nature and its desire to counteract the painful sacrifices demanded by civilization.⁷¹ In terms of their psychical origins, however, religious ideas are illusions: they are not oriented toward reality and are instead "derived from human wishes."⁷² As he had earlier done with totemism, Freud now connects religion to obsessional neurosis, arguing that just as most children grow out of their propensity to magical thinking, so civilization should grow out of its dependence on religious illusions.⁷³ Doing so is part and parcel of a civilizational "education to reality," the goal of which is to compel human beings to accept their finitude and their insignificance in the universe.⁷⁴

To be sure, Freud's articulation of his official position on civilizational development is not so omnipotent that he fails even to consider the question of whether science might not itself be an illusion grounded in a wishful faith in the power of reason. Although he acknowledges that he cannot completely rule out this possibility in advance, nevertheless he insists that, insofar as it is internally self-correcting, science is distinct from religion and thus "no illusion."⁷⁵ He also expresses a deep faith in the power of reason to win out in the long run: "The primacy of the intellect lies, it is true, in a distant, distant future, but probably not in an *infinitely* distant one."⁷⁶ We may be far from its realization, but, insofar as it is not impossible, we can still hope to attain the dictatorship of reason.

Although Brickman does not distinguish explicitly between Freud's official and unofficial positions on social and cultural development or progress, a version of this distinction implicitly structures her discussion. Thus, even as she tracks the influence of racialized models of civilizational development on Freud's account of the primitive, she maintains that his account was more complex and ambivalent than the evolutionary anthropological model on which it was based. For Freud, unlike for the evolutionary anthropologists, previously superseded "primitive" stages of mental development persisted in the unconscious, where they constantly threatened to break through the veneer of civilization.⁷⁷ Therefore, Brickman maintains, Freud's conception of primitivity was highly ambivalent, representing both a "universal feature of the psyche of all humankind (rather than a characteristic of savages only)" and "an evolutionarily prior and therefore—by the logic of the evolutionary anthropology from which he borrowed—a racially indexed category."⁷⁸ On the one hand, Brickman contends that even in his most developmentalist moments—and precisely as a result of the interlocking psychic and civilizational aspects of primitivity—Freud was mindful that earlier, more "primitive," psychic and cultural forms are never fully eliminated or superceded. Thus his official position is less triumphalist than it might at first seem. On the other hand, however, she reminds us that insofar as Freud's trenchant critique of European civilization consists in pointing out the persistence and ineliminability of "primitive" psychic and social forces in mature individuals and civilizations, it, too, rests on racially indexed notions of civilizational development. To the extent that this is the case, Brickman maintains that the "emancipatory intent of Freud's project" is "racially ambiguous."[79]

Brickman's analysis not only complicates Whitebook's distinction between the official and unofficial positions by suggesting what we might call an "unofficial" aspect of the official story; it also reveals the degree to which Freud's Eurocentric Whiggishness pervades not just the official position but also Whitebook's version of the unofficial position as well. To the extent that the latter remains committed to defending the developmental model of civilization as the overcoming of omnipotence (in however chastened, modest, and fallibilist a manner), it remains tied to the racialized notions of primitivity that Brickman's work painstakingly exposes. This, in turn, suggests that confronting Freud's Eurocentric Whiggishness requires a more radical challenge to the interlocking developmentalist conceptions of individual and civilization that undergird his official position.

Freud's Unofficial Position on Civilization and Progress

The foregoing discussion poses a number of hurdles that a psychoanalytically informed critique of notions of historical progress and civilizational development would need to clear. If it is to avoid being mired in Eurocentric racist modes of thinking, such a critique would have to go beyond Whitebook's postsecular defense of the developmental, social-evolutionary model of civilization. It would also have to go beyond questioning whether or not civilization is worth the effort required to sustain it and pointing out that "primitive" modes of experience continue to exist alongside more mature developmental forms, at both the individual and the cultural levels. Why? Because these positions retain, whether explicitly or implicitly, a commitment to the superiority of modern, secular, scientific, rational forms of life and subjectivity and the concomitant devaluation of "primitive" forms of life and experience. If it is truly to break free of the racialized subtext of the notion of the primitive, a psychoanalytic critique of progress would need to break with such developmental-historical modes of thinking altogether. As I see it, Freud's unofficial position on civilization and progress—which emerges in his late masterpiece, *Civilization and Its Discontents*—provides the outlines for just such a critique. Reconstructing the critique of progress in this text enables us to see that Freud's unofficial position on civilization entails a radical epistemological challenge to the very idea of reading the history of societies and cultures as a story of progress—or regress.

Civilization and Its Discontents is framed as an answer to the question of the meaning or purpose of life. Freud demurs on this question, suggesting it doesn't admit of an answer, but he does say that he knows quite well what most people show, through their actions, what they take to be the purpose of life—namely, the pursuit of happiness, understood as the program of the pleasure principle.[80] And yet the pleasure principle finds itself opposed by the universe at every turn, which means that it must give way to the more modest reality principle. The three primary sources of unhappiness, and thus the three dimensions of reality to which the pleasure principle must yield, are the frailty of our own bodies, the dangers of the natural world, and our interactions with other people. While Freud takes the first two to be ineliminable because, he assumes, we will never be able to completely master nature, including our own bodies, the third at least seems as if it should be solvable. The fact that it has thus far proven to be intractable, and that, instead, our relations with other human beings cause perhaps the most acute suffering of all, suggests to Freud that "a piece of unconquerable nature may lie behind" this particular type of suffering: a piece "of our own psychical constitution" that places us at odds with the demands and constraints of civilization.[81] This realization—an oblique reference to the recently discovered death drive—leads Freud to consider the "astonishing contention" that "what we call our civilization is largely responsible for our misery, and that we should be much happier if we gave it up."[82]

The discovery of the death drive has profound implications for Freud's thinking about progress, but these emerge slowly over the course of his discussion and are not fully evident until the closing pages of the text. Indeed, *Civilization and Its Discontents* opens with a definition of civilization that recalls Freud's official position. Civilization, Freud writes, refers to "the whole sum of the achievements and the regulations which distinguish our lives from those of our animal ancestors and which serve two purposes—namely to protect men against nature and to adjust their mutual relations."[83] It is a human achievement that sets us apart from nature through the progressive mastery and control of nature, both inner and outer, and of each other. As a mechanism of control or mastery, civilization is antithetical to freedom or liberty, in particular the freedom to satisfy one's basic drives in an unimpeded manner. Because freedom of this sort inevitably leads to conflicts, civilization requires—indeed, to a large extent, consists in—submitting these drives to the control of the "higher psychical agencies, which have subjected themselves to the reality principle."[84] But the challenge, as Freud sees it, is that "the feeling of happiness derived from the satisfaction of a wild instinctual impulse untamed by the ego is incomparably more intense than that derived from sating an instinct that has been tamed."[85] The allure of unsublimated drive satisfaction remains high, as does the potential for conflict between the drives and the demands of civilization.

However, not all drives are alike when it comes to their potential to create conflict and their need to be mastered by civilization. Although Freud starts his discussion with the conflict between the pleasure principle and the demands of civilization, as the discussion goes on, it becomes clear that the real problems arise *beyond* the pleasure principle. For, as Freud argues in chapter 4 of *Civilization and Its Discontents*, love and necessity (Eros and Ananke) are the twin foundations of human communal life. Necessity creates the compulsion to work, which prompts human beings to master nature, and love binds men to their sexual objects and women to their children, creating families. Love, in other words, is a foundation of civilization; its function is to bind people together into unities. Eros is pro-civilization, prosocial. To be sure, conflicts arise between sexual or family unions and the needs of the larger civilization; and civilization demands the restriction of sexual life through mechanisms such as the incest taboo, monitoring the sexual lives of children, and the compulsion of heterosexual monogamy. Still, at the most basic level and in the broadest sense, there is no necessary conflict between Eros—defined by Freud as the drive to "preserve living substance and to join it into ever larger units"—and civilization.[86]

Things look rather different when we get to the pivotal fifth chapter of *Civilization and Its Discontents*. Here, the central challenge and conflict between the drives and the demands of civilization emerges, and it is rooted not in Eros but in the death drive. Civilization requires affective, even erotic, bonds and cooperative relationships between large groups of individuals. However, Freud famously continues, "men are not gentle creatures who want to be loved, and who at the most can defend themselves if they are attacked; they are, on the contrary, creatures among whose instinctual endowments is to be reckoned a powerful share of aggressiveness."[87] As evidence for this claim, Freud cites the combination of the basic life experience of the individual and the collective experience of recorded history and asks, reasonably enough, "Who, in the face of all his experience of life and of history, will have the courage to dispute this assertion?"[88] It is the death drive that disrupts our relations with other human beings, continually threatening civilization with disintegration and forcing us to take steps to control it.[89]

Freud insists in his late work that the death drive, although often entwined with Eros in the form of sexual sadism, also operates independently. As he puts it, "Even where it emerges without any sexual purpose, in the blindest fury of destructiveness, we cannot fail to recognize that the satisfaction of the instinct [to aggression] is accompanied by an extraordinarily high degree of narcissistic enjoyment, owing to its presenting the ego with a fulfillment of the latter's old wishes for omnipotence."[90] If Eros is prosocial and pro-civilization, and if the aggressive drive is opposed to Eros's unifying project, then the history of civilization becomes a process of struggle between Eros and Thanatos working itself out through the human species.[91]

To be sure, Freud maintains that civilization has means at its disposal to inhibit or at the very least redirect the aggressive instincts. By far the most effective of the means that it employs to this end is the development of the superego, which is formed through the introjection or internalization of aggression.[92] Through the constitution of the superego, civilization "obtains mastery over the individual's dangerous desire for aggression by weakening and disarming it and by setting up an agency within him to watch over it, like a garrison in a conquered city."[93] With the development of the superego comes the sense of guilt, rooted not only in the child's fear of doing something bad but also in their fear of wishing for or phantasizing something bad. Indeed, Freud goes so far as to identify "the sense of guilt as the most important problem in the development of civilization" and to conclude that "the price we pay for our advance in civilization is a loss of happiness through the heightening of the sense of guilt."[94] This leads Freud to critique both the individual superego and the "cultural superego" of ethics and to suggest that the point of psychoanalysis is to work, both therapeutically and culturally, to loosen their excessive, unfulfillable demands.[95] The problem with ethics, according to Freud, is that, like the excessively demanding superego, "it, too, does not trouble itself enough about the facts of the mental constitution of human beings. It issues a command and does not ask whether it is possible for people to obey it."[96] In other words, one might say, the problem with ethics is that it lacks a realistic conception of the person and that, as a result of this lack, it trades in a problematic moralistic idealism.[97] Moreover, according to the logic of Freud's argument, the tendency toward moralistic idealism is itself an expression of the very aggressive drive the existence of which idealists so vigorously deny.

It is here, at the end of Freud's text, that the various scattered clues as to his unofficial position on civilization and progress are gathered together into a coherent statement. Freud first notes that he has attempted to be impartial in his analysis of civilization, to be neither prejudiced in its favor, viewing civilization as the path to perfection, nor biased against it, understanding civilization as not worth the monumental effort required to hold it in place. "My impartiality," he notes wryly, "is made all the easier to me by my knowing very little about these things. One thing only do I know for certain and that is that man's judgments of value follow directly his wishes for happiness—that, accordingly, they are an attempt to support his illusions with arguments."[98] To those who would find his analysis of civilization disheartening or devoid of solutions, Freud admits that he "can offer them no consolation."[99] All that he can do is to pose what he calls "the fateful question for the human species": "Whether and to what extent their cultural development will succeed in mastering the disturbance of their communal life by the human instinct of aggression and self-destruction"— and, we might add, at what cost?[100]

In these closing pages, Freud sketches the outlines of a nonteleological, nondevelopmental, nonprogressive way of reading history, a historical stance that above all remains agnostic on the question of whether the achievements of civilization are worth the repression and internalized domination necessary to achieve them. In stark contrast not only to his official position but also to Whitebook's more chastened, humble, and postsecular version of the unofficial position, Freud declines to offer any defense, however modest, of the achievements of modern, secular, scientific, enlightenment rationalism. Moreover, by taking this position, Freud is simply consistently following out the logic of his own argument. His conception of the death drive and its role in the generation of the superego lead him to locate the very foundation of morality in aggression. As such, for the late Freud as much as for Nietzsche, the roots of morality are "soaked in blood thoroughly and for a long time."[101] With this argument, Freud implicitly calls into question the very possibility of a context-transcendent normative point of view from which something could be identified as a civilizational or developmental advance at all—at least if we understand "advance" in normative terms. As he says, we have to be "careful not to fall in line with the prejudice that civilization is synonymous with perfecting, that it is the road to perfection pre-ordained for men."[102] We have to be careful, too, of the extent to which our backward-looking, historical judgments about what constitutes progress and whether it has been achieved up to now, in the historical process that has led to our own form of life, are simply, as Freud might have said, an attempt to support our harmonistic illusions with arguments.

So, what, then, is Freud's unofficial stance toward civilization and progress? I agree with Whitebook that Freud is best understood as a thinker of the dark enlightenment, but I would characterize the implications of this stance for his unofficial conception of progress differently.[103] Freud offers a tragic, unreconciled vision of the conflicts between the death drive and the demands and constraints of civilization, one that unsettles our harmonistic illusions by problematizing our own tendency toward complacent and self-congratulatory conceptions of progress.[104] To say that Freud's late vision is tragic is not to say that he believes that moral or political progress is in principle impossible. Rather, it is to say that he holds steadfast to an unreconciled reading of history, one that refuses to take sides with either the cheerleaders or the enemies of civilization, with either the defenders or the critics of the Enlightenment. Freud's profession of impartiality on the question of whether civilization is the best thing that ever happened to us or not worth all the bother suggests precisely this: *any* attempt to read history as having a clear normative direction, whether that direction is construed progressively or regressively, constitutes an attempt to support one's illusions—be they optimistic or pessimistic—with arguments. Freud's unofficial position can thus be read as a form of problematizing critique of our present, precisely insofar as it refuses either to vindicate or to subvert the historical path that led up to it.

To the extent that Freud's unofficial position on civilization undermines teleological readings of history, whether positive or negative, it entails a more radical break from his official position than Whitebook imagines. However, to the extent that Freud's unofficial position unsettles the progressive-developmental conception of history that undergirds theories of social evolution, it also implicitly pulls the rug out from under the racialized conception of primitivity in which his official position—and Whitebook's formulation of the unofficial position—remains mired. More radically still, by calling into question the conception of freestanding normativity from which judgments of civilizational progress would have to be made through his revelation of the rootedness of normativity in aggression, Freud's unofficial position also provides some resources for a powerful psychoanalytic critique of the pernicious racialized legacy of the notion of historical progress. In his unofficial position, Freud not only reveals the source of the aggression and violence bottled up within judgments of relative civilizational value; he also holds up an unflattering mirror to our desire to sustain our self-congratulatory illusions of cultural superiority and progress with social-evolutionary arguments. This feature of his unofficial position may explain why Freudian psychoanalysis has proven to be so productive for work in critical philosophy of race despite the evident developmental, Eurocentric racism of Freud's official position.[105]

Klein's Antidevelopmentalism

Freud's unofficial position on civilization has seemed to many readers to leave him mired in a conservative cultural pessimism that denies the possibility of any meaningful improvement in the human condition.[106] Although I respond to this worry more directly in the next chapter, one complication that emerges in the course of Whitebook's discussion of this issue requires comment here. Although he describes the late Freud as a cultural pessimist, Whitebook also attributes Freud's pessimism to his acceptance of the official position on the psyche.[107] The thought here is that Freud's pessimism about progress is rooted in his view that the psyche is founded on structures of repression and internalized domination made necessary by the deep, intractable conflict between the drives and the demands of civilization—that is, precisely, in his official position on the psyche. As I've already suggested, I think there is more motivating what I would characterize as Freud's skepticism rather than his pessimism about progress than simply the point about internalized domination, but there's no doubt that the latter is an important aspect of Freud's story, even as I've presented it. So, what gives? Why would Freud present the clearest statement of his unofficial position on progress in the context of a staunch and uncompromising version of his official position on the psyche? Does this admission not undermine my reading of *Civilization and Its Discontents* as a statement of Freud's unofficial position on civilization?

Not necessarily. At the risk of pointing out the obvious, the distinction between official and unofficial positions is not explicit in Freud's work, and what Whitebook calls his unofficial position on the psyche is never worked out in the kind of depth and detail that marks his account of the official position. This is even more true of his unofficial position on civilizational progress, which is admittedly a minor theme as compared to the bulk of his work in social and cultural theory. Perhaps, just as Freud struggled through much of his late work to incorporate his discovery of the death drive into his theory, he never quite saw how his radical critique of civilizational progress—by undermining the phylogenetic logic that underpins the recapitulationist thesis—calls for a more radical reconceptualization of the psyche that moves beyond developmental models altogether.[108] Such a radical reconceptualization is precisely what can be found in the work of Klein.

To see why this is the case, let's return to Whitebook's description of the unofficial position. On this account, the strength of the ego is measured in terms of its capacity to expand its "associative web." Integration in this context refers to the enrichment of the ego through the incorporation of more and more unconscious content, the synthesis of this material into larger and more differentiated unities, and the ability to tolerate the resulting incompatible ideas. As should be clear from my discussion in the previous chapter, this description of the unofficial position corresponds in several crucial respects with Klein's account of ego integration. To review, for Klein, to strengthen the ego is to enhance its capacities for integration, where this means being able to incorporate previously split off unconscious contents and to tolerate the resulting ambivalence without resorting to splitting and other manic defenses. Ego integration, for Klein, refers to an ongoing, open-ended, and incomplete process of expansion, augmentation, or enrichment of the personality.

Moreover, Klein's articulation of the unofficial position is arguably preferable inasmuch as it does not rely on fantasies of the archaic mother or of primary fusion, both of which play a crucial role in Whitebook's account. According to Whitebook's version of the unofficial position, the psyche starts out in a state of primordial unity or primary fusion with the "archaic mother." For Whitebook, among the reasons that the unofficial position is preferable to the official position is that the former acknowledges the crucial importance of pre-Oedipal, maternal object relations in the development of the psyche. Although I agree with Whitebook that the post-Freudian emphasis on early, pre-Oedipal phases of development has profound implications, I am nonetheless skeptical of his account of Freud's unofficial position. The problem is not only that talk of the archaic mother runs the risk of essentializing or idealizing the mother-infant relationship or the maternal body (though, to be clear, this is an important problem). But even if one were to be assiduous in noting that the maternal object need not be a biological mother, a woman, or a female, there is still a problematic idealization of early object relations lurking in the background of this story. To see why, we need only recall Whitebook's first criticism of Freud's official position: If the psyche is monadic and completely self-contained, then how can it experience the disappointment that motivates its turn to reality? And insofar as the infant psyche can experience such disappointment, can it ever have truly been self-sufficient in the first place? But notice that this conceptual argument applies with equal force to the idea of a self-contained, isolated, individual psyche as it does to a wholly merged, undifferentiated mother-infant dyad. Indeed, recall that, even on Freud's official position, the infant can be viewed as a self-enclosed psyche only when taken together with a maternal caregiver, which already suggests that the appeal to primary fusion cannot provide the solution to this conceptual problem. As Lacan puts this point in his critique of Michael Balint's version of the primary fusion story: "There has to be intersubjectivity at the beginning, since it is there at the end."[109]

By contrast, Klein's claim that the infant is object-related from the very beginning of life implies a rejection of both primary narcissism and primary fusion. If the infant is object-related from the very beginning of life, then it never exists in either monadic isolation or a state of merger; in order to relate to objects as objects, it must have a rudimentary—even if incoherent, unstable, and fragmented—ego from the very beginning. This means that, even if the young infant's experience of its objects, both internal and external, is filtered through the (often distorting) lens of phantasy, it makes no sense to describe the primary object relationship as one of merger or fusion.[110] Furthermore, although Klein places great importance on the relationship between infant and primary caregiver, her emphasis on primary aggression and the resulting ambivalence that necessarily marks all of the subject's relations to its objects makes it impossible, I think, for her to fall into the tendency to idealize that relationship, much less the archaic mother.

Thus, the Kleinian version of the unofficial position emphasizes the expansion and enrichment of the ego through the incorporation of unconscious content and the toleration of ambivalence while avoiding both the monadic solipsism of the official position and the problematic implications of primary fusion or narcissism. Moreover, as Brickman argues, the undifferentiated merger experiences that form the foundation of theories of primary fusion tend to be coded as not only feminine but also as "primitive."[111] By breaking with the theories of primary narcissism and primary fusion, Klein could be seen as providing a psychoanalytic model that avoids the assimilation of the unconscious to ideologies of primitivity. As Brickman notes, "If the unconscious can be released from a developmental framework in which subjectivity is premised exclusively on repudiation or separation, then it need not be imagined as an abjected, inaccessible primitivity."[112] The key, she suggests, is to figure out how to disengage "the unconscious from an evolutionary-developmental discourse" in order to "dis-articulate representations of subjectivity from the racially indexed map to which it has been correlated."[113] My suggestion is that Klein offers just such a conception of subjectivity.

To be sure, this is not to deny that Klein herself has some deeply problematic things to say about colonialism.[114] Nor is it to deny that she often uses the language of primitive defenses, or that she occasionally draws on social-evolutionary accounts of phylogenesis.[115] As Meira Likierman points out, Klein even makes use of the comparative method in her early work.[116] In this vein, for example, Klein writes that "as the individual repeats biologically the development of mankind, so also does he do it psychically. We find, repressed, and unconscious, the stages which we still observe in primitive people: cannibalism and murderous tendencies of the greatest variety."[117] However, Likierman also argues that, in her later work, Klein moves away from this developmental conception of subjectivity—and, we might add, in so doing leaves behind the associated racially coded view of primitivity.[118] Although Likierman doesn't emphasize this point, this move goes hand in hand with the emergence of the positional model of psychic development for which Klein is justly famous. As I discussed in chapter 1, the paranoid-schizoid and depressive positions are not developmental stages that one passes through and leaves behind, but rather configurations or constellations of object relations, anxieties, and defenses that can and do persist and recur throughout life.[119]

That said, there is a sense in which Klein's positional model retains a conception of psychic development or maturation, though this conception is extremely complex and even, as Likierman insists, ultimately tragic. The move from the paranoid-schizoid position to the depressive position is a developmental achievement that enables the subject to overcome its tendencies toward splitting, idealization, and demonization and its related experience of itself as fragmented and incoherent. With this move, the subject experiences its objects and itself in more integrated ways—as both good and bad at the same time. Although some Kleinians read the achievement of the depressive position as the end point of psychic development, and, as a result, valorize the depressive position while denigrating the paranoid-schizoid position, Likierman maintains that Klein's position is more complicated: "Klein herself did not regard psychic growth as a move from a negative paranoid-schizoid position to a depressive position which is a purely positive phenomenon." Rather, Likierman insists, the depressive position is "both developmentally progressive and positive" and, at the same time "a dangerous crisis point which sets in motion ambivalence, a catastrophic sense of loss and also, psychotic anxieties and defences, all of which need to be overcome."[120]

However, as Likierman also admits, Klein's notion of overcoming is complex, such that overcoming the depressive position does not mean leaving it behind altogether. Rather, as Likierman explains, "overcoming in the texts applies to a level of depressive experience that is submerged in the process of growth but that continues none the less to represent a powerful psychical reality. As such, it affects the more evolved mode of psychical functioning that replaces it."[121] In her elaboration of this point, Likierman distinguishes two implicit strands in Klein's account of the depressive position that she calls the tragic and the moral. The tragic refers to the "irrevocable loss" of the loved object at the heart of the depressive experience;[122] the moral, by contrast, refers to the capacity to withstand that loss and the guilt that accompanies it, and to preserve the object through acts of reparation.[123] The moral thus represents an experiential reversal of the tragic strand of the depressive position: when the psyche enters the reparative mode, it no longer experiences the object as irrevocably lost but as restored and protected.[124] However, even in the moral mode, the tragic element of depressive experience never really goes away; the psyche doesn't overcome or leave behind tragic experience so much as it learns to live with it and to go on by transforming loss into creative repair. The tragic and the moral thus represent two inextricably entangled strands of depressive experience: the subject's ability to take up a moral, reparative stance is a permanent possibility that opens up only on the basis of tragic loss.

"Overcoming" the depressive position, for Klein, thus means not that the tragic aspect of experience is eliminated or left behind but that the moral strand moves to the forefront. In other words, as Likierman explains, "a dialectical tension needs to be maintained in the mature psyche, which neither annihilates nor completely succumbs to the significance of primitive tragic anxieties. Such a tension is itself an inseparable aspect of the moral level of the depressive position."[125] This is not the same as staying at the level of the tragic. As the moral strand takes center stage, tragic emotions are no longer experienced in a catastrophic way that threatens to overwhelm the psyche and trigger its manic defenses but instead in a more mediated and tolerable form.[126]

Likierman is right, I think, to insist that Klein tends to describe the depressive position in these two strikingly different ways without explicitly distinguishing between the two strands of depressive experience. This suggests that readings of Klein that stop short with a valorization of the depressive position are too simplistic. However, once we appreciate what is meant by overcoming the depressive position, it becomes clear that this "overcoming" is more accurately described as a different way of inhabiting the depressive position than as moving beyond it—in other words, as the ongoing, never-ending task of working through.[127] "Overcoming" the depressive position refers, then, to successfully navigating the transition from its tragic, early phase, where depressive anxiety and the tendency toward manic modes of reparation are at their height, to the later, moral mode of depressive integration, characterized by a greater ability to withstand ambivalence and to transform loss into reparative creativity.

Likierman's complicated account of the trajectory through the depressive position supports Jacqueline Rose's contention that Klein does not offer "a developmental paradigm in any straightforward sense."[128] Rather, for Rose, "the movement is constantly in two directions—progression being constantly threatened by the mechanisms that move it on."[129] Or, to translate this thought into Likierman's terminology, the progression to the moral mode of depressive experience is continually threatened by the tragic mode that makes it possible in the first place. On Rose's reading, Klein's emphasis on negativity leads to the radical self-subversion of developmental normativity: "The value of the stress on negativity would then reside in the trouble it poses to the concept of a sequence, the way that it acts as a bar, one could say, to what might elsewhere (and increasingly) appear as normative and prescriptive in the work and followers of Melanie Klein."[130] Likierman's more modest reading, by contrast, retains a commitment to a developmental normativity that moves from the paranoid-schizoid position through tragic to moral depressive modes of experience. Whatever one might think of Rose and Likierman's implicit disagreement about developmental normativity, Klein's model does not—as far as I can see, at any rate—map onto any existing hierarchical stage model of civilizational development. After all, splitting and the accompanying tendencies toward idealization and demonization clearly remain rampant in "advanced" societies, while instances of integration and reparation in the Kleinian sense can be found in many cultures, including indigenous ones.[131] As such, whatever sort of residual developmentalism may remain in Klein's work, this is decidedly not the problematically Eurocentric racist version that underpins Freud's official position.

❊ ❊ ❊

David Eng's important essay "Colonial Object Relations" offers a crucial rejoinder to the argument of this chapter. Situating his essay within the broader project of exploring the intersection of race, colonial modernity, and psychoanalysis, Eng seeks to cast the recent resurgence of Klein's work in affect theory in a new light by excavating the racialized and colonial subtext of Klein's account of love and reparation. In contrast to affect theorists who describe Klein's account of reparation as "a psychic road map for the preservation of love, albeit a love born out of hate and the psychic negativity of infantile life"[132] and as an "ethical detour of Freud's death drive that allows intersubjective relations under threat to persist and endure,"[133] Eng instead interrogates the "psychic limits of reparation."[134] The Kleinian conception of reparation, he contends, is predicated upon a differential deployment of love and hate that produces and reproduces a split between good and bad objects that maps onto the divide between liberal European subjects and their colonized others.

Eng's argument makes two key moves. First, he follows Judith Butler in reading morality in Klein as the effect as opposed to the cause of the reparative impulse.[135] As he glosses this point: "The ego repairs the object on which it depends for its own survival, and in this way, the infant's precarious life takes precedence over the precarious existence of the (m)other."[136] On the basis of this reading, he claims that Kleinian reparation is not an ethical detour of the death drive that founds a genuine responsibility for the other but, rather, an expression of the infant's irrational and ultimately self-interested fear for their own survival. Although I think it is correct to say the fear born of excessive dependence is part of what motivates the emergence of reparation for Klein, this is far from the whole story. The urge for reparation emerges not only out of the infant's fear and dependence but also from the realization that they have harmed the object of their *love*. Klein herself makes this clear when she says that "even in the small child one can observe a concern for the loved one which is not, as one might think, merely a sign of dependence upon a friendly and helpful person.... In the depths of the mind, the urge to make people happy is linked up with a strong feeling of responsibility and concern for them."[137]

This, however, leads to Eng's second move, which turns on who gets defined as an object of love in the first place. On Klein's model, in order for the urge toward reparation to emerge, there must first be the loss of a loved object, for without the acknowledgment of a prior love relationship there would be no depressive guilt. But what, Eng asks, of those objects that are "left to perish in the dark regions beyond the circle of love and repair?"[138]

Through a close reading of several passages in her 1937 text "Love, Guilt, and Reparation," Eng traces Klein's acknowledgment and even justification of a kind of affective segregation that structures the infant's expanding world of objects. As the child learns to transfer their love for their mother to others and thus to expand the circle of their object relations to include first siblings, then schoolmates, then members of her broader community and social world, they also separate those objects into good, loved objects and bad objects, who become the legitimate repository of their hatred. As Klein has it, this separation of love from hate in both our intimate and our broader social relationships "affords relief, both because the 'good' person is spared and because there is satisfaction in hating someone who is thought to be worthy of it."[139] The stronger our hatred and aggression, the greater our need to protect goodness and love by cordoning it off into an idealized figure; conversely, "together with the idealization of certain people goes the hatred against others, who are painted in the darkest colours."[140] In this context, Klein makes the eyebrow-raising link between the love of one's mother and the idealization of one's motherland.[141] Worse still, her discussion culminates in the extremely problematic claim that the European colonists' repopulation of the "New World" with "people of their own nationality" can be seen as an instance of reparation for the commission of acts of cruelty and aggression against the native population.[142]

Without attempting to justify or even to explain Klein's bizarre and deeply problematic reading of settler colonialism as an instance of reparation, which Eng quite rightly eviscerates, I nevertheless worry that his indictment of her conception of reparation on the basis of these passages goes too far. *Love, Guilt, and Reparation* is in many ways a transitional text, written during the period in which Klein was still developing her mature metapsychology. Indeed, it is noteworthy that although Klein uses the term "reparation" repeatedly here, the terms "paranoid-schizoid position" and "depressive position" do not appear. Moreover, her discussion does not reflect the deep connection between reparation and the overcoming of paranoid-schizoid tendencies toward splitting, idealization, and demonization through the achievement of depressive integration that is so prominent in her mature view. Indeed, when read in light of her later accounts of the links between depressive integration and reparative tendencies, Klein's account in this text seems more like the description of a pathological repetition of a paranoid-schizoid dynamic of splitting, idealization, and demonization as the subject expands its object world than the prescriptive account of reparation that Eng takes it to be. From this point of view, it seems odd to read these passages as instances of genuine reparation at all, despite the fact that Klein uses this term to describe them, precisely because they don't reflect the emphasis on overcoming splitting and tolerating ambivalence that Klein later takes to be hallmarks of the depressive position and thus prerequisites for reparation.

Thus, without minimizing the force of Eng's powerful critique of this particular text, I think that it is too strong to conclude on the basis of this reading that "reparation in Klein cannot be thought of as a moral response to or concerted self-reflection on violence. It cannot prefigure any synthesis of liberal guilt into the ethical assumption of historical response and responsibility,"[143] or that her understanding of reparation is so bound up with the justification of colonialism that it is guilty of "foreclosing . . . any possibility for *racial* reparation and redress."[144] Making this case would require arguing that Klein's concept of reparation per se depends upon or requires the split that Eng uncovers in this text between loved European objects and the colonized subjects who they deem unworthy of their love and repair. To say that I don't think Eng has made that case is not to deny the importance of his critique of this aspect of Klein's work; it is simply to maintain that her mature account of subject formation, unlike Freud's official position, does not *depend on* her obviously deeply problematic, Eurocentric, racist remarks about colonialism. The point is not to condemn Freud for his blind spots and failings on the issue of race while excusing Klein for hers, but rather to acknowledge both of their blind spots and failings while asking which model of psychic subjectivity does justice to the richness, complexity, and ambivalence of psychic life without relying upon Eurocentric, racist, or colonial notions of primitivity and developmental progress.

4

The Cure Is That There Is No Cure

Psychoanalysis and the Idea of Progress

The ambivalent philosophical anthropology found in Freud's late work and developed more fully by Melanie Klein is closely bound up with assumptions about the philosophy of history and the prospects for reading history in progressive terms. In the previous chapter, I argued that the deep tension between Freud's official and unofficial positions on the psyche is mirrored by a split between his conceptions of historical progress and development. While Freud's official position on progress remains mired in problematically Eurocentric and racist forms of developmental thinking, his unofficial position not only shows the way out of such developmentalism, but also offers a radical epistemological critique of the very idea of reading history teleologically. Klein moves further in this direction insofar as her later work breaks free of developmental stage models of the psyche. This strand of psychoanalytic thinking—from the unofficial Freud to the official Klein, we might say—relies neither on developmental-historical social evolutionary models nor on potentially self-congratulatory (not to mention Eurocentric) backward-looking claims about historical progress as a "fact" in order to explicate its conception of psychic integration.[1]

However, psychoanalysis is also bound up with progress in the forward-looking sense of the possibilities for individual and social improvement. Insofar as it aims to bring about some sort of change for the better in the analysand, psychoanalysis is implicitly committed to a forward-looking notion of progress at the level of the individual, though how exactly to characterize what constitutes progress in this domain is highly contested. On one prominent interpretation of psychoanalysis, its aim is to cure analysands of their psychological illness or neurosis, restoring them to health and normality. This interpretation was reinforced by the medical model that dominated psychoanalytic treatment in the United States until late in the twentieth century, and it is connected to an image of psychoanalysis as an agent of social normalization that links progress with conformity to prevailing notions of psychological health and normality—however oppressive and restrictive those notions may be.[2] The long and ignominious history of the psychoanalytic profession's homophobia and transphobia offers perhaps the most glaring example of the dangers of this normalizing interpretation.

To be sure, this interpretation of psychoanalysis is arguably a misinterpretation—one characteristic of the "revisionism" of the ego psychology approach that was prominent in post–World War II American psychoanalysis—that betrays Freud's own best insights.[3] But, even if we reject this normalizing interpretation, the question of how to understand the process of individual transformation made possible by psychoanalysis remains open. From the perspective of the individual, then, the question of the implications of psychoanalysis for thinking about progress (in a forward-looking sense) is this: What sort of progressive transformation does psychoanalysis attempt to bring about in individuals? If psychoanalysis aims to enable individuals to live a better life, what constitutes "better" from a psychoanalytic point of view? Finally, what constraints are imposed on the prospects for progressive transformation, and what possibilities are opened up, by the realistic conception of the person explored in earlier chapters?

This question of the implications of psychoanalysis for thinking about progress recurs at the social level as well. From this perspective, acceptance of the death drive in particular is often presumed to entail the impossibility of social progress understood as the attempt to improve the human condition. The following passage from Klein captures the thought well: "The repeated attempts that have been made to improve humanity—and in particular to make it more peaceable—have failed, because nobody has understood the full depth and vigour of the instincts of aggression innate in each individual. Such efforts do not seek to do more than encourage the positive, well-wishing impulses of the person while denying or suppressing his aggressive ones. And so they have been doomed to failure from the beginning."[4] Not surprisingly, then, initial skepticism about the prospects for fusing Marxism and psychoanalysis—one of the primary aims of the first generation of the Frankfurt School—turned precisely on the difficulties of integrating the death drive into the materialist conception of history. For example, Erich Fromm, in a fascinating discussion of Freud's philosophical anthropology, writes: "In the second phase of his work, after the first World War, Freud's picture of history became truly tragic. Progress, beyond a certain point, is no longer simply bought at great expense, but is in principle impossible. Man is only a battlefield on which the life and death instincts fight against each other. He can never liberate himself decisively from the tragic alternative of destroying others or himself."[5] Such skepticism about the implications of the death drive for the prospects of social progress was not limited to critical theorists. From within the psychoanalytic movement, the pioneering early female analyst Karen Horney put the point succinctly when she claimed that the death drive "paralyzes any effort to search in the specific cultural conditions for reasons which make for destructiveness. It must also paralyze efforts to change anything in these conditions. If man is inherently destructive and consequently unhappy, why strive for a better future?"[6]

But is the death drive in fact incompatible with any and all claims about the possibility of social or political progress in the future?[7] This chapter addresses this question by first discussing the most sustained and well-developed attempt from within the Frankfurt School tradition to reconcile progress with the death drive: Herbert Marcuse's *Eros and Civilization*. Although I am skeptical of Marcuse's speculative, utopian vision of progress beyond the performance principle, I contend that his work offers some important clues for reconciling the possibility of progress with the persistence of the death drive. These clues can be further developed by turning from Marcuse's account of Eros and the aesthetic dimension as celebrations of regression to the polymorphously perverse pleasure principle to Klein's conception of reparation and creativity as expressions of the work of mourning. Drawing on this discussion and putting Klein into conversation with Freud and Lacan, I sketch a less speculative, more negativistic conception of progress as an ethical-political imperative, one that is, I argue, compatible with the assumption of the death drive.

Regression as Progress in Marcuse

Unlike those readers who choose the official or the unofficial Freud, either declaring him to be a staunch defender of the Enlightenment or denouncing (or celebrating) his Counter-Enlightenment pessimism, Marcuse consistently highlights the deep tension and fundamental ambivalence at work in Freud's philosophical anthropology. The Freudian conception of human nature is, for Marcuse, both "the most irrefutable indictment of Western civilization—and at the same time the most unshakeable defense of this civilization."[8] And yet Marcuse centers his reading of Freud on the claim that "civilization is based on the permanent subjugation of the human instincts," thus foregrounding what I have called, following Whitebook, Freud's official position.[9] Linking this account directly to the concept of progress, Marcuse reasons that if civilization is based on the subjugation of instinct, then the domination of inner nature is a precondition of progress, which means that greater progress necessarily entails greater domination and unfreedom.[10]

However, Marcuse famously questions not the *connection* between progress and domination in civilization but rather its *ongoing necessity*. Whereas Freud's official position held that the clash between drives and societal norms was the price that human beings must pay for the protection afforded by civilization, Marcuse argues that the interrelation between domination and progress is not the principle of civilization per se, but of a "specific historical organization of human existence."[11] Without disputing that the repression of instincts was necessary for the development of civilization up to now, Marcuse contends that it has become superfluous.[12] Reading Freud's late metapsychology as a concrete insight into "the *historical* structure of civilization," Marcuse argues, first, that Freud's own theory is at odds with his explicit denial of the possibility of a nonrepressive civilization; and, second, that, somewhat paradoxically, our repressive civilization has created the social and historical conditions of possibility for the abolition of repression.[13]

With this first argument, Marcuse aims to uncover what he calls "the hidden trend in psychoanalysis."[14] Marcuse argues that the central conflict in Freud's work and the key to its implications for social theory is the triumph of the reality principle over the pleasure principle. Although necessary for the functioning of civilization, this triumph is also "the great traumatic event in the development of man" at both the ontogenetic and phylogenetic levels.[15] Freud himself saw the struggle between the pleasure and reality principles as eternally antagonistic; thus, Marcuse claims, "the notion that a non-repressive civilization is impossible is a cornerstone of Freudian theory."[16] However—and this is the aforementioned hidden trend—Freudian theory also contains aspects that implicitly challenge this pessimistic conclusion. More specifically, Freud's metapsychology not only uncovers but also tacitly calls into question the necessity of the internal connection between progress and domination. The aim of Marcuse's second argument, then, is to exploit this hidden trend in psychoanalysis by historicizing Freudian concepts. Although Freud makes a valid historical generalization when he claims that up to now "civilization has progressed as organized *domination*," this does not justify the conclusion that such domination is necessary.[17] Thus, Marcuse proposes to unfold the historical content of Freud's concepts through the introduction of two key terms. First, the "performance principle" refers to the prevailing historical form of the reality principle, a capitalist imperative that requires individuals to delay gratification of their libidinal drives in order to engage in productive, alienated labor. Second, "surplus repression" denotes the amount of repression above and beyond the level required for the basic functioning of civilization that serves to maintain the structures of social domination unique to modern capitalism.

Unlike Freud, who, at least in his official position, seems willing to bite the bullet and accept that the progress of civilization proceeds through repression and domination (the triumph of the reality principle over the pleasure principle, the mastery of the id by the ego, the repression of sensuous drives by reason, the domination and subversion of freedom), Marcuse calls for a transformation of this dynamic, a "reversal of the direction of progress."[18] Whereas, up to now, progress has been conditioned upon the increasing domination of inner and outer nature and of other human beings, progress could, in the future, take the form of regression to the archaic, to imagination, to phantasy—in short, to pleasure. Noting that the pleasure principle "was dethroned not only because it militated against progress in civilization but also because it militated against a civilization whose progress perpetuates domination and toil," Marcuse identifies Eros—specifically, Eros understood as the polymorphous perversity of bodies and pleasures rather than as genital sexuality—as an explosive force that is in conflict with a repressive civilization.[19]

To be sure, there is a contradiction lurking here in Freud's account of Eros, one that threatens to destabilize Marcuse's argument. Freud defines Eros—and thus also sexuality, as a form or manifestation of Eros—as the force that binds things together in ever greater unities and as such makes civilization possible, while at the same time describing sexuality as an explosive force that is in conflict with civilization.[20] This makes Eros both the force that holds civilization together and the one that threatens to tear it apart. Marcuse's solution to this problem is to attribute this unreconciled tension in Freud's thinking to his insufficiently historicist sensibilities. He writes:

> Against [Freud's] notion of the inevitable "biological" conflict between pleasure principle and reality principle, between sexuality and civilization, militates the idea of the unifying and gratifying power of Eros, chained and worn out in a sick civilization. This idea would imply that the *free* Eros does not preclude lasting civilized societal relationships—that it repels only the supra-repressive organization of societal relationships under a principle which is the negation of the pleasure principle.[21]

In other words, Eros manifests itself as a form of sexuality that is in conflict with societal bonds only in the context of a sick civilization. Free Eros, Eros unchained from its constrained and constraining manifestation as genital sexuality, need not be in conflict with civilization at all.

But what more can be said about the nature of free Eros? Although one might expect someone with deep commitment to historicist principles to be cautious about characterizing the true nature of Eros (or of anything else, for that matter), Marcuse is undeterred. "Originally," he claims, "the sex instinct has no extraneous temporal and spatial limitations on its subject and object; sexuality is by nature 'polymorphous perverse.'"[22] As a result, the "perversions" provide us with a "*promesse de bonheur*," a glimpse of the happiness promised by "rebellion against the subjugation of sexuality under the order of procreation, and against the institutions which guarantee this order."[23] The perversions have a deep affinity with phantasy and with artistic imagination, such that all three enable us to challenge the rule of the performance principle and the surplus repression required for adherence to this principle. "Against a society which employs sexuality as a means for a useful end," Marcuse writes, "the perversions uphold sexuality as an end in itself; they thus place themselves outside the dominion of the performance principle and challenge its very foundation."[24] The liberation of Eros through the release of polymorphous sexuality and the related free play of phantasy and aesthetic imagination thus form the core of Marcuse's subversion and reversal of existing conceptions of progress, predicated as they are upon the domination and subjugation of instinctual drives, and the establishment of progress in a new direction.[25]

Unlike Freud, whose official position cast doubt on whether the direction of civilization could or should be reversed, Marcuse calls for a regressive conception of progress beyond the rule of the performance principle. Ironically, he notes, such a vision of progress has become possible only because of the achievements of the performance principle, which have allowed us to develop the technological and economic capacity to satisfy everyone's needs. Thus, progress in Marcuse's sense involves not so much a rejection as a self-overcoming of the performance principle, a negation of its negation: it is in this sense that progress lies *beyond* the performance principle. Contrasting this new sense of progress with what he calls repressive desublimation—the apparent liberation of sexuality that in fact serves to uphold the status quo by harnessing sexual libido for the reinforcement of capitalism[26]—Marcuse contends that the genuine liberation of Eros "would necessarily operate as a destructive, fatal force—as the total negation of the principle which governs the repressive reality."[27]

Under these conditions, Marcuse contends that regression behind the level of civilized rationality that was formed through the repressive imposition of the reality principle "assumes a progressive function."[28] Indeed, the regressive liberation of our libidinal, instinctual past enables a radical critique of our present: "The rediscovered past yields critical standards which are tabooed by the present."[29] By uncovering and invoking critical standards that are denied or ruled out in the present, with its focus on self-renunciation in the name of productivity, regression orients itself toward the future and becomes utopian. In the place of repressive desublimation we would have nonrepressive sublimation, the channeling of libidinal and erotic energies into all aspects of social life.[30] Whereas repressive desublimation reinforces social conformity by bypassing the superego, nonrepressive sublimation "preserves the consciousness of the renunciations which the repressive society inflicts upon the individual, and thereby preserves the need for liberation."[31] Nonrepressive sublimation harnesses the culture-building, prosocial dimensions of Eros—which has been transformed through this process from aim-inhibited, repressed, genitally organized sexuality into a polymorphous eroticism—in the service of the free, playful creativity of phantasy, the imagination, and the aesthetic.[32]

However, even if the conflict that Freud envisioned between civilization and the drives can be ameliorated in the case of libidinal drives via the transformation of genital sexuality into Eros, this still leaves the death drive for Marcuse to contend with. And here the stakes and degree of difficulty are much higher.[33] Again, Marcuse's strategy is to historicize Freudian concepts. As Marcuse sees it, the conflict between pleasure and reality principles, and the resulting repression of instincts, is rooted in Ananke, which he interprets as the struggle for existence in light of material scarcity.[34] The conflict between instincts and civilization is grounded in what Marcuse calls "*exogenous* factors" that "are not inherent in the 'nature' of the instincts but emerge from the specific historical conditions under which the instincts develop."[35] If these externally derived factors can be transformed, so too can the relationship between instincts and civilization, and even the instincts themselves. Thus, Marcuse contends that Freud's account implicitly opens the door to the radical transformation of the instincts.

Indeed, Marcuse contends that we live in an age in which civilizational progress has made it possible to eliminate material scarcity, which in turn undermines the force of Ananke.[36] As a result, the conditions that produce the conflict between the pleasure and reality principles have become increasingly "obsolete and 'artificial' in view of the real possibility of their elimination."[37] Moreover, this dynamic gives rise to a virtuous circle. If the death drive strives for a state of quiescence or absence of tension—if, in other words, we understand the death drive in classically Freudian terms as a manifestation of the "Nirvana principle"—then "this trend of the instinct implies that its *destructive* manifestations would be minimized as it approached such a state."[38] In other words, as we progressively employ the fruits of technological progress to reduce material want and scarcity, tension will increasingly dissipate and the resulting destructive manifestations of the death drive will melt away. At the end point of this process, "pleasure principle and Nirvana principle then converge."[39] At the same time, as the struggle for existence lessens, the repressive constraints that originally arose as a response to that struggle (i.e., the requirement to delay libidinal gratification in order to work to secure the means of subsistence) will collapse.[40] The result will be a genuinely liberated Eros, an Eros freed from surplus repression and expanded beyond the narrow constraints of genital sexuality, increasingly empowered to bind the death drive and to mitigate its most destructive effects.[41]

Marcuse's argument about the withering away of the death drive represents the flipside of his call for the liberation of Eros. Central to the latter account is Marcuse's discussion of unconscious phantasy and artistic imagination, both of which are distinct from reason, which is governed and enforced by the existing reality principle. In the current, repressive mode of psychic development, individuation is predicated on the "repressive utilization of the primary instincts," a process through which the instincts are "subdued" under the rule of the reality principle.[42] In this process, Marcuse writes, "reason prevails: it becomes unpleasant but useful and correct; phantasy remains pleasant but becomes useless, untrue—a mere play, daydreaming."[43] By contrast, imagination (phantasy) makes an implicit claim to reconciliation and wholeness; as such, it presents a taboo image of freedom that challenges the established principle of individuation.[44] Imagination "has a truth value of its own, which corresponds to an experience of its own—namely, the surmounting of the antagonistic human reality. Imagination envisions the reconciliation of the individual with the whole, of desire with realization, of happiness with reason."[45] The truth value of imagination stands revealed in art, which presents us with images of reconciliation and in so doing stages a protest against the performance principle and its repressive, dominating control of the instincts.

To be sure, the claim that imagination, polymorphously perverse eroticism, and art could form the core of a new, nonrepressive reality principle would likely have struck Freud as problematically, perhaps even hopelessly, utopian. And yet Marcuse insists that imagination plays the crucial critical function of refusal: "Refusal to accept as final the limitations imposed upon freedom and happiness by the reality principle, . . . refusal to forget what *can be*."[46] Imagination is thus crucial to Marcuse's infamous "Great Refusal," understood as the "protest against unnecessary repression, the struggle for the ultimate form of freedom—'to live without anxiety.'"[47] The emergence of this nonrepressive reality principle would indeed be a kind of regression, at least when considered from the viewpoint of our current understanding of progress, where progress is predicated on the repression and domination of the instincts in the service of civilization. However, far from a "relapse into barbarism," this "regression" would take place "in the light of mature consciousness and guided by a new rationality."[48] As such, it would constitute for Marcuse both the progress of liberation—the fulfillment of the possibilities for freedom that are implicit but as yet unrealized in our form of life—and the liberation of progress from its entanglement in repression and domination.

Although I am sympathetic to those Foucauldians who object strenuously to Marcuse's account of liberated Eros as a revolutionary force of refusal, the crucial point for my purposes lies elsewhere.[49] Marcuse's assumption that the destructive manifestations of the death drive could be thoroughly disarmed or dissolved through the elimination of material want or scarcity rests on a problematic understanding of Freud's notion of Ananke (reality or necessity). As Joel Whitebook explains, Ananke for Freud signals the fact that "through inevitable loss, physical pain, and death, nature will always rise 'up against us, majestic, cruel and inexorable' and remind us of our 'helplessness and weakness, which we thought to escape through the work of civilization.' Whatever level of abundance might be achieved—and material well-being is nothing to scoff at—human beings will still be confronted with the 'ineluctable,' which will always administer an insult to our self-esteem."[50] In other words, even if—and this is an enormous if, one that unfortunately looks less plausible with each passing day—the elimination of material scarcity through the satisfaction of the basic physical and economic needs of everyone is (ecologically, not to mention politically) possible, this would not mean the elimination of all tension in human life whatsoever.[51] A complete dissolution of all tension would require not only the elimination of the toil, struggle, and alienation currently required for the satisfaction of material needs but also the eradication of all loss, pain, tragedy, disappointment, and death. Even if such a state could be achieved, the result would so drastically transform the human condition as to make it unrecognizably human—which means, in turn, by the logic of Marcuse's own argument, that there is no basis for his hope that the death drive would, in fact, melt away.

Further problems arise from Marcuse's conception of the death drive itself. As I indicated earlier, Marcuse accepts Freud's speculative biological conception of the death drive as rooted in the Nirvana principle. As I argued in chapter 1, this is not the most productive way for critical theorists to understand the death drive, in part for reasons that Marcuse himself discusses—namely, that, on this account, the death drive and Eros actually seem to converge for Freud, because both are defined as the conservative striving for lack of tension[52]—and in part because this account fails to offer a compelling social and psychological account of aggression. By staking his utopian vision on the withering away of the death drive, Marcuse also falls into the fairly common tendency to assume that the death drive is necessarily bad, and that individuals and society would be better off without it. However, one might wonder whether the playful, creative, artistic, utopian vision of society that Marcuse sketches could be possible without usefully channeled aggression—artistic creativity absent all tension, want, striving, struggle, aggression, and even iconoclastic destructiveness being difficult if not impossible to imagine.

In the end, Marcuse is stuck in the untenable position of advocating a romantic liberation of Eros and dissipation of the death drive because he remains overly faithful to Freud's official position: he accepts without question the claim that the psyche is held together through internalized domination. This leads him to endorse an overly simplistic conception of emancipation understood as the liberation of repressed instincts—a view that has been rightly and resoundingly criticized by Foucault.[53] To be sure, Marcuse historicizes this Freudian conception, insisting that this is the ego structure that is predominant in late capitalist societies. However, rather than considering the possibility of other, less repressive forms of ego organization, Marcuse assumes that progress requires the overthrow of the dominating rule of the rational ego. As he puts it, "Phantasy (imagination) retains a truth that is incompatible with reason.... Phantasy is cognitive in so far as it preserves the truth of the Great Refusal, or, positively, in so far as it protects, against all reason, the aspirations for the integral fulfillment of man and nature which are repressed by reason."[54] Because of her nonrepressive understanding of ego integration, Klein offers critical theorists different resources for reconciling the death drive with the possibility of progress. In the place of the regressive liberation of polymorphously perverse Eros, Klein envisions love and reparation as forces that can mitigate and ameliorate the negative effects of the death drive without banking on its withering away; instead of an aesthetic utopian longing for the complete reconciliation of individual with society, Klein conceives of creativity as the unreconciled and necessarily incomplete work of mourning.

From Reconciliation to Reparation

In his groundbreaking work on Klein and critical theory, C. Fred Alford effects a similar turn from Marcuse to Klein, and for related reasons.[55] Alford contends that Kleinian love is more productive for critical theory than Marcusean Eros, insofar as the latter is inherently selfish, immature, and narcissistic.[56] In contrast to Marcuse's libidinal utopia, Klein provides a vision of love and reparation as forces capable of countering the negative effects of primary aggression. Although Alford doesn't explicitly link reparation to the notion of progress, I shall argue that Klein's account of love and reparation provides the basis for a realistic and nonutopian but still critical conception of the possibility of progress. Moreover, unlike Marcuse's conception of Eros, the Kleinian account does not depend on an illusory fantasy of complete reconciliation that rests on the elimination of the death drive but instead is predicated on the mature acceptance of the ubiquity and ineliminability of destructiveness and of loss.[57]

In order to understand Klein's account of reparation, let's return for a moment to her conception of psychic development. Recall that, for Klein, the mother or primary caregiver is the first object of the infant's love and desire, because they satisfy the baby's hunger and do so in a way that also gratifies the baby's libidinal desires, and also of the infant's hatred, because they inevitably frustrate that desire. This means that, from the very beginning, for Klein, "love is already disturbed at its roots by destructive impulses. Love and hate are struggling together in the baby's mind; and this struggle to a certain extent persists throughout life."[58] In the paranoid-schizoid position, the baby splits the primary object into good and bad breast and directs all of their love toward the former and all of their hatred and destructiveness to the latter. When the infant feels gratified by the breast, they have pleasant phantasies of a perfectly good, completely gratifying breast that always satisfies their desires, but, when they feel frustrated, they have destructive and aggressive phantasies of a terrifying, persecutory bad breast. As the infant moves into the depressive position, they become capable of recognizing their primary caregiver as a whole object, which compels the realization that the object that they have destroyed in phantasy is the same as the one that they love and depend upon—in other words, that the good breast and the bad breast are one and the same. Moreover, because of the omnipotence of thoughts characteristic of infantile thinking, the baby feels that they have really destroyed the primary object through their phantasied attacks, which leads to depressive anxiety and guilt. These, in turn, are the source of the urge to make reparation.

Thus, for Klein, the reparative tendency is an "essential corollary" of the depressive anxiety and guilt that come to the fore in the depressive position.[59] These painful feelings give rise to "an over-riding urge to preserve, repair or revive the loved objects: the tendency to make reparation."[60] Klein writes,

> The basis of depressive anxiety is the process by which the ego synthesizes destructive impulses and feelings of love towards one object. The feeling that the harm done to the loved object is caused by the subject's aggressive impulses I take to be the essence of guilt.... The urge to undo or repair this harm results from the feeling that the subject has caused it, i.e., from guilt. The reparative tendency can, therefore, be considered as a consequence of the sense of guilt.[61]

In other words, the urge or tendency toward reparation is rooted in depressive anxiety and guilt, which are, in turn, rooted in love, first and foremost, in the infant's love for the primary caregiver experienced as a whole object. The reparative impulse both reinforces and is reinforced by love. As Klein explains:

> It seems probable that depressive anxiety, guilt, and the reparative tendency are only experienced when feelings of love for the object predominate over destructive impulses. In other words, we may assume that recurrent experiences of love surmounting hatred—ultimately the life instinct surmounting the death instinct—are an essential condition for

the ego's tendency to integrate itself and to synthesize the contrasting aspects of the object.[62]

Love thus stands in a complex relationship to reparation. Reparation is made possible by love: first, in the sense that depressive guilt emerges as a response to the infant's fear that they have attacked and destroyed the object that they love, and, second, as I discussed more fully in chapter 1, in the sense that the move to the depressive position is made possible by the primary caregiver's love for the infant. More fundamentally still, however, reparation is made possible by love inasmuch as love is the unifying force that enables the psychic integration characteristic of the depressive position.

However, Klein's account of love is deeply ambivalent. To relate to the object as a whole object is to accept that the good breast that one loves and idealizes is one and the same as the bad breast that one hates and feels persecuted by—and to continue to love that object all the same. This dynamic sets up a challenge for the subject, who must, as Klein puts it, "find the way to bear inevitable and necessary frustrations and the conflicts of love and hate which are in part caused by them: that is, to find his way between his hate which is increased by frustrations, and his love and wish for reparation which bring in their train sufferings of remorse."[63] Even if love is the only force that can mitigate and repair the damage unleashed by aggression and destructiveness, depressive love is also in large part about living with, managing, and withstanding ambivalence. For Klein, ambivalence cannot be overcome precisely because the death drive is ineliminable. This is another way of saying that, for Klein, unlike for Marcuse, there is no possibility of complete and final reconciliation, no possibility of wholeness.[64]

Klein's distinction between manic and genuine or mature forms of reparation, discussed briefly in chapter 2, sheds further light on how her account differs from the strong notion of reconciliation envisioned by Marcuse. In manic reparation, the subject attempts to put the shattered object back together perfectly, as if it had never been destroyed, and in so doing denies its own responsibility for having attacked or destroyed the object in the first place. In this mode, reparation manifests as an obsessional need to control the object. As Klein puts it: "The reparative tendency, too, first employed in an omnipotent way, becomes an important defence. The infant's feelings (in phantasy) might be described as follows: 'My mother is disappearing, she may never return, she is suffering, she is dead. No, this can't be, for I can revive her.'"⁵⁵ Genuine reparation, by contrast, requires, as Hanna Segal explains, "learning to give up omnipotent control of this object and accept it as it really is."⁶⁶ If manic reparation is the attempt to restore the object in an omnipotent way, without admitting guilt or the reality of loss, genuine or mature reparation is, according to Segal, "the very reverse of a defense, it is a mechanism important both for the growth of the ego and its adaptation to reality."⁶⁷ Genuine reparation thus depends upon accepting the real or phantasied harm that one has done to the object, withstanding the fundamental ambivalence of one's relation to the object and to one's self, and integrating that complexity and ambiguity into one's ego. This, in turn, entails accepting that neither the damaged object nor oneself can ever be made fully whole—indeed, that complete reconciliation is an omnipotent illusion.

In one of her relatively rare discussions of overcoming the depressive position, Klein suggests that this process entails moving from manic to genuine forms of reparation. As she puts it: "When the child's belief and trust in his capacity to love, in his reparative powers and in the integration and security of his good inner world increase as a result of the constant and manifold proofs and counter-proofs gained by the testing of external reality, manic omnipotence decreases and the obsessional nature of the impulses towards reparation diminishes, which means in general that the infantile neurosis has passed."⁶⁸ Although, as I discussed in chapter 3, the depressive position can never be finally overcome but instead must be continually worked through, if anything lies "beyond" the depressive position, it is reparation, the urge to mend things that have been destroyed, fragmented, or torn to bits by the operation of the death drive. But, precisely because the death drive is ineliminable and destructiveness and aggression are ongoing, reparation can never be complete but instead must be continually reactivated and reengaged. Reparation may be able to mitigate the effects of primary aggression, but it can never, on Klein's view, eliminate, defuse, or bind the death drive entirely. Rather, the richly integrated ego "again and again brings together and synthesizes the split off aspects of the object and of the self."⁶⁹ Furthermore, this process helps the ego to bring its internal (psychic) and external (social) realities into closer alignment, which, in turn, brings about a change in the ego's experience of its own frustration and aggression. As the infant is better able to distinguish internal and external reality, their capacity to distinguish between external frustration and "phantastic internal dangers" is enhanced.[70] This leads, in turn, to a greater trust in its objects and to "a more realistic and objective method of dealing with his own aggression, which rouses less guilt and ultimately enables the child to experience, as well as to sublimate, his aggression in a more ego-syntonic way."[71] In this way, psychoanalysis offers important resources for managing the destructive effects of the death drive. Even if, as Klein admits, we cannot hope to "altogether do away with man's aggressive instinct as such," psychoanalysis can, "by diminishing the anxiety which accentuates those instincts, break up the mutual reinforcement that is going on all the time between his hatred and his fear."[72]

Klein's perspective thus offers important resources for understanding how we can deal with the death drive both ethically and politically. Indeed, for Klein, ethics not only remains possible in the face of the death drive but in fact can be understood as *emerging from* the death drive. Judith Butler's recent engagement with Klein makes this point very powerfully. Butler aims to develop an ethics of nonviolence from a starting point that both recognizes and reckons with the ineliminability of the death drive. As she states: "No position against violence can afford to be naïve: it has to take seriously the destructive potential that is a constitutive part of social relations, or what some call 'the social bond.'"[73] Starting from this recognition, she asks how can we hope to alleviate violence without setting for ourselves the impossible task of eliminating a constitutive part of the psyche. Although Butler does not discuss Marcuse in this context, his utopian vision is clearly implicated in her critique. But perhaps Marcuse is drawn to this quixotic project in part because he believes, incorrectly, that ethics and the death drive are fundamentally opposed. It does not occur to him to entertain the possibility of rethinking ethics as an *expression* of the death drive.

To be sure, as I discussed in the previous chapter, Freud had already in some sense understood ethics as an expression of the death drive. However, for him, ethics and the death drive come together in the superego, a turning inward of the death drive that enforces adherence to moral and social norms. Butler contends that accepting the Freudian account leaves us stuck in a conservative position, capable of upholding ethics only by siding with the cruelty and severity of the superego. This position is also ultimately paradoxical precisely because it requires the superego to enlist the forces of aggression in the attempt to contain aggression. Turning to Klein to think beyond this impasse, Butler's work demonstrates that an ethical orientation toward reparation is not only compatible with but emerges from primary aggression. For Klein, the ability to identify with or put yourself in the place of the other—an ability that is fundamental to ethics—is generated within the dynamics of dependency, frustration, aggression, loss, and guilt that characterize early childhood. As Butler writes, "We cannot understand the reparative trajectory of identification without first understanding the way that sympathetic identification, according to Klein, is wrought from efforts to replay and reverse scenes of loss, deprivation, and the kind of hatred that follows from nonnegotiable dependency."[74]

Because Klein conceives of our primary object relation as a complicated mixture of dependence, love, and hate, on her view, destructiveness gives rise to guilt and the urge for reparation. When the child moves to the depressive position and experiences their primary caregiver as a whole object, they realizes that the object they hate and have attempted to destroy whether in reality or in phantasy is also the object that they love and on whom they depend. This means that guilt and the drive for reparation needn't be imposed *from without* in the form of strict moral rules and laws that must be anchored in a superego through a process of internalization and aggressive self-beratement; they emerge *from within*, as an internal consequence of the move to the depressive position. Furthermore, when I engage in reparative acts, as Butler postulates, "I do not disavow my destructiveness, but I seek to reverse its damaging effects. It is not that destructiveness converts into repair, but that I repair even as I am driven by destructiveness, or precisely because I am so driven."[75]

The profound political implications of Klein's notion of reparation have been explored recently in David McIvor's book *Mourning in America*.[76] McIvor draws on Klein to discuss truth and reconciliation commissions (TRCs) as potential sites for a democratic politics of mourning. While acknowledging that such commissions are far from perfect, McIvor reads them as entities that have the capacity to help communities work through traumatic events and violent pasts without appealing to impossible and potentially exclusionary ideals of social unity, harmony, or integration. Leaning on Klein's distinction between manic and genuine forms of reparation, McIvor cautions us against understanding the "reconciliation" pursued in TRCs as the manic attempt to overcome all social conflict—in which case such commissions could easily become instances of a problematic "sentimental humanitarianism."[77] Following Klein's account of genuine reparation, McIvor instead envisions TRCs as contributions to an open-ended, ongoing, never-ending task of social and political integration. As McIvor understands them, TRCs are "less a collective form of healing or forgiveness than the possibility of ongoing interactions across social divides through which democratic norms and practices might extend and deepen their reach."[78] Drawing on Klein, McIvor thus reimagines reconciliation as an ongoing democratic practice by means of which communities can form and reform a fractured, fractious, and internally contested—and thus incomplete, open-ended, and unreconciled—whole.

As McIvor's work shows beautifully, Klein's work supports a more realistic account of political integration, an alternative to the Marcusean utopia of full, harmonious reconciliation, one that does not depend on the withering away of the death drive. Together, Butler and McIvor show how Klein's account of reparation yields a realistic yet still critical ethical and a political vision. Reparation, understood as the ongoing responsiveness to destructiveness, supports an ethical and political commitment to continually mitigating and repairing the harm that inevitably results from primary aggression entirely distinct from the utopian vision of complete reconciliation, harmony, and wholeness found in Marcuse. From the Kleinian perspective, such utopian visions rest on an omnipotent denial of the reality and ubiquity of loss. Reparation for Klein, by contrast, is internally fragmented, ambivalent, incomplete, open-ended, and, thus, ongoing.

Creativity as the Work of Mourning

Like Marcuse's conception of reconciliation, Klein's account of reparation is also closely bound up with creativity, imagination, and the aesthetic. For Klein, however, unlike for Marcuse, creativity and the aesthetic are not celebrations of regression to polymorphous perversity but rather expressions of the work of mourning. The difference in their views can be attributed, in part, to their differing understandings of sublimation. On the classical Freudian account, which Marcuse accepts, sublimation is so tightly linked with repression as to be virtually indistinguishable from it. Freud defines sublimation as "a process that concerns object-libido and consists in the directing itself toward an aim other than, and remote from, that of sexual satisfaction."⁷⁹ The deep problem with this definition is that it does not clearly differentiate sublimation from neurotic symptoms, which are also formed through the redirection of repressed sexual drives. As a result, Freud vacillates between two very different understandings of sublimation: as a *species of* and as an *alternative to* repression.⁸⁰ His attempts to distinguish the latter from the former tend to rest on potentially ad hoc—and unpsychoanalytic—claims that sublimation is the channeling of libidinal drives into "higher" aims or pursuits, such as artistic or intellectual endeavors. This is part of the reason that Lacan complains about "the virtually absurd difficulties that authors have encountered every time they have tried to give a meaning to the term 'sublimation.'"⁸¹

Because he hews so closely to Freud's official position (even as he reinterprets it in historical terms), Marcuse preserves this link between sublimation and repression and inherits its internal contradictions. "Sublimation," Marcuse writes, "demands a high degree of autonomy and comprehension; it is mediation between the conscious and the unconscious, between the primary and secondary processes, between the intellect and instinct, renunciation and rebellion. In its most accomplished modes, such as in the artistic *oeuvre*, sublimation becomes the cognitive power which defeats suppression while bowing to it."⁸² In other words, the capacity for sublimation is predicated on renunciation and suppression. Hence repressive desublimation, by providing direct and immediate satisfaction of certain narrowly circumscribed sexual drives, "frees the instinctual drives from much of the unhappiness and discontent that elucidate the repressive power of the established universe of satisfaction."⁸³ In other words, repressive desublimation flattens out the opposition between the drive for individual libidinal satisfaction and the demands of social reality, thus creating a happy consciousness that all too readily conforms to the status quo.

This diagnosis, however, leaves Marcuse stuck between two problematic poles: on the one hand, a conservative longing for the return of more repressive modes of individuation on the grounds that such modes at least foster the development of autonomy, and, on the other hand, a radically utopian Great Refusal. More uncomfortably still, it seems to leave him with the idea that the former is a necessary precondition for the latter—in other words, that the negative, transgressive refusal of existing social relations that fuels great art and political protest is possible only on the basis of the (repressive) antagonism between society and individual. Repressive sublimation thus becomes the condition of possibility for nonrepressive sublimation.[84]

Klein, by contrast, provides an account of sublimation that is not modeled on repression. Indeed, as I discussed previously, Klein is relatively uninterested in repression, preferring to focus on a range of more primordial psychic mechanisms—including splitting, manic defenses, idealization, projection, introjection, and projective identification.[85] This goes hand in hand with her focus on the deepest layers of the psyche and their associated fundamental anxieties about, as Hinshelwood has it, "the formation or disintegration of the ego and of its objects."[86] Accordingly, sublimation for Klein entails not the redirection of repression toward higher aims, but the ongoing integration, enrichment, and expansion of the personality. Although she is highly attuned to the dynamics of ambivalence, Klein does not leave us in the uncomfortable position of longing for our own repression as a precondition of our freedom.

As Hanna Segal makes clear, the ego grows and is enriched through a process of working through loss: "Through the repetition of experiences of loss and recovery, felt partly as destruction by hatred, and recreation through love, the good object becomes gradually better assimilated into the ego, because, in so far as the ego has restored and recreated the object internally, it is increasingly owned by the ego and can be assimilated by it and contribute to its growth. Hence the enrichment of the ego through the process of mourning."[87] By linking mourning to the enrichment of the ego, Klein once again follows in Freud's footsteps, though here, as elsewhere, she takes her cue from Freud's later work. Recall that, in "Mourning and Melancholia," Freud famously contrasts melancholia with mourning: although both of these psychic states are responses to the loss of a loved object that are characterized by painful sadness, lack of interest in the world, and difficulty moving on, Freud depicts mourning as a normal reaction to an experience of loss that is overcome in due course while portraying melancholia as a pathological state in which the subject gets stuck. The melancholic internalizes the lost object, forging an identification with it; thus, the melancholic subject never truly gives up the lost object but instead sets it up inside its ego, replacing object love with identification. Its object loss is translated into ego loss, which explains why melancholia—unlike mourning—is accompanied by feelings of extreme worthlessness and self-beratement.[88]

Later, however, Freud rethought this pathologization of melancholia. In an important passage at the beginning of chapter 2 of *The Ego and the Id*, he acknowledges that he previously "did not appreciate the full significance of this process and how typical it is," adding that he has since come to realize that "this kind of substitution has a great share in determining the form taken by the ego."[89] He now admits that the process of melancholic identification may in fact be the "sole condition under which the id can give up its objects."[90] As a consequence, for the later Freud—and this idea has an important resonance with Klein's work—the character of the ego is best understood as "a precipitate of abandoned object-cathexes" that "contains the history of those object-choices."[91] In other words, the ego itself has a melancholic structure: it is forged through and in response to an experience of loss.

In "Mourning and Its Relation to Manic-Depressive States," Klein explicitly links her understanding of the depressive position to both mourning and melancholia, without distinguishing between the two. Indeed, the depressive position is "depressive" precisely because it is a response to an experience of loss, the result of a process of mourning. The infant in the depressive position mourns the loss of the good breast, which they feel they have destroyed through their aggressive phantasied attacks.[92] To be sure, in an important sense, the good breast never existed, precisely because it was a phantasied part-object: an overly idealized, wholly gratifying, never disappointing caregiver. But what matters is the infant's perception that it has been lost as the result of their own destructiveness. The infant thus mourns the loss of the wholly good breast that they never had. To be sure, there is another sense in which the infant doesn't lose the good breast after all; rather, the good breast is internalized and, Klein says, forms the core around which the ego develops.[93] As the internal representative of the life instinct, the internalized good breast thus enables the creation of psychic structure, and therefore of symbolization, language, and creativity.[94] But in order to gain access to these things, the child must first give up their idealized phantasy of the purity of the good breast. In this sense, too, the depressive position is predicated upon loss.

However, the internalization of the good breast isn't sufficient for the development of the capacity for creativity. The integration of the ego also depends on the ability to manage and withstand the ambivalence of love and hate that emerges with the experience of the object as a whole object. Klein explains the matter as follows:

> The more the ego can integrate its destructive impulses and synthesize the different aspects of its objects, the richer it becomes; for the split-off parts of the self and of impulses which are rejected because they arouse anxiety and give pain also contain valuable aspects of the personality and of the phantasy life which is impoverished by splitting them off. Though the rejected aspects of the self and of internalized objects contribute to instability, they are also at the source of inspiration in artistic productions and in various intellectual activities.[95]

In other words, creativity for Klein is not only a matter of working through loss; it is also a process of harnessing and usefully channeling the energy and instability of previously split-off, painful, and anxiety-provoking unconscious impulses and aspects of experience. Relatedly, the work of analysis aims to enhance the creativity of the analysand by allowing for the kind of integration and enrichment of personality that involves incorporating previously split-off parts of the self. Insofar as Klein connects creativity with the good breast and claims that the good breast forms the core of the developing ego, this suggests that the project of enriching the ego by working through the depressive position and engaging in acts of reparation is in itself a creative act—perhaps the original creative act.

Whitebook brings out the relationship between mourning and creativity beautifully in his discussion of Freud's notion of resignation. As I suggested, in his discussion of Ananke, Whitebook emphasizes the immutable fact of our own finitude and thus the ubiquity and inevitability of loss. As Whitebook presents it, resignation is the mature and sober acceptance of the painful reality that I and everyone I care for will die, while the desire for transcendence or immortality is, by contrast, an infantile, omnipotent response. Painful though resignation may be, it can also spark genuine creativity as the psyche works to metabolize its losses. Similarly, for Klein, the psyche in the depressive position is forged through the acceptance of painful reality and is engaged in a process of working through the loss of idealizations entailed by this acceptance. To be sure, there is an important difference here: the painful reality in question for

Klein is not so much human finitude but rather the fundamental ambivalence of all human relationships due to the ineliminability of the death drive. Thus, Klein's is less an existential form of resignation than a social and relational one. However, both accounts of resignation are linked to a strong critique of idealization. Idealization, for Klein, is a mode of paranoid-schizoid defense against persecutory anxiety, a way of protecting one's good objects by splitting them off from the bad and thus attempting to keep them pure and safe.[96] As such, it is a relatively immature and omnipotent attempt to cope with a reality that is all too messy, complicated, and ambivalent.

Creativity for Klein is therefore, first and foremost, a productive response to constraints imposed upon the human condition by the death drive. In this picture, the death drive is figured in negative terms: as a feature of existence and human sociality that may be mitigated through acts of reparation and creativity but that is primarily something to be suffered and borne. However, some contemporary Kleinians urge a less wholly negative view of the death drive. Thomas Ogden, for instance, argues that Klein herself was too quick to "valorize the depressive mode and villainize the paranoid-schizoid mode."[97] Ogden claims that these two modes are dialectically related in the sense that each serves to redress the dangers inherent in the other. Although the depressive position enables reparation and integration, thereby mitigating the dangers posed by the paranoid-schizoid position, Ogden notes that it can also lead to "certainty, stagnation, closure, arrogance, and deadness."[98] The paranoid-schizoid position, by contrast, "provides the necessary splitting of linkages and opening up of the closures of the depressive position, thus reestablishing the possibility of fresh linkages and fresh thoughts."[99] Aggression thus has a distinctive value, of particular importance for creative pursuits: it clears space for something new by destroying existing structures, modes of thought, and patterns of relationship.

There is a tantalizing but very brief and underdeveloped suggestion of something like this more positive conception of aggression in Klein's work. In a footnote to "Love, Guilt, and Reparation," Klein notes that even in individuals who have a highly developed capacity for love, aggression and hatred remain active. "In such people," she writes, "both aggression and hatred . . . [are] used very greatly in constructive ways ('sublimated,' as it has been termed). There is actually no productive activity into which some aggression does not enter in one way or another."¹⁰⁰ The examples she offers involve activities like politics, law, and criticism (and, we might add: philosophy!) in which people debate and argue with each other for a living; games and sports that involve attacking one's opponent; and even housekeeping insofar as it entails a never-ending assault on dirt and disorder. In this manner, Klein points toward the productivity of aggression, its potential for sublimation, and the intrinsic link between destruction and creation.

Segal's discussion of Kleinian aesthetics clearly illuminates the connections between mourning, reparation, creativity, and ambivalence.¹⁰¹ Segal argues that the depressive position makes sublimation possible insofar as it gives rise to the urge for reparation, which is, fundamentally, an urge to create and recreate. On her Kleinian view, "All creation is really a re-creation of a once loved and once whole, but now lost and ruined object, a ruined internal world and self. It is when the world within us is destroyed, when it is dead and loveless, when our loved ones are in fragments, and we ourselves in helpless despair—it is then that we must re-create our world anew, reassemble the pieces, infuse life into dead fragments, re-create life."¹⁰² Segal also highlights the importance of the sublimation of both aggressive and erotic drives in Klein's account of creativity. For Segal, the artist's achievement lies in the ability to express the conflictual union of life and death, beauty and ugliness, destructiveness and unity.¹⁰³ The creative sublimation that opens up with the working through of the depressive position has ambivalence—the conflict of the life and death drives, beauty and ugliness, harmony and disharmony—at its core.

All of which suggests that the work of art, for Klein, presents not so much an image of complete reconciliation and harmony—as Marcuse put it, the image of "the reconciliation of the individual with the whole, of desire with realization, of happiness with reason"—as a representation of deep tension, conflict, and ambivalence.¹⁰⁴ Similarly, artistic creativity for Klein is less a Marcusean expression of unbridled, liberated Eros than it is a loving, creative attempt to repair a shattered object, coupled with the mature acknowledgment that what has once been shattered can never be made fully whole.¹⁰⁵ Reparation and creativity for Klein are not about restoring a phantasied state of wholeness; rather, they are about reassembling the shattered pieces of a ruined, lost object and world in a way that acknowledges the depth of the loss and nonetheless resolves to make meaning and beauty out of the remaining fragments.

Progress (Without a Cure)

What, if any, conception of progress in a forward-looking sense is possible on the basis of the preceding discussion of reparation and creativity? Especially in light of my emphasis on resignation—the importance of resigning ourselves not only to our finitude but also to the ineliminability of the death drive and thus of ambivalence—one might think that this conception of psychoanalysis leaves us wallowing in conservative, pessimistic despair. And yet nothing could be further from the truth. To say, with Klein, that the death drive is ineliminable is not necessarily to say that no such thing as progress is possible, and this is not only because, from a Kleinian perspective, it is a mistake to presuppose that the death drive is wholly negative. If, as Klein argues, the sublimation of aggression is crucial for creativity and art, then Marcuse's utopian vision of a libidinal utopia in which the death drive has withered away not only looks internally incoherent but also intrinsically undesirable. But, even if we restrict our focus to the negative effects of the death drive, to say that the death drive is ineliminable does not mean that there is nothing for us to do. Klein contends not only that it is possible to mitigate or redress the negative, destructive effects of the death drive by engaging in the work of reparation, but also that efforts to promote progress as a forward-looking moral or political imperative that are predicated on a denial of the death drive are grounded in a kind of wishful thinking that dooms them to failure.[106] In this way, the failure to do justice to the death drive might itself constitute an impediment to progress.

In her critique of positive utopian visions of a world beyond the death drive, Klein's work connects to a strand of psychoanalytic theory that runs from the unofficial Freud to Lacan.[107] This conception is fundamentally at odds with the normalizing interpretation of psychoanalysis understood as the cure of mental or psychological illness that aims at achieving a state of psychic health or normality. The core idea of this alternative, nonnormalizing, and nonutopian conception of psychoanalysis is summed up well in Lacan's repeated insistence in his Seminar 7, *The Ethics of Psychoanalysis*, that Freud was a humanitarian but he was no progressive.[108] Given the deep tension between Freud's unofficial and official positions on progress that I explored in the last chapter, this might seem like a curious claim. Clearly in at least some aspects of his work Freud was an ardent defender of both the reality and the possibility of progress, understood as the progressive rational mastery of the ego and the related rise of secular science. So, when he insists that Freud was a humanitarian but not a progressive, what could Lacan mean? At the risk of stating the obvious, Lacan stakes his reading on what I have called, following Whitebook, the unofficial Freud.[109] On the basis of this reading, then, Lacan is saying that although psychoanalysis aims in some sense at relieving or ameliorating suffering—and in that sense it is humanitarian—it should not pretend to be able to cure the subject by making it whole and thus eliminating or filling in its lack—and, in that sense, because it doesn't aim at the realization of a positive utopian end, it isn't progressive.

The idea that psychoanalysis does not aim at the realization of a positive utopian end is summed up well in the Lacanian slogan that there is no cure.[110] In other words, for the Lacanian, there is no possibility of filling in one's lack in being or of achieving wholeness. And yet one needn't be a Lacanian to endorse some version of this claim. As I've already suggested, Klein too rejects the possibility of complete reconciliation or wholeness, linking it to a manic, omnipotent illusion that denies the reality and ubiquity of loss and the persistence of ambivalence. Moreover, as Joel Whitebook—himself a trenchant critic of Lacan—reminds us, psychoanalysis considers utopianism to be an undesirable expression of infantile omnipotence and a disavowal of the conflictual and incomplete nature of human existence.[111] Accepting this antiutopianism necessitates a different conception of the aims of psychoanalysis, according to which its aim is to facilitate the analysand's attainment of a sense of vitality, enrichment, and an opening up of possibilities that is grounded in the acceptance of this reality.

Freud had already sounded a skeptical note about the very idea of an analytic cure in one of his earliest protopsychoanalytic works, *The Studies on Hysteria*, where he famously proclaims that psychoanalysis aims not at happiness but rather at "transforming. . . . hysterical misery into common unhappiness."[112] To be sure, in his more official mode, Freud often talks in the language of illness, treatment, and even cure, and he occasionally expresses great optimism regarding the long-term therapeutic prospects of psychoanalysis.[113] By contrast, his residual, unofficial skepticism regarding such prospects receives full articulation in his late essay "Analysis Terminable and Interminable," one of his final statements on analytic technique. The skepticism that Freud expresses here—both about the practical limits of the power of analysis to transform the analysand and about the epistemic limits of the analyst's ability to know when analysis should be terminated—stems from his discovery of the death drive, in which the resistances that impede analytic transformation and the negative transference to which they give rise are rooted. "No stronger impression arises from the resistances during the work of analysis," he writes, "than of there being a force which is defending itself by every possible means against recovery and which is absolutely resolved to hold on to illness and suffering."[114] Such forces, he continues, "are unmistakable indications of the presence of a power in mental life which we call the instinct of aggression or of destruction," and they work at cross purposes to the erotic power of the positive transference that psychoanalysis mobilizes to bring about individual transformation.[115]

This unofficial strand of Freud's understanding of the aims of psychoanalysis, a strand that is present almost from the beginning but becomes more prominent in his late work, finds more consistent articulation in Lacan. Indeed, Lacan argues in Seminar 7 that psychoanalysis demands the "radical repudiation of a certain ideal of the good."[116] Thus psychoanalysis entails not only a beyond the pleasure principle but also a "beyond-the-good principle."[117] This is part of the lesson that Lacan draws from his reading of Sophocles's *Antigone*, for Antigone shows us what it means to make an absolute choice, one that is not motivated by any good.[118] Lacan goes on to say: "The question of the Sovereign Good is one that man has asked himself since time immemorial, but the analyst knows that it is a question that is closed. Not only doesn't he have that Sovereign Good that is asked of him, but he also knows there isn't any. To have carried an analysis through to its end is no more nor less than to have encountered that limit in which the problematic of desire is raised."[119] In other words, the aim of psychoanalysis is neither psychological normalization nor rationalizing moralization nor happiness; analysis has nothing to do with what Lacan calls the "service of goods."[120] Rather, the aim of psychoanalysis is to bring the analysand to accept that there is no cure, no possibility of achieving psychic wholeness, and along with this to accept and perhaps even embrace the idiosyncratic and ultimately obscure nature of their own desire, refusing to give ground with respect to it.[121] In this Lacanian rewriting of amor fati, the psychoanalytic "cure" is nothing more—but also nothing less—than the embrace of the realization that there is no cure.[122]

Although Klein's talk of psychic integration and strengthening the ego might seem to suggest a vision of psychoanalysis starkly at odds with Lacan's, as I discussed in chapter 2, Klein understands integration not in terms of wholeness or reconciliation but as an expansion and enrichment of the personality that comes from experiencing oneself and one's objects as whole persons—both loved and hated, with good and bad parts to them—and from withstanding the ambivalence that inevitably results. Kleinian integration is thus both open-ended and internally fractured in ways that mitigate against Lacanian concerns about narcissistic fantasies of wholeness. Moreover, as I discussed earlier, the Kleinian subject has a melancholic structure in that it is founded on an experience of loss. Although this is not quite the same as the Lacanian account of the subject as founded on a lack-in-being, it means that Klein shares with Lacan the sense that psychoanalysis can never make anyone whole, can never eliminate the loss that founds the subject; at best it can offer ways to negotiate this loss productively, creatively, and ongoingly.[123]

However, Lacan's ethics of psychoanalysis emphasizes the individual ethical act and the refusal to give ground with respect to one's desire even when this requires breaking social bonds and relationships. This is not to say that Lacan's ethical act is necessarily antisocial or that his theory is simply antirelational (though it is often interpreted in that way). It is to say, instead, that his discussion of the ethical act and of the ethics of psychoanalysis emphasizes the individual's idiosyncratic desire and advocates taking one's distance from the demands of the Big Other.[124] Klein, by contrast, leads us in a different direction, one that is perhaps more productive for a critical social theory. If psychoanalysis can "break up the mutual reinforcement that is going on all the time between . . . hatred and fear," then it can help us to find better ways of managing the destructive effects of primary aggression without indulging in the utopian fantasy of eliminating the death drive. Insofar as Kleinian drives are inherently directed toward objects, this process of reworking the drives necessarily entails remaking our relationships with others. In other words, Klein helps to ground an ethics of intersubjectivity and a realistic politics of nondomination.

In this strand of psychoanalytic theory from Freud through Klein to Lacan, we can discern a distinctive conception of progress (in a forward-looking sense). Lacan is correct to emphasize the antiutopian implications of Freud's unofficial position, but this does not mean that psychoanalysis does not aim at some sort of improvement.¹²⁵ Whether that improvement is understood as turning neurotic misery into ordinary unhappiness or breaking up the vicious self-reinforcing cycle of aggression and anxiety or engaging in the ongoing work of individual or political reparation or refusing to give ground with respect to our desire, there is a shared vision here of a *realistic, negativistic*, and *open-ended* conception of progress. *Realistic* because this strand of psychoanalysis converges not only on the postulation of the death drive but also on resignation to the inevitability of finitude, loss, and lack. *Negativistic* in the sense that progress consists not in achieving a state of psychic health, normalcy, or cure but rather in ameliorating or negating an experience of suffering. *Open-ended* in the sense that, instead of a preconceived end or state of affairs, its aim is an ongoing enrichment of the personality that opens up new possibilities, enabling the analysand to feel more vibrant and alive. Bruce Fink captures this idea beautifully when he contends that, for Lacan, the aim of analysis is to enable analysands to turn dead ends into through streets.[126]

❏ ❏ ❏

What, if anything, does this realistic, negativistic, and open-ended conception of the individual "progress" that can be achieved through psychoanalysis have to do with social or political progress? To return to the contrast between Klein and Marcuse that has structured this chapter, it is clear that Klein's realistic philosophical anthropology puts constraints on how much and what sort of social and political progress we can hope to achieve. As Alford explains, whereas for Marcuse "in the end it is only humanity who stands in the way of utopia; but for the way to be cleared humanity must be utterly transformed, down to its instincts," Klein's view "holds out little hope for such a transformation. Nevertheless it finds in human nature as it is currently constituted cause for hope—a hope, to be sure, that remains tragically unfulfilled."[127] On the Kleinian account, progress in the future would consist in nothing more—but also nothing less—than working to ameliorate the aggressive tendencies toward splitting and the mirror image processes of demonization and idealization, hallmarks of the paranoid-schizoid position, that fuel the dynamics of domination.[128]

Accordingly, the social-political analogue of the Kleinian conception of progress sketched here would need to be realistic, negativistic, and open-ended: realistic in that it would accept that to the extent that relations of domination are fueled by primary aggression, there is no possibility of a power-free utopia; negativistic in that it would orient itself to the critique, transformation, and amelioration of relations of domination in the present; and open-ended in that it would aim not at the achievement of a positive utopian state, but at the transformation of fixed and static relations of domination into open-ended, fluid, mobile, and reversible relations of power.[129] In this way, one can accept that there is no cure and nonetheless retain a critical conception of the possibility of progress.

Moreover, recall Klein's suggestion that heretofore efforts to promote progress as a forward-looking moral or political imperative tend to be predicated upon a wishful denial of the death drive or of primary aggression that dooms them to failure. In this way, the utopian faith in the possibility of eliminating the death drive becomes an impediment to progress. Here Klein's vision dovetails with that of Adorno, specifically with his claim that in the current historical context the harmonistic illusions of the defenders of utopian visions are actually an impediment to progress precisely because they blind us to the depth of the challenges that we face. As such, they serve the interests of the status quo. As Adorno put it, "That one is to speak from the bright and not from the dark side of individual and society, suits exactly the official and acceptable and respectable ideology."[130] In this way, Klein could be placed alongside Nietzsche, Freud, and the Marquis de Sade, those dark Enlightenment thinkers who make progress possible precisely through their ruthless critique of its alleged instances. Here we have a different way of understanding the explosive content of psychoanalysis, distinct from Marcuse's account of the revolutionary, utopian potential of uninhibited Eros. The explosive content, on this reading, consists in the ability to break through respectable ideology, to fracture existing social reality, and in so doing to make room for its radical critique. In this sense, then, we might think that at the social and political level as well, the cure that psychoanalysis offers us is nothing more (but also nothing less) than the realization that there is no cure.

5

Transference

Psychoanalysis and the Methodology of Critique

The early Frankfurt School turned to psychoanalysis not only for a social psychology that could explain why the masses chose fascism over communist revolution, but also for a model of critical method. Although the idea of modeling critical theory on psychoanalytic method received its most explicit and systematic articulation in Jürgen Habermas's early work *Knowledge and Human Interests*, this connection was also central to the work of Adorno. Indeed, as Susan Buck-Morss notes in her magisterial study, "Adorno was struck by psychoanalysis as a cognitive model" very early in his career.[1]

Buck-Morss argues that the core of Adorno's negative dialectics, his focus on nonidentity and particularity, is at least partly inspired by his reading of psychoanalysis. The corollary of Adorno's critique of identity thinking—a critique that can be encapsulated in his insistence on what he called the "untruth of identity," which is to say that objects do not go into their concepts without remainder[2]—is the thought that nonidentity is the "locus of truth."[3] If, for Adorno, "the whole is the false," in the sense that the real and the rational have not been reconciled precisely because social reality is thoroughly irrational, then the converse also holds: concrete particulars contain important glimmers of truth.[4] Although Adorno mostly resisted demands that he clarify his critical method, to the extent that he can be said to have had one, it consisted of a micrological reading of the seemingly insignificant artifacts of bourgeois culture and philosophy for their unintentional truths—that is, for what they reveal about social reality despite themselves. In this respect, his method drew inspiration from psychoanalysis, with its focus on the parapraxes, slips of the tongue, everyday cases of losing or forgetting, mishearing or misreading something, and so forth, what Adorno, citing Freud, called the "dregs of the phenomenal world."[5] Like Freudian psychoanalysis, Adorno focused his critical method on what Buck-Morss characterizes as "the smallest, seemingly insignificant details" and on the "ruptures, the logical gaps in appearances as the place where truth appeared in unintentional configurations."[6] In other words, just as psychoanalysis concerns itself with the "dregs of the phenomenal world" that other sciences pass over as unimportant, negative dialectics concerns itself with what Adorno calls "the dregs of the concept, …in what is not itself concept."[7]

Because the nonconceptual is necessarily defined and delimited, at least negatively, by concepts, precisely as what is excluded from them, the philosopher can approach the nonconceptual only with great difficulty. Adorno draws a comparison here to Freud's account of repression, which similarly impedes the psychoanalyst's approach to the unconscious. "There is such a thing as societal repression," Adorno writes,

> and one of the organs of the philosophically inclined—if indeed we may speak of an organ in this context—is the ability to sense something of this repression, to sense what has been repressed in certain objects by the general consciousness, and to be attracted by the very things that pass unobserved or by what people prefer to regard as undeserving of scrutiny. If the method I am trying to describe to you constantly tends toward micrology, in other words to immerse itself in the minutest details, it does so not out of philosophical pedantry, but precisely so as to strike a spark.[8]

That is to say, just as the analyst immerses herself in the fragments and gaps of the analysand's speech, assembling them into interpretations that may offer transformative clues to the latter's unconscious, the critical theorist immerses herself in the blind spots and waste products of history, assembling them into constellations that can strike a spark that lights up social reality in a new and practically transformative way.

In his early work, Habermas takes up this analogy between psychoanalysis and the methodology of critical theory, transforming it to cohere with his more rationalistic vision. In Habermas's hands, the conception of psychoanalytic and critical method shifts from the striking constellation of fragments of experience to the motivational power of rational insight, and the deep and arguably intractable problem of doing justice to the non-conceptual is (at least ostensibly) solved through the model of communication. In this chapter, I argue that Habermas's approach to this analogy—an approach that he himself abandoned in the early 1970s, but that has been more recently rehabilitated by critical theorists such as Axel Honneth and Robin Celikates—rests on a flawed understanding of how psychoanalysis works. A common thread running through the work of Freud, Klein, and Lacan is that analysis works (if and when it does work) first and foremost through the transference, not through the power of rational insight. This is not to say that rational insight is completely beside the point; there is an important sense in which psychoanalysis aims at enhancing and expanding one's self-understanding. But it is to say that transference is a necessary precondition for such insight to be effective. Thus, any attempt to model critical theory on psychoanalytic method must grapple with the role of transference in the distinctive type of self-transformation that analysis aims to bring about. Although stressing this point might seem to undermine the analogy between psychoanalytic and critical theoretical method (for it is admittedly difficult to see, at least at first glance, what could serve as the analogue within critical theory for psychoanalytic transference), I will argue that the proper understanding of transference shows that this is not the case. However, it does point in the direction of a different understanding of the methodology of critical theory, one that is closer to Adorno's than to Habermas's.

In what follows, I first examine the analogy between psychoanalysis and critical method as it is developed in Habermas's early work and subsequently taken up by Honneth and Celikates. Although these three versions of the analogy differ in their details, I argue that they rest on a rationalistic (mis)interpretation of psychoanalysis that fails to take seriously enough the role of the transference in analytic method. Next, I reconstruct the role of transference in analytic technique and its relationship to rational insight in the work of Freud, Klein, and Lacan. This reconstruction makes it clear that self-transformative rational insight is only possible on the basis of the affectively imbued, desire-laden process of establishing and working through the transference. This, in turn, demands a different understanding of the analogy between psychoanalytic and critical method, which I develop by drawing on Jonathan Lear's account of transference understood as the structural process of bringing an idiosyncratic world into view, thus opening it up for transformation. Finally, I return to Adorno's account of philosophy as interpretation to rethink the relationship between transference and rational insight in more consistently psychoanalytic terms.

Psychoanalysis as Model of Critique

In *Knowledge and Human Interests*, Habermas reads psychoanalysis as a science of "methodical self-reflection."[9] On his interpretation, psychoanalysis is a form of depth hermeneutics that aims to analyze those aspects of the self that have been alienated from the self and yet in some sense remain a part of it. To speak of alienated or split-off parts of the self is to refer to what Freud once called the "internal foreign territory" of the unconscious.[10] In his early work, Habermas understands the individual psyche in communicative terms; hence, for him, unconscious wishes are those that have been "exclude[d] from public communication," or "delinguisticized,"[11] but that continue to disrupt the subject's internal self-communication in the form of dreams, slips of the tongue, and other interruptions.[12] The job of the analyst, on this view, is to help the subject learn to "comprehend his own language" and, in so doing, to restore a broken internal dialogue.[13] Psychoanalysis, for Habermas, thus aims at a reflective act of self-understanding, specifically of those portions of our life history that have been alienated, split off, or repressed; its goal is that of making the unconscious conscious by translating it into a communicable language.

Habermas acknowledges that reflective self-understanding is both a cognitive process of coming to understand the resistances to making the unconscious conscious and an affective process of dissolving those resistances, and he discusses extensively the role of transference and working-through in Freud's account of these processes. Nevertheless, his account of psychoanalysis emphasizes and places conceptual and temporal priority on the role of linguistic interpretation and rational insight in the process of self-reflection.[14] This emphasis is evident when Habermas concludes from his discussion of Freud that psychoanalysis "is critique in the sense that the analytic power to dissolve dogmatic attitudes inheres in analytic insight. Critique *terminates* in a transformation of the affective-motivational basis, just as it *begins* with the need for practical transformation. Critique would not have the power to break up false consciousness if it were not impelled by a passion for critique."[15] In other words, on Habermas's account, although psychoanalysis begins with a felt desire for change that compels individuals to enter analysis and (at least ideally) leads to a practical transformation of the analysand's affects and motivations, the transformative work is done by analytic *insight*. That is to say, for Habermas, psychoanalysis works, if and when it works, through the medium of insight. This remains the case even as he acknowledges that analytic knowledge is "impelled onward against motivational resistances by the *interest in self-knowledge*."[16] The analysand's pretheoretical, anthropologically deep-seated interest in self-knowledge may be what draws her into analysis, but the analytic relationship is understood in communicative terms as facilitating a process of enlightenment that, in turn, leads to heightened self-reflection and self-understanding.

On the basis of this interpretation of psychoanalysis, Habermas offers an analogous conception of critique as the diagnosis and cure of social pathologies. Like psychoanalysis, critique begins and ends with a felt need for practical change—the desire for social change compels individuals to engage in critique, and the insight gained through critique, when mediated through political struggles for institutional change, (ideally) leads to practical transformation—but it works, if and when it works, through the medium of rational insight. Crediting Freud with this idea, Habermas writes: "For the social system, too, the interest inherent in the pressure of suffering is also immediately an interest in enlightenment; and reflection is the only possible dynamic through which it realizes itself."[17] Therefore, critique becomes the process of methodical self-reflection applied at the level of the social whole; it is the attempt to restore a broken or distorted internal dialogue within a society, by restoring open and free communication with those parts that have been internally split off or alienated. It may be guided by an emancipatory interest—that is, an interest in overcoming social suffering or political domination—and it may, if all goes well, result in practical social and political transformation, but critical power inheres in critical insight, specifically in a process of communicative, rational enlightenment.

To be sure, Habermas himself abandoned this analogy between critique and psychoanalysis—and the whole idea of anthropologically deep-seated knowledge-constitutive interests with which it was intertwined—not long after the publication of *Knowledge and Human Interests*. Around the same time, he also abandoned psychoanalysis altogether, replacing Freud with the cognitive and moral developmental psychology of Jean Piaget and Lawrence Kohlberg, respectively.[18] Recently, however, this analogy has been revived by two prominent critical theorists, Axel Honneth and Robin Celikates.[19]

Honneth's account of critical theory as the critique of a social pathology of reason implicitly resuscitates certain key features of the Habermasian understanding of the psychoanalytic model of critique. On Honneth's view, critical theory starts from a stance of negativity, from the identification of injustices and other forms of social harm and suffering. These forms of suffering are experienced as such insofar as they violate legitimate expectations of the social conditions that are necessary for individuals to lead a good life. In such circumstances, Honneth claims that the cause of those negative experiences is understood as a "deficit in social rationality," or a social pathology of reason.[20] The idea of a social pathology of reason necessarily presupposes a conception of intact social rationality, for it is only against the background of such a conception that a pathology of reason can be identified as *pathological*. Although different members of the critical theory tradition have expressed this idea in different ways, Honneth insists that "the innermost core of the entire critical theory tradition" is the idea that the process of social rationalization unique to modern capitalism generates pathologies of reason.[21]

Here is where psychoanalysis enters Honneth's picture of the distinctive methodology of Frankfurt School critical theory. Critical theorists, on Honneth's account, not only share the diagnostic premise that contemporary capitalism represents a deficient or pathological form of social rationality, one that impedes the realization of the rational potential inherent in modern institutions and practices; they also share a conception of the proper therapy for this social pathology of reason. "The forces that contribute to the overcoming of the social pathology," Honneth writes, "stem from precisely that reason whose actualization is impeded by the form of organization present in capitalist society."[22] Honneth credits Freud with this idea, maintaining that Freudian psychoanalysis inspires the critical theoretical insight that "social pathologies must always express themselves in a type of suffering that keeps alive the interest in the emancipatory power of reason."[23]

Given the internal connection between theory and practice that is essential to this tradition, critical theory takes the practical overcoming of social pathologies to be essential to its goals. In order to envision how critique might be effective in bringing about the kind of social and political transformation that it recommends or envisions, critical theory must, according to Honneth, take up the standpoint of the intact social rationality that has been distorted—but not entirely obviated—by the social pathology.[24] Modern rationality may be deformed or pathological, but it is not *wholly* deformed, and, moreover, individual subjects are intrinsically motivated to attempt to more fully realize that rationality that is only partially actualized in their current social order. This latter claim rests on two further points, both of which Honneth finds in Freud. First, pathologies of reason lead to individual suffering because human beings "cannot be indifferent about the restriction of their rational capacities."[25] This claim is inspired by the Freudian idea that "every neurotic illness arises from an impairment of the rational ego and must lead to individual cases of stress from suffering."[26] Second, the method for overcoming this suffering involves the mobilization of the very same rational capacities that have been impeded by the existing pathology.[27] Just as psychoanalysts must presuppose a desire to be cured of neurotic suffering as what motivates analysands to enter analysis, critical theorists must presuppose a desire for the healing of social suffering on the part of pathological societies—in other words, they must presuppose the existence of what Habermas called "the emancipatory interest." Moreover, just as analysis cures neurotic suffering through the reactivation of the very same rational powers that have been impeded by neurosis, critical theory must cure social pathologies through a reactivation of the rational powers that those pathologies have impeded.

On Honneth's reading, psychoanalysis rests on an individual interest in rational enlightenment and self-realization that parallels the emancipatory interest that fuels social critique. Thus, psychoanalysis serves as a model for critical theory insofar as the emancipatory *aim* of each is the achievement of a more rational mode of self-relation or society. This enhanced rationality is understood as the fuller realization of the rational potential that is inherent in both the individual and in the modern social order, but deformed by neurosis, in the former case, and capitalism, in the latter. Moreover, for Honneth, the *method* for achieving this emancipatory aim—in both psychoanalysis and critical theory—is the reactivation and mobilization of the very rational powers that have been distorted either by neurosis or by social pathologies of reason. On this view, psychoanalysis and critical theory work by mobilizing rational, reflective insight and processes of critical self-understanding whereby previously split off components of the personality or the society are integrated into a rational psychic or social whole.[28]

In his more recent work, Honneth has distanced himself from some aspects of Habermas's early work on psychoanalysis, leading him to reformulate his conception of the psychoanalytic model of critique. In particular, he questions Habermas's understanding of the emancipatory interest as an anthropologically basic, deep-seated interest akin to the cognitive interest in transforming nature and the practical interest in communication. The principal problem with this understanding of the emancipatory interest is that it rests on a dubious social-ontological conception of the human species as a macrosubject that has a shared interest in its own emancipation.[29] This focus on the species as a whole leads Habermas's account "to sever the connection between practical critique and an opposition between groups or classes."[30] In response to this worry, Honneth reconceptualizes the notion of emancipatory interest by rooting it in an account of struggles or conflicts *between* social groups, conflicts that give rise to distinctive epistemic interests for members of subordinated social groups. Specifically, because their needs, interests, and experiences are not reflected in hegemonic interpretations of norms, such groups have an epistemic interest in denaturalizing and exposing the ideological bases of those interpretations.[31]

However, Honneth's new interpretation of the emancipatory interest does not abandon the psychoanalytic model of critique altogether. On the contrary, Honneth notes that the model of psychoanalysis remains "surprisingly helpful" for the task of articulating "the characteristic methodology of those kinds of knowledge, which serve to satisfy the emancipatory interest in a systematic way."[32] Specifically, Honneth maintains that what is "worth preserving" in the "methodology outlined by Habermas" is "the thought that critical social theories should proceed in a 'reconstructive' fashion so as to identify idealized developmental paths that can be conceived of as actualizations of already accepted norms and which can then be used to diagnose the deviations that mark *de facto* developmental processes."[33] In other words, Honneth preserves his conception of the emancipatory aims—overcoming social-pathological deviations from idealized developmental paths—and methods of critical theory as analogous to psychoanalytic method.

Robin Celikates has also defended the early Habermas's analogy between psychoanalysis and critical theory in order to clarify his own, reconstructive conception of critique. Celikates's main contention is that "psychoanalysis can help us to understand the constructive, normative, dialogical and critical aspects of reconstruction, and to make them more precise regarding both aims and procedures."[34] By emphasizing reconstruction, Celikates counters the assumption that critique is a form of expert knowledge constructed from a privileged epistemic position distinct from everyday practices of justification. On Celikates's pragmatic, reconstructive conception, critique is a social practice that is in constant dialogue with everyday practices and discourses of justification. Reconstructive critique is critical and emancipatory in both its aims and its methods: it aims to empower ordinary agents by enhancing their already existing capacities for reflection and critique; its method involves treating ordinary agents not as objects of social scientific knowledge or as cultural dopes hopelessly caught in the grips of a totalizing ideology, but rather as social agents capable of reflexivity and critique. Building on the insights of Habermas's earlier work, Celikates argues that psychoanalysis provides a compelling methodological model for this conception of reconstructive critique.

For Celikates, the aim of psychoanalysis, like that of critical theory, is the enhancement of the analysand's autonomy, understood as "the subjects' ability to lead their lives in a self-determined, reflective and critical way, and to decide for themselves what this might mean."[35] Both psychoanalysis and critical theory understand autonomy procedurally, meaning that rather than appealing to substantive values or conceptions of the good life, they are oriented by a "conception of reflexivity, that is, by the capacity to confront one's own wishes, opinions and modes of behavior. . . . and to take up a reflective attitude towards them."[36] As such, psychoanalysis and critical theory ultimately aim at their own overcoming, in the sense that they strive to enable analysands and social agents to carry on the work of analysis and critique themselves.[37] This in no way commits Celikates to a utopian notion of a psyche or of a society that is no longer in need of psychoanalysis or critique, however; self-reflexivity requires that "one must constantly appropriate it anew, never sure that one possesses it."[38] Moreover, like Honneth, Celikates assumes that agents cannot be indifferent to the restriction of their capacities for autonomy and self-reflexivity because these capacities are constitutive for their self-understanding as agents. Therefore, the motivation for engaging in the work of analysis and critique is built into agency itself. Both psychoanalysis and critical theory are best understood as attempts to overcome "structural reflexivity deficits" that are at odds with constitutive features of the self-understanding of agents qua agents.[39]

Celikates further argues that this conception of the aims of psychoanalysis and critical theory puts constraints on the methods appropriate to these endeavors. If the aim of both practices is the enhancement and promotion of autonomy and self-reflexivity, then this "can be achieved only by means of a procedure in which the subject is considered, from the very beginning, capable of actually taking up this role."[40] Individuals can count as addressees of psychoanalysis or of critical theory only if they are already taken to have some capacities for reflection, however blocked or distorted those capacities may be at present. Both psychoanalysts and critical theorists may well draw on specialized theoretical vocabularies that are initially unfamiliar to analysands and social agents as they engage in the practice of analysis or critique, but only on the assumption that the latter can learn to appropriate those vocabularies. Whatever hypotheses the analyst or critical theorist may form on the basis of their theoretical knowledge—about the sources of the analysand's neurotic conflict or the causes of certain social pathologies—"depend for their criterion of adequacy on the self-understanding of the addressees."[41] In other words, the proof is always in the pudding, in whether the analytic or critical-theoretical dialogue initiates a process of reflective self- or social transformation.

Although reflexivity clearly plays a key role in Celikates's account, this transformative process is not merely a cognitive one:

> Just as little as it suffices in psychoanalysis to present the patient with a certain interpretation of his disorder without confronting its causes, social critique will be inadequate if it merely points out reflexivity deficits in agents without analyzing their causes (which in critical theory will

be understood as structural) and ensuring that these can be reflected on by the addresses. Neither psychoanalysis nor social critique are purely epistemic or cognitive projects; they cannot bring about transformations solely by imparting knowledge. Rather, they constitutively depend on a dialogical transformation of the addressees' self-understanding.[42]

Still, even if Celikates admits that the aims of psychoanalysis and critical theory are not exhausted by the enhancement of autonomy understood as the capacity for self-reflexivity, the latter is a necessary precondition for whatever further practical self- or social transformation these practices may hope to bring about—say, for example, transforming the causes of an analysand's neurotic conflicts or of agents' reflexivity deficits.[43] Self-reflection, for Celikates, is thus central to the aim and method of psychoanalysis and of critical theory: both practices aim to facilitate and enhance capacities for autonomy through a reflexive process of psychoanalytic or critical-theoretical reconstruction.

Psychoanalytic Method

Although these three versions of the analogy between critique and psychoanalysis differ in their details, each rests on a rationalist interpretation of psychoanalytic method. For Habermas, psychoanalysis is a process of enlightenment that works through the medium of critical insight; for Honneth, it is the repair of a distorted form of rationality; for Celikates, it is the enhancement of the analysand's capacities for critical self-reflection.[44] Even as all three authors acknowledge, to varying degrees, that analysis is not merely cognitive but also affective, motivational, and practical in character, they converge on the assumption that psychoanalysis works, if and when it does work, through the medium of rational insight or reflection. It is this assumption that we should pause to consider.

This is not to say that there is no textual evidence for a rationalistic reading of Freudian technique. As I've discussed in previous chapters, there is undoubtedly a strong rationalistic current running through much of Freud's work, and there are, moreover, versions of psychoanalytic theory and practice that resonate deeply with such a conception of its aims and methods.[45]

Nonetheless, the rationalist interpretation of psychoanalytic method is at the very least problematically partial insofar as it obscures the ultimately rather limited role that Freud's writings on clinical technique gave to rational insight and the corresponding emphasis that he placed on transference.[46]

Freud recognized the limitations of the talking part of the talking cure and the importance of transference as early as 1910. As he puts it in his paper "'Wild' Psychoanalysis": "It is a long superseded idea, and one derived from superficial appearances, that the patient suffers from a sort of ignorance, and that if one removes this ignorance by giving him information. . . . he is bound to recover. The pathological factor is not his ignorance itself, but the root of this ignorance in his *inner resistances*."[47] After all, if mere knowledge about the unconscious were as transformative as people sometimes think it is, then reading books about psychoanalysis would suffice to treat neurosis. But simply reading about psychoanalysis has as much of an impact on the neurotic's symptoms as "a distribution of menu-cards in a time of famine has upon hunger."[48] Moreover, and more problematically, offering the patient insights into his unconscious "regularly results in an intensification of the conflict in him and an exacerbation of his troubles."[49] Analysts should, Freud therefore suggests, refrain from offering interpretations until two preconditions are met: first, the analysand has already "reached the neighborhood of what he has repressed," and, second, a transference relationship has been established between analyst and analysand.[50]

To be sure, Freud was at times guilty of overestimating the effectiveness of insights and interpretations in analysis. As he explains in the important paper "Remembering, Repeating, and Working Through," his thinking about analytic technique went through a series of transformations, from an early reliance on hypnosis to bring about catharsis, to a later emphasis on interpretations to generate insight into the cause of repressions, to a mature focus on the importance of working through the transference relation. On this latter conception of the analytic situation, the analysand does not, as Freud had previously assumed, *remember* anything about the fact that he has repressed something, much less about the content of that repression. Rather, he *repeats* what he has forgotten and repressed, but without being aware that he is doing so. Freud offers some memorable examples here: the analysand who has repressed her defiance toward her parents' authority acts defiantly toward the doctor; the one who felt ashamed of his infantile sexuality now feels shame in the face of the analyst and can't offer productive associations, and so on. As Freud puts it, "As long as the patient is in treatment he cannot escape this compulsion to repeat; and in the end we understand that *this is his way of remembering*."[51] Indeed, the transference relation is itself a kind of repetition, a replaying of dynamics of the affective relationship to the primary caregiver—primarily of love, but also, Freud acknowledges, of hate as well.[52]

Psychoanalysis, for the mature Freud, provides a context in which the psychic traumas and deficiencies of that primary relationship can be affectively relived and negotiated. Here is Freud:

> The main instrument for curbing the patient's compulsion to repeat and for turning it into a motive for remembering lies in the handling of the transference. We render the compulsion harmless, and indeed useful, by giving it the right to assert itself in a definite field. We admit it into the transference as a playground in which it is allowed to expand in almost complete freedom and in which it is expected to display to us everything in the way of pathogenic instincts that is hidden in the patient's mind.[53]

The goal, then, is to replace the analysand's actual neurosis with a transference neurosis, which can be dynamically worked through in the context of the analysis. This process involves something altogether different in character from analytic knowledge or insight. Indeed, Freud acknowledges that offering insight into the analysand's resistances only makes them that much stronger.[54] The key to overcoming resistance is thus not more or better analytic insight but rather allowing "the patient time to become more conversant with this resistance with which he has now become acquainted, to *work through* it, to overcome it, by continuing, in defiance of it, the analytic work."[55]

Jonathan Lear highlights this aspect of analytic technique in his masterful overview of Freud's work. Although Lear characterizes the aim of psychoanalysis as that of "*facilitating the development of self-conscious thought* in the analysand," he doubts that rational self-reflection is the proper method for this facilitation.[56] The key to understanding this point lies in how we conceptualize the unconscious. Lear contends that the unconscious is best understood not simply as a repository of repressed wishes or instinctual impulses, but rather as "a peculiar *form of thinking*," one that is subject to its own distinctive rules: governed by logics of condensation and displacement, exempt from the principle of noncontradiction, and timeless in character.[57] These features of unconscious thinking enable the development of certain core unconscious fantasies that serve to organize the individual's experiences and that are remarkably stable and impervious to counterevidence. As an example, Lear considers an individual who developed as a child the rudimentary unconscious fantasy "I am the unloved one." Given the rules that govern unconscious thinking, this fantasy is timeless and incapable of being contradicted, which means that whenever the individual is confronted with instances of being loved, they will reinterpret those experiences through the framework of being unloved ("She doesn't really love me, she is just using me"). In so doing, the fantasy of being the unloved one becomes, as Lear puts it, "effective in organizing and unifying the psyche, in ways that often bypass—and sometimes distort—rational, self-conscious thought. These fantasies have a way of infiltrating our self-conscious thinking—*inclining* our judgment—so as to make it appear rational that we are 'the unloved one.'"[58] The acknowledgment that unconscious fantasies can infiltrate and distort our very experience of rational self-reflection, however, calls into question the capacity of rational reflexivity to bring about psychic transformation.[59]

On Lear's understanding, psychoanalysis aims at enabling the analysand to gain a deep understanding of the structure of their unconscious. This means not merely a cognitive grasp of that structure but, crucially, the acquisition of *"practical mastery over its fractal nature."*[60] For this type of practical mastery to be possible, the analyst telling the analysand the content or structure of their unconscious is clearly insufficient. Instead, the analyst and analysand must work together in such a way that "the analysand can experience the unconscious emerging in the here-and-now and can thus incorporate a practical understanding of it."[61] By contrast, mere rational or cognitive insight or self-reflection can all too easily become a form of psychic defense that "block[s] the self-understanding it purports to deliver"[62] or an "empty intellectualization" that impedes this process of achieving genuine self-understanding.[63] Psychoanalytic method is thus best understood not as a process of achieving rational insight or heightening reflexivity but as "the building up of a practical-cognitive skill of recognizing the fractal nature of one's unconscious conflicts as they are unfolding in the here and now—and of intervening in ways that make a satisfying difference."⁶⁴ This is how Lear understands the Freudian concept of working-through.⁶⁵

Although Lear's primary frame of reference is Freud, his account of analytic technique resonates in important respects with that of Klein and Lacan. Klein offers a succinct overview of her conception of analytic technique in a short text she wrote in the context of her debate with Anna Freud.⁶⁶ Klein insists, contra Anna Freud, that a transference relation, whether positive or negative (or both), is active from the very beginning of an analysis, in both children and adults.⁶⁷ As she explains: "In my experience, the transference situation permeates the whole actual life of the patient during the analysis. When the analytic situation has been established, the analyst takes the place of the original objects, and the patient, as we know, deals again with the feelings and conflicts which are being revived, the very defences he used in the original situation."⁶⁸ This does not mean, however, that the analysis focuses solely on the here and now of the analytic situation and ignores the analysand's past and present experiences; rather, consistent with her account of unconscious phantasy, those experiences "are seen again and again through the medium of the transference situation."⁶⁹ The transference situation gives expression to the ongoing interplay between conscious and unconscious mental processes, between the analysand's perception of reality and their unconscious phantasies, between what I have called in previous chapters the intersubjective and the intrapsychic dimensions of experience. To analyze the transference is thus to analyze this complicated set of processes and relationships.

Moreover, Klein emphasizes that "the figures whom the analyst comes to represent in the patient's mind always belong to specific situations, and it is only by considering those situations that we can understand the nature and content of the feelings transferred on to the analyst."⁷⁰ Accordingly, transference "is not just a one to one relation between patient and analyst, but something more complex."⁷¹ Klein stresses that "it is by keeping the two things together in the transference—feelings and phantasies on the one hand and specific situations on the other—that we are able to bring home to the patient how he came to develop the particular patterns of his experiences."⁷² Analysis of the transference aims to reveal to the analysand how their experience of their object world (both inner and outer) came to follow a certain pattern, and it is by bringing this home to the analysand that transformation becomes possible.

Hanna Segal suggests that technique plays a crucially important role in Klein's work because her entire approach was rooted in a "technical invention"—namely, her pioneering technique of child analysis. It was this technical invention that enabled Klein to access the more primordial, even psychotic, layers of mental experience and the anxieties and defenses specific to those layers.[73] Segal emphasizes the importance of transference for Klein, given her emphasis on unconscious phantasy and the dynamics of projection and introjection. As she puts the point: "Since the analyst comes to stand for the internal figures, all the material that the patient brings contains a dynamic element of transference."[74] On Segal's view, the aim of Kleinian analysis is "to free the ego and enable it to grow and mature and establish satisfactory object relations."[75] In order to achieve this, Segal insists that one needs both analytic insight and a "corrective object relationship" that enables the analyst to be the good object for the analysand, thus promoting the enrichment and integration of the ego (in Klein's distinctive sense). As she explains: "These two factors are inseparable because it is only in the security of the analytical relationship with the analyst as a partner who does not project or react but aims at understanding, that true insight can develop. On the other hand, it is only through insight into one's own psyche that a better object relationship can be established in relation to both internal and external reality."[76]

Lacan similarly emphasizes the importance of transference as a precondition for the effectiveness of analytic interpretation. He writes: "If [analytic] speech hits home. . . . it is because transference is involved in it."[77] Indeed, Lacan cautions analysts against understanding too quickly or offering interpretations prematurely; for him, "the space occupied by not understanding is the space occupied by desire," and the aim of analysis is unraveling the distinctive structure and object of the analysand's desire.[78] For Lacan, psychoanalysis works through the medium of transference, where transference is understood on the model of love. Crucially, however, for Lacan, love is not a relationship of intersubjectivity; it is a relationship between a subject and an object, a lover and a beloved, and, as a result, its structure is fundamentally asymmetrical and nonreciprocal.[79] This asymmetry is reflected in the structure of the analytic relationship. The analysand comes to analysis seeking knowledge of the most intimate aspects of their experience, and yet the analysand assumes that the analyst—who is, after all, a stranger—has this intimate knowledge of the analysand's desire. "How," Lacan asks, "does this situation generate something—as a first approximation—akin to love?"[30] Bruce Fink helpfully explains the dynamic this way:

> Analysis automatically places the analysand in the position of the beloved. The analysand, by speaking demands to be found lovable, and we as analysts take the analysand as someone who is important and listen to him in a way that no one else has ever listened to him before. . . . By asking the right questions, we highlight the lack in the analysand, who then comes to believe that we ourselves must have the answers since we have asked the questions . . . Not finding the answers in himself, he projects them onto us, and comes to love us as possessors of knowledge. . . . For the analysand, we become the "subject supposed to know," as Lacan dubs it—the subject whom he assumes has the knowledge he is seeking.[81]

Fink contends that the analyst must harness the analysand's love so that it becomes the driving force of the work of analysis, but that they must do so without seeking to be the object of the analysand's love. In other words, "*The analyst must love without wanting to be loved in return.*"[82]

However, as Mari Ruti explains, the ultimate aim of Lacanian analysis is "to break the transferential dynamic by which the patient comes to regard the analyst as a *sujet-supposé-savoir*, as an expert who holds the key to her desire."[83] As the transference love blossoms, Lacan notes that an "inversion" takes place "which turns the search for a possession into the realization of desire."[84] The analytic process aims not at increasing the subject's self-knowledge but rather unraveling "what is fundamentally irreducible in the subject's relationship to the signifier."[85] In other words, by working through the transference, the analysand finds nothing more than the distinctive track of their desire, and therefore their lack. All love, for Lacan, transference love included, emerges at the site of the shift or reversal that accompanies the realization that desire will always exceed its objects—that no object will ever fully satisfy the subject's desire, for to do so would be to fill in its constitutive lack.[86] Transference brings the analysand face to face with the fact that the analyst cannot give them the knowledge that they seek because the analyst does not have it: "Love," Lacan claims enigmatically, "is giving what you don't have."[87] Thus, love represents precisely the limits of knowledge that aspires to self-transparency (*epistéme*).[88]

Despite obvious divergences between Freudian, Kleinian, and Lacanian understandings of analytic technique, they converge on the claim that psychoanalysis doesn't work, if and when it does work, through rational insight. Indeed, as Lear emphasizes, rational insight is often an *impediment* to the work of analysis, insofar as it heightens resistances and serves as one of the ego's prime modes of defense. In a similar vein, Lacan notes that "any premature mode of interpretation can be criticized inasmuch as it understands too quickly, and does not perceive that what it is most important to understand in the analysand's demand is what is beyond that demand. The space occupied by not understanding is the space occupied by desire."[89] To be sure, Habermas, Honneth, and Celikates acknowledge that analysis doesn't work through rational insight *alone*, and they admit that self-transformation requires a certain kind of relationship between rational insight and affective, motivational, and practical transformation. However, they neither attend to the dangers of rational self-reflection nor take seriously enough the role of transference in analytic transformation; hence they do not consider how a less rationalist understanding of psychoanalysis impacts the analogy with critical method. Freud, Lear, Klein, and Lacan suggest that it is not sufficient to maintain that rational insight or reflection serves as a precondition for affective or motivational transformation without also acknowledging the reverse: that psychoanalytic power inheres in the dynamic working-through of internal conflicts and repetition compulsions on the terrain of the transference relationship, and that this affectively laden, practical process is a necessary condition for the effectiveness of rational insight. Even if we agree that the aim of this process is a more unified, integrated, rational, and autonomous self, the method for achieving this aim is neither solely nor even in the first instance a rational one. Psychoanalysis is not a process of enlightened, self-reflective insight that in turn brings about an affectively imbued, practical transformation, as the Habermasian model suggests. Self-transformative rational insight has as its practical condition of possibility the affect- and desire-laden process of establishing and working through the transference.

Transference and Critique

Focusing on the role of transference in the analytic relationship might seem to raise a serious problem for the analogy between psychoanalytic and critical method. What, after all, could it possibly mean to say that critique, like psychoanalysis, works through the establishment of a transferential dynamic that enables analytic insight to hit home? Two distinct but not unrelated sets of questions emerge here. First, does this mean that critical theorists should somehow aim to establish an affective bond with the members of social movements with whom they are in partisan if not uncritical dialogue?[90] And does such a vision not suggest a deeply problematic—not to mention highly implausible!—image of the critical theorist as charismatic guru? Second, where does the analyst or critical theorist stand in relation to this transferential dynamic? Does the analogy between psychoanalytical and critical method rest on a problematic authoritarian and elitist conception of the analyst, according to which the analyst occupies an objective stance, unaffected by the neurotic and affective disturbances that they aim to diagnose and treat? If so, then does this imply a similarly authoritarian and elitist conception of the critical theorist who takes up an objective, external stance on the social practices, structures, and institutions that she aims to criticize? And is not such a conception of the theorist at odds with critical theory's commitment to immanent critique?

To address the first concern, let's return to Lear, who helpfully distinguishes between two conceptions of transference in Freud. In Freud's original conception, transference refers to the transferral of an emotion or an affective state from one object to another. On this view, a transference relation is established within the analysis when the analysand transfers their feelings for their primary object to the person of the analyst. Here, the analysand's interpersonal world is taken to be more or less fixed or given, and what is transferred is simply the attachment to their primary object.

In Freud's later work, however, Lear contends that a new conception emerges, one in which the structure of the analysand's interpersonal world is no longer taken for granted, but instead becomes the primary focus. On this view, transference is not merely the transferral of feelings from one object to another; rather, it is the "repetition of an entire orientation to the world"[91] or "*an idiosyncratic world coming into view* in the analytic situation."[92] Through the establishment of the transference in the analytic situation, analysands "can come to recognize their own activity in creating structures that they have hitherto experienced as an independently existing world."[93] Through this process, Lear writes,

> the analyst and analysand jointly come to recognize that there are a structured set of responses that orient [her] emotional life. When done well, this is not an intellectual exercise; it is an emotionally vivid reality that analyst and analysand are trying to grasp as such.... As [the analysand] herself comes to recognize [the various positions and interrelations that make up this reality], she begins to grasp the world of meanings that she has hitherto used to interpret experience and orient herself. This is what it is for that world to start to open up. For in grasping the constricted nature of the possibilities that she has mistaken for reality, she opens up new possibilities for life.[94]

The aim of analysis is thus to create a transference world that the analysand can experience *as* a transference world. That is to say, although they have up to now experienced the structure of this world as given, they now come to experience it at least in large part as a function of their own construction. This experiential shift opens their world up for transformation.

Although neither Klein nor Lacan refers explicitly to Lear's distinction between relational and structural conceptions of transference, both seem to adopt something closer to the latter than the former. Klein contends that transference concerns not just the one-to-one relationship between analyst and analysand but a more complex situation that represents the analysand's entire world of internal and external object relations; similarly, Lacan insists that we must be careful not to reduce transference to the "the analysand's feelings for the analyst"—a conception that is reflected in the use of terms such as "positive" or "negative transference."[95] To understand transference in this way is to remain at the level of the imaginary.[96] Instead, he writes, "we must begin with the fact that transference, in the final analysis, is repetition compulsion."[97] Situated at the level of the symbolic, transference is a spontaneous construction of the past within the present that is accessible to interpretation and directed to the Other. Transference "manifests itself in a relationship with someone to whom one speaks," and, through speech, it reveals the distinctive structure of the analysand's desire.[98] In other words, transference is best understood as the repetition within the analysis of the distinctive track of the analysand's desire, with the analyst taking the place of desire's distinctive object. Lacan suggests as much when he says that, through transference, "the analyst is situated in the position of he who contains the ágalma, the fundamental object involved in the subject's analysis, as linked and conditioned by the subject's vacillating relationship that I characterize as constituting the fundamental fantasy, inaugurating the locus in which the subject can be fixated as desire."[99]

Reading the discussion of transference offered in the previous section through the lens of Lear's distinction helps to show why the first worry outlined is misplaced. If we understand transference as bringing into view the analysand's distinctive and idiosyncratic way of experiencing the world (for Klein, the structure of their object relations; for Lacan, the distinctive, idiosyncratic track of their desire) and revealing that way to be contingent, thereby opening it up to transformation, then we are no longer subject to the danger of positioning the critical theorist, by analogy, as a charismatic figure to whom social movement actors need to become affectively attached. Instead, to establish something like a transference relationship in the context of critical theory would mean simply to bring into view, through the interaction between critical theorists and social actors, the actors' distinctive, idiosyncratic way of experiencing the world as precisely that: a way of experiencing the world that they themselves have had a hand in constituting. Doing so thus reveals this structure of experience as something that is open to practical transformation.

By opening up a new way of understanding the analogy between psychoanalysis and critique, this structural conception of transference also points to a distinctive conception of critical theory: what I have called elsewhere, following Colin Koopman, "critique as genealogical problematization."[100] Indeed, for anyone with even a basic knowledge of Michel Foucault's work, the description of transference probably already sounds somewhat familiar. Consider Foucault's description of his critical method in his late essay "What Is Enlightenment?":

> Criticism. . . . is genealogical in its design and archaeological in its method. Archaeological—and not transcendental—in the sense that it will not seek to identify the universal structures of all knowledge or of

all possible moral action, but will seek to treat the instances of discourse that articulate what we think, say, and do as so many historical events. And this critique will be genealogical in the sense that it will not deduce from the form of what we are what it is impossible for us to do and to know; but it will separate out from the contingency that has made us what we are, the possibility of no longer being, doing, or thinking what we are, do, or think.[101]

Like the structural conception of transference, Foucault's critical method aims to reveal an idiosyncratic, historically specific way of ordering things or structuring the world as contingent and made up by a set of complex social practices thereby opening that mode of experience up to the possibility of practical transformation.[102] To be sure, unlike Habermas, Foucault never developed the analogy between psychoanalysis and the methodology of critique in a systematic way. Nevertheless, particularly in his early work, he embraced such an analogy, suggesting that his critical-historical method aims to disrupt the presumptions of continuity, unity, and progressive self-realization that underlie traditional views of history in much the same way that psychoanalysis disrupts the traditional philosophical conception of subjectivity.[103] Although this analogy is no longer referenced explicitly in Foucault's middle and later work, I don't think it is entirely misplaced either—perhaps because, unlike other commentators, I see more continuity than rupture in the various phases of Foucault's work.[104] Throughout the various articulations of his method, Foucault's distinctive aim is to bring to awareness those unconscious aspects of experience that structure our current ways of interpreting the world, to reveal them as contingent ways of ordering things that have been constituted through specific historical processes, and in so doing, to open them up to practical transformation.

However, this attempt to develop the analogy between psychoanalysis and critique by connecting the structural conception of transference to problematizing genealogy might seem to heighten the second concern raised earlier about the role of the analyst/critical theorist in the transferential dynamic. After all, although Foucault is not unique in critiquing psychoanalysis for its authoritarian conception of the analyst, he does offer a particularly powerful version of this critique. In a nutshell, the concern is that psychoanalytic method rests on a hierarchical authoritarian relationship between analyst and analysand that trades on the putative moral authority of the analyst who is taken to be both the representative and arbiter of "normality." This criticism is summarized well in Foucault's early critique of psychoanalysis, in *History of Madness*:

> Freud... exploited the structure that enveloped the medical character: he amplified his virtues as worker of miracles, preparing an almost divine status for his omnipotence. He brought back to him, and to his simple presence, hidden behind the patient and above him, in an absence that was also a total presence, all the powers that had been shared out in the collective existence of the asylum; he made him the absolute Gaze, the pure, indefinitely held Silence the Judge who punishes and rewards in a judgment that does not even condescend to language; and he made him the mirror in which madness, in an almost immobile movement, falls in and out of love with itself.[105]

In other words, although Foucault's broader argument credits Freud with attempting to reinstate the dialogue with unreason that had been broken off by positivist psychiatry—and for this reason we must "do justice to" him[106]—in the end he maintains that Freud reinscribed the power structures characteristic of the asylum (silence, the gaze, and moral judgment) within the doctor-patient relationship—specifically, within the transference relationship itself ("the mirror in which madness... falls in and out of love with itself").[107]

Greater attention to the dynamics of the transference and the way that the analyst is necessarily implicated therein (often referred to under the heading of countertransference) help to dispel this worry. Although the concept of countertransference is never systematically developed in Freud's own work—indeed, he seemed to understand it primarily as an obstacle to be overcome—it has become a prominent theme in post-Freudian psychoanalysis.[108] Similarly, although Klein says very little about countertransference in her published writings, and she seems to understand it mostly as a hindrance to analytic work, later Kleinians and post-Kleinians have made countertransference central to their understanding of analytic technique.[109] Whitebook contends that this development provides psychoanalysis with a compelling response to Foucault's critique of the authoritarian nature of the analytic relationship. With the concept of countertransference, the analyst's own unconscious and affective responses to the analysand become as much at issue in the analysis as the transference; this, in turn, has the effect of undermining the very distinction between "the normal, healthy doctor and the sick patient" on which the authoritarian image of the analyst, so trenchantly criticized by Foucault, rests.[110]

To be sure, Lacan was critical of the concept of countertransference because of his insistence on the asymmetry of the transferential relationship.[111] Still, Lacan does not totally reject the idea of countertransference. Instead, consistent with his critique of a simplistic model of transference that focuses solely on the emotional or affective relationship between analyst and analysand, he rejects an understanding of countertransference that "consists of the analyst's feelings in analysis, which are determined at every instant by his relations with the analysand."[112] Indeed, Lacan insists that his structural account of transference allows for a better understanding of the phenomenon typically referred to as countertransference:

> What is presented to us here as countertransference, whether normal or not, in fact has no reason to be specially qualified as such. What is at work is but an irreducible effect of the transference situation itself. By the sole fact of transference, the analyst is situated in the position of he who contains ágalma, the fundamental object involved in the subject's analysis, as linked and conditioned by the subject's vacillating relationship that I characterize as constituting the fundamental fantasy, inaugurating the locus in which the subject can be fixated as desire. This is a legitimate effect of transference. There is no need to bring in countertransference, as if some aspect of the analyst himself were involved, and a faulty aspect to boot.[113]

In other words: what other analysts call countertransference has nothing to do with the analyst's feelings for the analysand and everything to do with the structure of desire that is being repeated in the analytic situation, a structure in which the analyst is necessarily always already involved.[114]

Lacan's insistence on the asymmetrical nature of the analytical relationship, however, should not be taken to imply that he defends the objective authority of the analyst. After all, the whole point of Lacanian analysis is for the analysand to reject the analyst's authority as the *sujet-supposé-savoir* and to accept that the analyst doesn't have the knowledge that they seek. Moreover, Lacan acknowledges that the fact that analysis consists in transference understood as the repetition compulsion places it on difficult epistemic terrain: "Under the normal conditions of analysis.... transference is interpreted on the basis of and using the instrument of transference itself. It is thus impossible for the analyst not to analyze, interpret, and intervene in the transference from the position bestowed upon him by transference itself."[115] Instead of objective, authoritative knowledge of the analysand's unconscious or the truth of their desire, what the analyst has to offer is "nothing other than his desire ... with the difference that it is experienced desire."[116] In other words, the analyst has no moral authority over the analysand, nor do they represent normality or health; all that they have is the experience of having engaged in the process of working through their own desire to the point of having encountered its limit. At best, the analyst, by virtue of having gone through a training analysis, "knows, in some sense, how to play [his unconscious] like an instrument"; they have not "a raw unconscious.... but rather a supple unconscious, an unconscious plus experience of that unconscious."[117]

Thus, if critical theory is to be understood on the model of psychoanalysis, this need not imply that the theorist is positioned as an external authority who claims to have objective knowledge of the social practices and institutions that they criticize. Taking seriously the way that the analyst is necessarily implicated in the transferential relationship suggests by analogy a view of the theorist as an engaged *participant* in ongoing social and political struggles.[118] What the critical theorist might bring to such struggles is nothing more—but also nothing less—than the experience of having undergone a change in their relationship to their social world, having come to understand that world as in large part a contingent construction that is open to internal transformation.

Philosophy as Interpretation

In light of the preceding argument about the role of transference in analytic interpretation, what role remains for rational insight in this process, and, analogously, in critical theory? Does my argument suggest that rational insight is irrelevant or beside the point? If not, then how does it relate to the work of the transference? And how can the role of insight be preserved without falling back into the rationalistic interpretation of psychoanalysis criticized here?

Habermas claims that critique is impelled by a passion for critique—that is, that individuals are motivated to engage in critique because of their suffering, which provides them with a passion for or practical interest in emancipation. If we take seriously the idea that transference is a necessary precondition for analytic insight to hit home, this suggests a more complex sense in which critique might be related to a passion for critique: namely, that critique can't possibly be effective unless the way has been affectively prepared for it. The implication of this would be that insofar as critical theory is a understood solely as a project of generating and deploying rational insights, it is not only insufficient for motivating emancipatory political praxis—a point that would be difficult to dispute—but that it may actually be counterproductive. In other words, the critical project of offering rational interpretations of social pathologies may serve either to deepen a society's resistances to the contents of those insights or to mobilize a society's internal defense mechanisms, to allow it to claim to have overcome its pathologies through rational insight and understanding while clinging to them all the more fervently. This would be the social-theoretical analogue of what Jonathan Lear calls "the illusion of reflective distance."[119] This is not, of course, to say that critical theory is responsible for the social suffering and pathologies that it attempts to diagnose, but that, insofar as critical theory works solely through the mechanism of rational insight, it might become a surface-level defense mechanism that enables social pathologies to remain rooted at a deeper affective and practical level.

Does this mean that critical theory must abandon the goal of offering rational insights into social problems? Not at all. Recall that the line of criticism developed here does not contend that rational insight or interpretation is irrelevant for the work of psychoanalysis—just that it can only be effective when the way has been prepared for it by working through the transference. Therefore, keeping the analogy between psychoanalysis and the methodology of critique firmly in view, the question is this: How can the rational aspect of critique be understood differently, in a way that coheres with the critical-genealogical analogue of the conception of transference discussed earlier? What model of critique preserves the power of rational insight while avoiding the potential pitfalls of a purely rationalistic model that downplays or misunderstands the passion for critique?

The outlines of such a conception can be found in Adorno's early programmatic essay "The Actuality of Philosophy." Here, Adorno advocates a conception of philosophy as interpretation modeled implicitly and explicitly on psychoanalysis, one that provides a compelling alternative to the rationalistic interpretation offered by Habermas and that coheres well with the critical-genealogical analogue of transference developed previously. Adorno's essay opens with a reflection on the failures of the idealist project of grasping the "totality of the real" with the "power of thought."[120] Philosophical idealism has failed, for Adorno, because present social reality is thoroughly irrational Any philosophical position that holds that the real is the rational and the rational is the real only serves to obscure the deeply antagonistic, contradictory, and irrational nature of current social reality and thus to justify the status quo.[121] In order to make this contradictory reality visible, philosophy requires a different, nonidealist method. After criticizing various contemporary philosophical attempts to respond to the crisis of idealism—including neo-Kantianism, *Lebensphilosophie*, Husserlian phenomenology, Heideggerian ontology, and logical positivism—Adorno offers his account of philosophy as interpretation. Distinguishing his account from philosophical hermeneutics, Adorno insists that interpretation does not decipher the meaning that lies behind perceptible reality. To find a meaning in reality is to justify it—and this is decidedly not the goal of interpretation, as Adorno understands it. Moreover, reality as such has no reason and thus no meaning; it is not produced intentionally. The task of philosophy of interpretation is "to interpret unintentional reality."[122]

The method for interpreting unintentional reality is the construction of constellations—trial combinations of the minute fragments of experience—that "fall into a figure which can be read as an answer, while at the same time the question disappears."[123] Adorno contends that these unintentional fragments are drawn from the empirical social sciences. Indeed, he insists that philosophy as interpretation "always remains bound" to the social sciences "because its power of illumination is not able to catch fire otherwise than on these solid questions."[124] Philosophy as interpretation turns to the empirical sciences not in search of grand theories of the social totality—philosophy as interpretation must "learn to renounce the question of totality"[125]—but for a reservoir of the "small and unintentional elements" out of which constellations are constructed.[126] In this connection, Adorno notes that "turning to the 'refuse of the physical world' which Freud proclaimed, has validity beyond the realm of psychoanalysis" and contributes to the project of authentically materialist knowledge.[127]

Although this is the only explicit reference to psychoanalytic method in the essay, Susan Buck-Morss has suggested that Adorno's constellative method for the critique of society is modeled directly on psychoanalysis:

> Both focused on the smallest, seemingly insignificant details, which Adorno, following Freud's formulation, referred to as the "refuse of the world of appearance." Both looked to the ruptures, the logical gaps in appearances as the place where truth appeared in *unintentional* configurations. Both solved the riddles of these configurations by reconstructing the inner logic governing their paradoxical appearance. Reification and ideology distorted the outer world, as repression and rationalization distorted the inner one. In both cases, knowledge as a process of discovery was itself an act of liberation, and in both cases the model for that process was a dialectical experience.[128]

Indeed, the very choice of the term "interpretation" for Adorno's conception of philosophy is telling. Although Adorno's use of this term is, as Martin Saar has noted, "vague" and "metaphorical," it can be made more concrete by reading it as implicitly modeled on psychoanalytic interpretation.[129] Just as psychoanalytic interpretation, when offered under the right conditions and at the right time, can light up the analysand's idiosyncratic world of object relations or structure of desire in a new way, enabling the analysand to practically transform those structures, philosophical interpretation can light up social reality in a new and strikingly conclusive way, thus enabling its transformation.

Recall Jonathan Lear's claim that the aim of psychoanalysis is to enable the analysand to acquire practical mastery over the fractal nature of psychic life. By fractal nature, Lear seems to have in mind the ways in which deep and intricate psychic patterns are unconsciously repeated across different scales of our psychic experience, giving a coherent if deeply implicit structure to events that would otherwise appear chaotic and random. "Without analysis," he contends, "the psychologically sensitive person is not in a position to grasp this fractal quality of life. For it is analysis that teases out the recurring structures—in the microcosmic details of life as well as the macrocosmic structure of one's life."[130] By experiencing the emergence of their unconscious conflicts in the context of analysis—that is, through the transference—the analysand comes to experience the fractal nature of those conflicts and is able to develop the practical-cognitive skill required to intervene in them in productive and satisfying ways. In this context, Lear describes a good psychoanalytic interpretation as "simply a form of words that accurately grasps those conflicts at the right level for the analysand to make a conscious, efficacious intervention in her own thinking and acting—and thereby augments this practical skill."[131]

For Adorno, social experience too has a fractal nature. Although he is highly critical of any philosophical system that aims to theorize the social totality—on the grounds that such systems fail to take seriously the deep and pervasive irrationality of the real and mirror the totalitarian logic of identity thinking by attempting to subsume all particulars within themselves—his turn to the unintentional fragments of subjective experience that are left in the wake of the decay of such systems does not leave the question of the social totality behind altogether. For Adorno, these fragments contain within them keys to interpreting the social totality; like Leibnizian monads, they hold up a windowless mirror to the contradictory nature of social reality.[132] As such, these particular fragments provide a point of entry into that contradictory reality that cannot be found through systematic philosophy. As Adorno puts it in *Negative Dialectics*, "Only a philosophy in fragment form would give their proper place to monads, those illusory idealistic drafts. They would be conceptions, in the particular, of the totality that is inconceivable as such."[133] If the totality is "inconceivable as such," then it can be approached only through the interpretation of its fragments as assembled in constellations.

Adorno makes a similar point in the context of his discussion of the relationship between psychoanalysis and sociology. "The isolated individual," he writes, "the pure subject of self-preservation, embodies in absolute opposition to society its innermost principle. The jarring elements that make up the individual, his 'properties,' are invariably also moments of the social totality. He is, in the strict sense, a monad, representing the whole and its contradictions, without, however, being at any time conscious of the whole."[134] In other words, the individual is a "contradictory microcosm" of the antagonistic society.[135] For Adorno, the fractal structure of subjective experience justifies the turn to psychoanalysis, which, insofar as it is "alive to the clash of psychic forces," is in a better position to illuminate "the objective character especially of economic laws as against subjective impulses" than theories predicated on the denial of fundamental antagonism or conflict.[136] In other words, psychoanalysis offers insight not only into the individual psyche but also into the social totality, inasmuch as the individual serves as a contradictory microcosm of the antagonistic whole.

Philosophy as interpretation assembles the small, unintentional fragments of subjective experience—the dregs of the concept—into trial combinations, constellations, that light up social reality in a new way. Its focus on fragments is necessitated by the failure of idealism, which is incapable of reading the "incomplete, contradictory, and fragmentary" text of social reality.[137] And yet, because of the fractal nature of social reality, the way that its contradictory, antagonistic, and oppressive patterns are repeated across multiple scales, the assembly of fragments into constellations yields a new perspective on the contradictory whole, inducing a transformative effect. Like a good psychoanalytic interpretation, a good philosophical interpretation illuminates the contradictory, antagonistic structure of social reality in such a way that enables social actors to make an effective intervention in their own ways of thinking and acting.

What relationship, if any, does this Adornian conception of critique as interpretation have to do with the Foucauldian account of problematizing genealogy that I discussed in the previous section? Although it might be going too far to claim that Adorno is himself a genealogist full stop—this would be to underplay the specifically dialectical nature of his thinking—I do think it is fair to say that there is a significant genealogical element in his work. One can see this quite clearly in Adorno's Lukácsian conception of "second nature," which refers to the totality of existing social structures or social reality that have been produced through a process of historical mediation but that have come to take on an appearance of naturalness and givenness.[138] For Adorno, as for Foucault, revealing the contingent historical mediations that have congealed into second nature has the effect of freeing us up in relation to them. Consider, for example, his remarks on what we stand to gain from simply raising the question of how the type of reified consciousness that gives rise to the authoritarian personality develops:

> Simply posing such questions already contains a potential for enlightenment. For this disastrous state of conscious and unconscious thought includes the erroneous idea that one's own particular way of being—that one is just so and not otherwise—is nature, an unalterable given, and not a historical evolution.... Above all [reified consciousness] is a consciousness blinded to all historical past, all insight into one's own conditionedness, and posits as absolute what exists contingently. If this coercive mechanism were once ruptured, then, I think, something would indeed be gained.[139]

To be sure, Adorno is a deeply dialectical thinker for whom the flipside of unmasking the historical dimensions of second nature is uncovering the ways in which history is "natural." Although I don't think that Adorno's critical naturalism is necessarily incompatible with Foucauldian genealogical commitments (provided that both positions are properly understood), arguing this point is not necessary for my purposes here.[140] My suggestion is simply that Foucauldian genealogy and Adornian critique fit together as interconnected parts of a broader critical methodology that takes the analogy with psychoanalysis seriously while at the same time reading psychoanalysis less rationalistically than Habermas and post-Habermasian critical theorists, and this does not require a full-scale assimilation of their theoretical perspectives. Problematizing genealogy brings an idiosyncratic, contingently structured social world into view in such a way that opens that world up to practical transformation. Philosophy as interpretation provides a form of words that, by revealing the contradictory and incoherent yet fractal quality of social experience, lights up social conflicts or problems in a new way, enabling social actors to make conscious, effective transformations in their modes of thinking and acting. Together, they provide the backbone of a critical methodology that is rational without being rationalistic, attuned to the ambivalences and contradictions of social reality, and oriented to practical transformation.

❊ ❊ ❊

Given the emphasis on transference and interpretation in my reading of psychoanalysis and, by extension, in my understanding of critique, what, you may be wondering, could possibly count as the criterion for success in either domain?

Although Freud's views on this topic, as on many others, changed over time, one of his last words on the subject suggests two criteria: first, the alleviation of the symptoms that brought the analysand to analysis, and, second, the analyst's judgment that enough unconscious material has been worked through "that there is no need to fear a repetition of the pathological processes concerned."[141] This does not mean, however, that analysis can serve a prophylactic function, such that having gone through a thorough analysis will inoculate the analysand from the emergence of further neurotic conflicts in the future. To assume that this is the case would be to assume that it is possible to resolve an unconscious conflict "definitively and for all time"—an assumption that Freud once entertained but later came to regard as overly optimistic.[142]

This account of what constitutes analytic success is noteworthy in two respects. First, whether we understand success narrowly, as Freud does here, as the alleviation of symptoms, or more broadly, as later analysts have emphasized, as the enhancement of the analysand's sense of vitality and aliveness, whether or not success has been achieved is a judgment to be worked out between analyst and analysand in the context of the analytic work. There is no objective or neutral standard of health or normality that, once met, signifies the end of the analysis.

Adorno makes a strikingly similar claim with respect to critical theory. Given that the task of philosophy is the interpretation of unintentional reality, constellations cannot be judged by how well or poorly they correspond to objective reality; they "are legitimated in the last analysis alone by the fact that reality crystallizes about them in striking conclusiveness."[143] One finds a similar thought in Max Horkheimer's programmatic early essay "Traditional and Critical Theory": "There are no general criteria for judging the critical theory as a whole, for it is always based on the recurrence of events and thus on a self-reproducing totality. Nor is there a social class by whose acceptance of the theory one could be guided."[144] Insofar as critical theory is influenced solely by its "concern for the abolition of social injustice," it may well appear biased against prevailing modes of thought and in favor of victims of injustice.[145] Moreover, because critical theory awaits its realization in a future just society, it cannot point to immediate practical results; indeed, it may, at first, intensify rather than resolve social struggles.

In light of this, Horkheimer asks, how can we possibly know that critical theory is bringing about the emancipatory transformation at which it aims? The answer is that we can't: "There can be no corresponding concrete perception of it [i.e., of the essential kind of change at which the critical theory aims] until it actually comes about."[146] In other words, the proof can only be in the pudding, and what constitutes success must be ongoingly negotiated between critical theorists and the social actors and movements with whom they are in partisan if not uncritical alliance.[147]

Second, just as there is no possibility of an analysis that can inoculate us against the possibility of all future neurotic conflicts or crises, there is no possibility of a critical theory that can foresee and protect against all future injustices or forms of oppression. Just as the work of analysis is interminable, the work of critique is necessarily ongoing. Or, as Foucault put it, as far as critique goes, "we are always in the position of beginning again."[148]

Conclusion

From Theory to Praxis

In the introductory chapter, I offered three reasons that critical social theory in the Frankfurt School tradition stands to benefit from a renewed engagement with the strand of psychoanalytic drive theory that stretches from Freud through Klein to Lacan. Although this list is not intended to be exhaustive, psychoanalysis offers critical theory at least the following: a realistic conception of the person that can mitigate critical theory's tendencies toward normative idealism; the possibility of rethinking the developmentalist conceptions of individual and social evolution that pervade critical theory; and the resources to understand critical theory's conception of the aims and methods of critique beyond problematic forms of utopianism and rationalism. Subsequent chapters have explored each of these reasons in greater detail.

Chapter 1 focused on the realistic conception of the person found in Kleinian theory. After laying out the core features of Klein's mature metapsychology, I argued that Klein brings together intrapsychic and intersubjective dimensions of experience in a uniquely productive way. Her emphasis on primary aggression, unconscious phantasy, and ambivalence makes her view "realistic" in the relevant sense, giving her understanding of intersubjectivity its richness and complexity. At the same time, her commitment to the idea that subjects are object-related from the start and her conception of the drives as relational passions render her intrapsychic model compatible with critical theory's methodological commitments to sociality and historicity.

Chapter 2 turned to the question of developmentalism, starting at the individual level, with the problem of the ego. I argued that Klein offers a unique conception of ego strength and integration that moves beyond the model of the ego's progressive domination of inner nature, and thus beyond Adornian and Lacanian critiques of the rational ego as narcissistic, paranoid, and oppressive. Klein's vision of ego integration as the expansion and enrichment of the personality through the incorporation of unconscious content not only echoes Adorno's fleeting remarks about genuine reconciliation; it is also linked to her complex and ambivalent conception of intersubjectivity. Thus, Klein's noncoercive, nondominating, and open-ended conception of ego integration provides a compelling alternative to the Habermasian model of individuation through socialization. Chapter 3 addressed the question of developmentalism at the level of social evolution. After reviewing the Eurocentric racism that pervades the Freudian conception of "the primitive," and thus Freud's official conception of social and cultural progress, I argued that his unofficial position, properly understood, radically subverts progressive, developmental models of the self and of civilization, and that Klein's nondevelopmentalist conception of the psyche provides a compelling articulation of this unofficial Freudian view. Despite Klein's own early commitment to social evolutionary theories and her deeply problematic remarks about colonialism, her mature metapsychology does not rely upon Eurocentric, racist, or colonial notions of primitivity and developmental progress for its rich, complex, and ambivalent conception of psychic life.

Chapter 4 turned to the task of rethinking the aims of critique in light of the realistic conception of the person articulated in earlier chapters. Following on a critical assessment of Marcuse's attempt to reconcile the possibility of progress with the death drive, I argued that Klein's accounts of creativity and reparation as the ongoing work of mourning offer an attractive alternative to Marcuse's utopian vision of complete reconciliation via regression to the polymorphously perverse pleasure principle. Drawing on Freud, Klein, and Lacan, I put forward a realistic, negativistic, and open-ended conception of progress as an ethical-political imperative. Chapter 5 took up the methodology of critique. While agreeing with the early

Habermas, Honneth, and Celikates that psychoanalytic method offers a compelling model for critique, I raised concerns about their overly rationalistic and cognitivist understanding of how analysis works. Highlighting the importance of working through the transference in analytic technique as a preparation for the effectiveness of analytic insight, I then sketched an analogous conception of critique that combines genealogical problematization with the construction of interpretive constellations.

Although chapter 5 began to consider questions of analytic technique and the practice of critical theory, for the most part this book has focused on abstract, metatheoretical reasons that critical theory needs psychoanalysis. The central claim has been that a renewed engagement with a certain strand of psychoanalysis can help to address problems that have arisen within critical theory as an intellectual project: normative idealism, developmentalism, utopianism, and rationalism. However, in critical theory, as in psychoanalysis, theory and praxis are indelibly intertwined. An argument that critical theory needs psychoanalysis thus could not be complete without further discussion of the up to now mostly implicit practical and political implications of the interpretation of psychoanalysis offered in this book.

Indeed, one might well think that the need to make sense of the deep irrationality of contemporary politics provides the most pressing justification for a renewed engagement between critical theory and psychoanalysis. After all, the recent resurgence of authoritarian politics around the globe, but especially in the United States and Europe, has left critical theorists scrambling for explanations. Although it seems clear that any sufficient analysis of this phenomenon has to take into account the global financial crisis of 2008 and its aftermath—and in that sense I wholeheartedly agree with those who have argued that a critique of neoliberal capitalism must come back to the center of critical theory—there is also a felt sense that this account on its own is insufficient.[1] The emergence of Trumpism, Brexit, the Alternativ für Deutschland, Marine Le Pen, and the like in the context of relatively stable, on the whole still prosperous liberal democracies seems so irrational, so tied to a politics of ferocious anger, violence, xenophobic hatred, and a destructive willingness to drive Euro-Atlantic democracy off a cliff, that it seems to many critical theorists that we need psychoanalytic resources to diagnose the situation and to identify prospects for progressive transformation.[2]

To be sure, not all critical theorists favor such a return to psychoanalysis. For example, in his trenchant assessment of the contemporary relevance of the authoritarian personality study in the wake of the 2016 election of Donald Trump, Peter Gordon suggests that the main lesson we should take from this study today is that psychoanalysis is no longer relevant for a critical theory of society. Gordon contends that, although the official discovery of this study is that of a new authoritarian personality type, the unofficial lesson is a more radical claim about the authoritarian character of modern society itself.[3] Although the authoritarian personality study may seem vulnerable to a charge of methodological self-referentiality—on the grounds that its fundamental distinction between an subject with a high F score and a "true individual who is apparently immune to typological thinking" is rooted in the very kind of stereotypical thinking that the study identifies as pathological—the real problem cuts much deeper.[4] As Gordon explains, Adorno "identified stereotypical thinking and authoritarianism with general features of the modern social order itself."[5] In other words, in our social world, true individuals are increasingly scarce, replaced by types. As a result, what might at first appear to be a flaw in the study's research methodology is in fact a problem in the social order. In this context, the individual psyche threatens to dissolve, suggesting, in turn, "that psychoanalysis too was beginning to lose its salience, while the behaviorists reductive model of the self as a mere 'bundle of reflexes' was assuming the status of objective truth."[6] That is to say, under the conditions of mass culture, which constitute a kind of psychoanalysis in reverse, the psychoanalytic model of autonomous depth becomes "objectively false and . . . ideological in the technical sense."[7]

Ultimately, according to Gordon, this leads Adorno to claim that the tendency to embrace fascism and authoritarianism is not a psychological disposition at all, but rather "a generalized feature of the social order itself."[8] Moreover, Gordon identifies important lessons from this facet of the study that apply to our diagnosis of Trumpism:

> Trumpism is not anchored in a specific species of personality that can be distinguished from other personalities and placed on a scale from which the critic with an ostensibly healthy psychology is somehow immune. Nor is it confined to the right-wing fringe of the Republican Party, so that those who self-identify with the left might congratulate

themselves as not being responsible for its creation.... Trumpism is not a social pathology but another instance of the general pathology that is American political culture.[9]

The lesson of Adorno's analysis of the authoritarian personality, for Gordon, is that Trumpism is not a pathology that affects *them*; it is *us*—all of us. It is rooted in what Gordon calls, echoing Arendt, "the thoughtlessness of the entire culture."[10]

Gordon is surely right to remind us that any diagnosis of Trumpism worth its salt must be rooted in a broader critique of the culture that produced Trump and made him popular enough to win the presidency in 2016 by however slim a margin. And he is rightly worried about the dangers of depoliticization that attend attempts to root the resurgence of authoritarian populism in individual personality structures.[11] Yet I think he goes too far in suggesting that, as a result of the rise of mass culture and the corresponding disappearance of true individuals, psychoanalysis is today losing its political relevance. As he puts it (in an admittedly exaggerated way): "Psychoanalytic categories remain valid only so long as we can plausibly speak of the psyche as a real referent. What passes for politics today in the United States has its etiology not in determinate forms of psychological character but rather in modes of mindless spectacle that may awaken doubt as to whether the 'mind' remains a useful category of political analysis."[12] Even if we grant Gordon the assumption that true individuals are disappearing under conditions of mass culture—bearing in mind that this is a rather big if, inasmuch as this claim rests on Adorno's problematic identification of rationality and autonomy with the coercive structure of the bourgeois ego and on his controversial critique of the culture industry—does this mean that we can no longer plausibly speak of the psyche as a referent? To be sure, Adorno is right to insist that individual psychology is historically, socially, and culturally conditioned, and Gordon is right to remind us of this. But the suggestion that it is no longer useful to refer to the psyche in our political analysis is plausible only on a very narrow, orthodox Freudian conception of the psyche (what I have called throughout this book, following Whitebook, Freud's official position) that we have ample reason to reject. Even then, I confess that I'm not so sure. Do we really think that, for example, infantile omnipotence, narcissistic ego structures, paranoid projections, the return of the repressed, and even Oedipal rivalries have no relevance whatsoever for contemporary politics? Be that as it may, I think that Klein's work provides an alternative here, precisely because her model of the psyche does not rest on the kind of bourgeois structure of Oedipalization that Adorno took to be constitutive of the psyche per se.

Gordon's more compelling worry, in my estimation, concerns the problematic triumphalism that he discerns in critical theorists' diagnoses of authoritarian (or other regressive) personality structures.[13] I fear that there is something of this tendency in Wendy Brown's contrasting—and in many ways extremely astute—analysis of the rise of authoritarian politics in the ruins of neoliberalism. Brown argues that although neoliberalism's devastations of economic and political security and its hollowing out of the public, social, and political conditions that sustain democratic politics are undoubtedly important factors in shaping our political present, they do not by themselves explain the affective energies that sustain right wing populist movements. Brown understands these affective energies as instances of the rancor, nihilism, and ressentiment of aggrieved power felt by whites (especially white men) whose privilege and status has been eroded.[14]

In order to diagnose these energies, Brown resuscitates Marcuse's analysis of repressive desublimation, understood as the selective but superficial release of libidinal energies in ways that uphold rather than challenge the status quo. For Marcuse, repressive desublimation constitutes subjects who reconcile the conflict between themselves and the demands of society by conforming their desire to those demands. This leads to a weakening of the superego—a strong superego is no longer needed to keep desire in check—which, in turn, undermines conscience, autonomy, and the capacity for critique. As a result, repressive desublimation is a reinforcement of the status quo masquerading as a form of freedom. The result of these changes in subjective constitution, Brown contends, is a new kind of politically reactionary subject, distinct from the authoritarian personality generated by previous iterations of capitalism. As Brown describes this distinctively neoliberal reactionary subject: "Malleable and manipulable, depleted of autonomy, moral self-restraint, and social comprehension, this subject is pleasure-mongering, aggressive, and perversely attached to the destructiveness and domination of its milieu."[15] In support of this analysis, she offers the following examples: the combination of "daring and disinhibition" "manifest in alt-right tweets, blogs, trolling, and performances"; the "wild, raging, even outlaw expressions of patriotism and nationalism that frequently erupt from the extreme right today"; and "the quality and intensity of aggression spilling from the right, especially the alt-right, amid its frenzied affirmation of individual freedom."[16]

Although Brown's description of the ethos of the alt-right seems apt, her account of the politically reactionary subject should give critical theorists pause. After all, is it really the case that "they"—those who inhabit these reactionary subject positions—are so heteronomous, so regressive, and so easily manipulated? Does such an analysis not at least implicitly position "us," the critics of right-wing and authoritarian movements, as autonomous, mature, and enlightened by comparison?[17] Even if we can shake off potential worries about methodological self-referentiality, should we ignore the fact that the awareness that "we" think "they" are backward and regressive is at least a part of what sustains the hatred of elites that fuels authoritarian politics?

In her recent discussion of capitalism with Rahel Jaeggi, Nancy Fraser rejects the temptation to take up a moralizing or dismissive stance toward right wing populist movements. As Fraser puts it: "The dismissive response is wrong—and, I would add, *counterproductive*. Right-wing populists *do* have genuine grievances, which deserve to be validated. And reactionary populist movements *are* responding to a real underlying crisis, which also requires acknowledgment."[18] On Fraser's analysis, to the extent that right-wing populism rejects not only the distributional effects of progressive neoliberalism but also its very *progressivism*, to respond to this critique by accusing populists of being regressive is politically counterproductive. This is not at all to deny that there are hard-core racists, white nationalists, misogynists, and homophobes who support right-wing populist movements. But it is to wager that there may be many Trump voters who do not fall into these categories and who thus could be part of a new, progressive political realignment against neoliberalism.

If Fraser's analysis is compelling, as I think it is, and if critical theorists would do well to follow Brown's lead and draw on psychoanalysis to understand the affective energies that fuel authoritarian movements, as I think we would, then we need a different kind of psychoanalytic language to help us understand the deep irrationality of our politics and the possibilities for moving beyond our current impasses. We need a psychoanalytic framework that can help us to understand what Fraser characterizes as the "deepening divisions, even hatreds, long simmering but recently raised to a fever pitch by Trump, which appear to validate the view, held by some progressives, that all Trump voters are 'deplorables'—irredeemable racists, misogynists, and homophobes. Also reinforced is the converse view, held by many reactionary populists, that all progressives are incorrigible moralizers and smug elitists who look down on them while sipping lattes and raking in the bucks."[19] Although Fraser herself would likely be reluctant to turn to psychoanalysis here, I contend that Kleinian theory can address these questions fruitfully, and better than Brown's Marcusean framework. The latter is limited not only because it arguably falls back behind the insights into the study of sexuality offered in Foucault's devastating critique of Marcuse in *The History of Sexuality, Volume 1*,[20] but also because, as I argued in chapter 4, Marcuse hews too closely to a classical Freudian developmental model of subjectivity. By linking the capacity for autonomy with the domination of inner (and outer) nature, Marcuse leaves us in a familiar bind: either we bite the bullet and throw our lot in with domination on the grounds that at least it gives us autonomy, or we accept Marcuse's utopian vision of the reversal of repression and release of erotic energies as the progressive solution. As I argued in more detail in chapters 2 and 4, I think that Klein's work provides a way out of this impasse.

Moreover, Klein offers resources for helping us to understand the divisiveness that fuels our politics without falling into the seductive comforts and satisfactions of pathologizing those on the other side. Drawing on Klein, critical theorists can, following Gordon, resist the temptation to use psychoanalysis as a tool for diagnosing *them*: their weak egos, their eroded superego, their unsublimated rage and aggression.[21] Recall that, for Klein, the descriptors "paranoid-schizoid" and "depressive" mark out positions—configurations or constellations of modes of relating to oneself and to others, together with their specific anxieties and defenses—rather than developmental stages. Although the depressive position does, to be sure, constitute a kind of achievement, and thus remains something to strive for, *everyone* has the tendency to fall back into the paranoid-schizoid mode, particularly under conditions of stress and heightened persecutory anxiety. Precisely because she is less wedded to rigid developmental schemas, Klein's framework is less pathologizing—her somewhat charged terminology (after all, "paranoid-schizoid" certainly doesn't sound like a compliment!) notwithstanding.

Contra Gordon, however, psychoanalysis can still provide insight into our *politics*; indeed, it might even contribute to the broader critique of the social order that Gordon calls for. In Kleinian terms, we might say that our politics is more and more often conducted in a paranoid-schizoid mode. The idea here is not to diagnose particular individuals, groups, or political movements or parties as being stuck in the paranoid-schizoid position. Rather, the suggestion is that Klein gives us a rich and resonant vocabulary for talking about certain logics that continually reemerge in and shape politics in the present. To inhabit the paranoid-schizoid mode, for Klein, is to experience a high degree of persecutory anxiety, which increases tendencies toward disintegration and splitting (demonization and idealization) and makes it more difficult to bring one's phantasied projections into line with reality.

Translating this into the register of politics, we might say that when right wing populist leaders stoke fears of being overrun from without by migrants or the forces of globalization or being attacked from within by rampant crime, they heighten and intensify persecutory anxieties, exploiting and enhancing the mutual reinforcement that Klein discerns between anxiety and aggression.[22] They do this, moreover, in the context of (to consider the example of the United States) a polity that is already under great stress from the economic devastation wrought by nearly forty years of neoliberal economic restructuring and global financialized capitalism, brought to a head by the financial crisis of 2008 and its aftermath, and that is already deeply split by racist structures of mass incarceration and the criminalization of immigration.[23] Under conditions of heightened persecutory anxiety, political communities further fragment and disintegrate, and polarization comes to the fore.[24] Politics devolves into what Noelle McAfee calls "a politics of Manichean divides" and is increasingly governed by a logic of splitting.[25] We may tend to demonize the dangerous others who we take to be attacking us, but even those who avoid this temptation are all too ready to demonize our political opponents, such that they appear to us not just wrong-headed but evil. Conversely, we tend to idealize the purity and rectitude of our own position. Moreover, while in this paranoid-schizoid mode, our perception is so distorted by phantasies of persecution and of revenge that it threatens to become untethered to reality at all. Only in such a post-truth context can concepts like "alternative facts" be invoked with a straight face.

Under such conditions, the recent resurgence of conspiracy theories, which are marked above all by their paranoid-schizoid logic, is little surprise. The more powerless, insecure, and disenfranchised a community feels, the more likely it would be to harbor persecutory anxieties, to feel itself constantly under attack from shadowy, nefarious, powerful forces.[26] With this in mind, we should expect to see conspiracy theories gain more ground among communities that feel particularly aggrieved or disenfranchised, regardless of whether that feeling is justified.[27] As Brown herself has argued, the politics of aggrieved ressentiment "emerges from the historically dominant as they feel that dominance ebbing—as whiteness, especially, but also masculinity provides limited protection against the displacements and losses that forty years of neoliberalism have yielded for the working and middle classes."[28] If this analysis is correct, as I think it is, then we should also expect that, although conspiracy theories have a long history in the American political landscape and come in right- and left-wing variations, at the moment conspiracy theories seem to wield the strongest influence on the right. Gaining strength from and in turn fueling increased political polarization, right-wing conspiracy theories exemplify clearly the demonization of opponents and the distorted orientation to reality that marks the paranoid-schizoid mode. As Robyn Marasco has argued perceptively, such theories are also marked by an idealization of power itself that goes hand in hand with persecutory anxiety: that is, by the assumption that power is all-encompassing, capable of achieving any and all of its ends, completely in control.[29]

If something like this Kleinian account of our paranoid-schizoid politics is compelling, then what, if anything, can be done? How can we work through the very real divides, hatreds, and basic lack of trust that mark our politics in order to build the new kind of inclusive progressive political movement that we so desperately need?

In the same way that the point of the Kleinian account is not to diagnose or pathologize particular individuals or political groups, the answer cannot be that those who support authoritarian forms of populism or subscribe to conspiracy theories need psychotherapy. Nor is it even that we all do—which is not to say that it wouldn't be beneficial for many of us! In this way, I part company with Adorno's own proposals for redressing the persistence of authoritarian personality structures. In two important late essays, "The Meaning of Working Through the Past" and "Education After Auschwitz," Adorno argues for combatting fascism and promoting enlightenment through pedagogy and the promotion of psychoanalytic treatment. On the pedagogy side, he envisions psychoanalytically trained educators being sent into schools across Germany to facilitate the development of more enlightened "cadres" that could, in turn, help to enlighten society as a whole.[30] Recognizing the obvious difficulties involved in scaling psychoanalysis up, Adorno nevertheless avers, "Although it is so difficult to carry out something like a mass analysis because of the time factor alone, nonetheless if rigorous psychoanalysis found its institutional place, its influence upon the intellectual climate in Germany would be a salutary one, even if that meant nothing more than taking it for granted that one should not lash outward but should reflect about oneself and one's relation to whatever obdurate consciousness habitually rages against."[31] Doubling down on his paradoxical defense of the strong ego, Adorno notes that education to enlightenment, autonomy, and critical reflection may not eliminate the unconscious impulses and anxieties that fuel fascist politics, but they could at least enable individuals to control them better.

Adorno favored this type of individualized solution to the pathologies that produced and reproduced fascism and authoritarian personalities because he believed that collective praxis was blocked. As he put it, "Since the possibility of changing the objective—namely societal and political—conditions is extremely limited today, attempts to work against the repetition of Auschwitz are necessarily restricted to the subjective dimension. By this I also mean essentially the psychology of people who do such things."[32] Without denying that the subjective, individualized solutions that he envisioned might be beneficial, and while acknowledging that there may still be good reasons to be pessimistic about the prospects for achieving radical progressive political change, still I think that there is more that critical theorists can say here and that Klein's work offers some compelling resources. The thought is that we might turn to Klein to learn how to practice democratic politics in a more depressive mode. If the paranoid-schizoid mode of politics is marked by disintegration, splitting, and a lack of orientation to reality, the depressive mode would be marked by enhanced (but still open-ended) integration, greater ability to withstand ambivalence, and the attempt to bring our perceptions in line with reality (including with the real experiences of other human beings).

As I discussed in chapter 4, the political implications of Klein's conception of depressive integration have been explored recently by David McIvor's analysis of truth and reconciliation commissions (TRCs).[33] The promise of TRCs, on McIvor's analysis, lies in their capacity to help communities to work through traumatic events and violent pasts without appealing to impossible and potentially exclusionary ideals of social unity, harmony, or integration. Drawing on Klein's account of reparation, McIvor envisions TRCs as sites for working through the open-ended, ongoing, never-ending task of social and political integration. Such processes at least have the potential to facilitate "ongoing interactions across social divides" and in so doing to "extend and deepen" the "reach" of democratic practices.[34] Drawing on Klein, McIvor thus imagines democracy as a depressive form of politics by means of which political communities can form and reform themselves as fractured, fractious, and internally contested—thus incomplete, open-ended and unreconciled—wholes.

In a similar vein, Noelle McAfee has recently drawn on Klein to offer a depressive model of democratic politics that highlights the role of ambivalence. As McAfee contends, democratic politics "calls for growing up, moving beyond the black and white of adolescence and toward a more mature understanding of the complexities and ambiguities in politics, and learning to live with ambivalence and uncertainty. This calls for radically questioning our own preconceptions and points of view and being willing to discover that the others in our midst, whom we were so sure were the devil, might possibly have a perspective, maybe even a point, we should consider."[35] In addition to requiring the overcoming of tendencies to splitting (and the resulting political Manicheanism) and the development of a greater capacity to withstand ambivalence (and the related rejection of demands for purity), democratic politics in a depressive mode also requires us to accept that politics inevitably entails losses and trade-offs that must be acknowledged and mourned lest they continue to haunt us in the future.[36]

Moreover, McAfee's expansive account of deliberative democratic practice highlights how democratic politics in a depressive mode can change our orientation toward others with whom we deeply and fervently disagree. On her view, the point of democratic deliberation is not so much that of changing people's views through the exchange of reasons. Although this may happen on occasion and although reasons are an important part of the content of deliberation, this is far from all there is to democratic deliberation. And, we might say, it's a good thing, too, as anyone who has ever tried to reason someone out of a fervently held belief in a conspiracy theory already intuitively knows. In a context where political argument is conducted in a paranoid-schizoid, conspiratorial mode, if reason is the only weapon we have, we may well already be doomed. The point of democratic deliberation, on McAfee's view, is to bring about a subtle but profound shift in our relationships to those with whom we disagree. It is, in other words, not so much to change people's views but rather, as she puts it, to "change their views of others and others' views."[37] At its best, democratic deliberation enables the depressive insight that those with whom we fervently disagree are not evil incarnate, but whole people, with good and bad parts. Crucially, this does *not* mean withholding judgments about views that we find abhorrent, whether white supremacist, misogynist, xenophobic, homophobic, transphobic, or what have you. It *does* mean trying to understand—not to justify, but to understand—what in someone's history, experience, or life circumstances might lead them to hold such views.[38] This, in turn, enables us to feel concern for them and to understand ourselves as coconstituting a shared, public world with them.[39] Doing so may not by itself generate political consensus—indeed it may not even reconcile all participants to the same interpretation of reality—but it just might foster the conditions of mutual trust and respect necessary to mitigate phantasmatic distortions and undermine the allure of alternative facts.[40]

From the Kleinian perspective, we will never be rid of the paranoid-schizoid mode of politics entirely. The paranoid-schizoid mode is a permanent possibility, always waiting in the wings, ready to return particularly under conditions of heightened anxiety and stress. And, to be sure, the depressive position is no picnic. It is, after all, depressive, melancholic, founded on loss: a letting go of comforting logics of purity that sustain political Manicheanism and of phantasies of pure reconciliation and complete integration. The continual, ongoing management of ambiguity, complexity, and ambivalence is exhausting, and the purity and simplicity of splitting and polarization remain constant temptations, as anyone who has ever reconciled himself to the painful loss of a lover by convincing himself that she's actually an evil bitch intuitively knows. To top it all off, shifting democratic politics into the depressive mode won't ever solve all of our problems. At best, it may help to foster conditions in which we will be better able to work collectively on solutions. But this is far from nothing.

Klein thus offers us resources for a realistic conception not only of the person, but also of democracy. As such, she can help critical theorists to avoid the twin temptations of democratic triumphalism and democratic defeatism. If the early Frankfurt School taught us anything, it is that authoritarianism can emerge *within* democracy just as it does in fascist and totalitarian contexts. It is precisely this emergence that we must think through anew today. But, in order to do so, we will have to bid farewell to the idealizing, triumphalist assumption that democracy is the unsurpassable horizon that carries the solution to all of our problems.[41] At the same time, letting go of this triumphalism does not commit us to a defeatism that casts democracy as mere neoliberal fantasy.[42] Both of these are positions defended by critical theorists within the last decade, and both seem problematic from a Kleinian point of view. Democracy may not be the solution to all of our problems, and the utopia of a fully rationalized democracy may be a dangerous fantasy, but democracy can enable us to negotiate ambivalence without resorting to hatred and demonization, cope with loss, and even productively channel aggression. It can support the ongoing painstaking, ongoing, open-ended work of building coalitions, constituting shared worlds, and sustaining communities across lines of difference and disagreement. Klein thus points us in the direction of a sober and realistic but still meaningful defense of democracy as, to echo McAfee, a politics for grown-ups.

❁ ❁ ❁

We find ourselves in a strikingly similar situation to the members of the early Frankfurt School, who first turned to psychoanalysis to supplement Marxism in order to understand the distinctive conjuncture of the failure of revolution in Germany and the fascism that rose in its wake. Indeed, it is worth remembering that the Frankfurt School project was born from an experience of prolonged and protracted social, political, and cultural breakdown and loss. The Institute for Social Research began its life as a Marxist reading group whose members came together in the early 1920s to try to comprehend the defeat of the revolutionary aspirations of German workers after World War I and the resulting splintering of the Left between communists and social democrats. What came to be known as the Frankfurt School later rose to prominence on the strength of its attempt to grapple with the catastrophic rise of European fascism, a rise facilitated by the support of the workers. The realization that early critical theory was forged in response to an experience of radical failure and loss might help us to understand how its initial revolutionary hopes, expressed especially in some of the programmatic texts of the 1930s, eventually gave way to gloomy resignation.

Understandable though that transition from revolution to resignation may be, the Kleinian perspective developed throughout this book offers critical theorists an alternative, one that avoids resignation without giving up the explosive content of psychoanalysis. Klein shows us that we need not accept arid rationalism and omnipotent developmentalism as the price that must be paid in order to avoid the failures and blind spots of early critical theory's engagements with psychoanalysis. Kleinian critical theorists can endorse the early Frankfurt School's critique of the paranoid, narcissistic structure of the authoritarian ego without being mired in paradox or consigned to vague utopian gestures. We can accept the sober and realistic psychoanalytic critique of utopianism without giving up on the possibility of progress, so long as this is understood in a negativistic and open-ended way. And, drawing on Klein's notions of creativity and reparation, we can begin to think about how to transform loss and failure into productive social and political transformation. Giving up on narcissistic and potentially exclusionary fantasies of revolutionary wholeness or complete reconciliation need not lead to political resignation. We can still strive to construct meaning, beauty, and political coalitions out of the fragments.

Notes

Introduction

1. Theodor Adorno, *Minima Moralia: Reflections on [sic] a Damaged Life*, trans. E. F. N. Jephcott (London: Verso, 2005), 49.
2. For helpful discussion of the philosophical and institutional connections between psychoanalysis and the early Frankfurt School, see Joel Whitebook, "The Marriage of Marx and Freud: Critical Theory and Psychoanalysis," in *The Cambridge Companion to Critical Theory*, ed. Fred Rush (Cambridge: Cambridge University Press, 2004), 74–75.
3. Martin Jay, *The Dialectical Imagination: A History of the Frankfurt School and the Institute of Social Research, 1923–1950* (Berkeley: University of California Press, 1996), 103.
4. On this point, see especially Theodor Adorno, "Sociology and Psychology (Part 1)," trans. Irving Wohlfarth. *New Left Review* 1, no. 46 (November–December 1967): 67–80; Theodor Adorno, "Sociology and Psychology (Part 2)," trans. Irving Wohlfarth, *New Left Review* 1, no. 47 (January–February 1968): 79–97; and Herbert Marcuse, *Eros and Civilization: A Philosophical Inquiry into Freud* (Boston: Beacon, 1955), 238–74.
5. As Marcuse explained in a 1978 interview: "The real reason for Fromm's departure from the Institute was his castration of Freudian theory, especially the revision of the Freudian concept of instinctual drives" (Herbert Marcuse, Jürgen Habermas, Heinz Lubasc, and Telman Spenglar, "Theory and Politics: A Discussion," *Telos*, 38 (1978–79): 124–53, 127). In an interesting twist, Fromm himself was also critical of the conformism of neo-Freudian analysis, though he centered his critique on the ego psychology of Heinz Hartmann and others. See Erich Fromm,

"The Crisis of Psychoanalysis," in *The Crisis of Psychoanalysis* (New York: Holt, Reinhart, Winston, 1970).

6. Marcuse et al., "Theory and Politics," 127. For insightful discussion of the Fromm-Marcuse debate, and interesting defense of Fromm, see John Rickert, "The Fromm-Marcuse Debate Revisited," *Theory and Society* 15 (1986): 351–400.

7. For a trenchant critique of this move, see Joel Whitebook, *Perversion and Utopia: A Study in Psychoanalysis and Critical Theory* (Cambridge, MA: MIT Press, 1995).

8. See Fromm, "Crisis of Psychoanalysis." Fromm notes the similarity between ego psychology and the cognitive developmental psychology of Piaget in that both emphasize the "rational aspects of adaptation, learning, will, etc." (27).

9. I'll come back to this issue; for incisive critical discussion of this aspect of Habermas's work on psychoanalysis, see Whitebook, *Perversion and Utopia*.

10. On this point, see Whitebook, "Marriage of Marx and Freud."

11. See Joel Anderson, "Situating Axel Honneth in the Frankfurt School Tradition," in *Axel Honneth: Critical Essays*, ed. Danielle Petherbridge (Leiden: Brill, 2011), 50–52.

12. On this point, see Axel Honneth and Joel Whitebook, "Omnipotence or Fusion? A Conversation between Axel Honneth and Joel Whitebook," *Constellations* 23, no. 2 (June 2016): 170–79.

13. Axel Honneth, "The Work of Negativity: A Psychoanalytical Revision of the Theory of Recognition," in *Recognition, Work, Politics: New Directions in French Critical Theory*, ed. Jean-Philippe Deranty, Danielle Petherbridge, John Rundell, and Robert Sinnerbrink (Leiden: Brill, 2007), 129.

14. See Honneth, "Work of Negativity." For extended critical discussion of his answer, see Amy Allen, "Are We Driven? Critical Theory and Psychoanalysis Reconsidered," *Critical Horizons* 16, no. 4 (2015): 1–18. As I discuss further on, I am not convinced that Honneth's interpretation of psychoanalysis actually accomplishes this goal.

15. Honneth, "Work of Negativity," 129. For Raymond Geuss's account of political realism, see Geuss, *Philosophy and Real Politics* (Princeton, NJ: Princeton University Press, 2008), 9–11.

16. Axel Honneth, *The Struggle for Recognition: The Moral Grammar of Social Conflict*, trans. Joel Anderson (Cambridge, MA: MIT Press, 1995), 96. In his early work, Honneth sought to integrate object-relations psychoanalysis with George Herbert Mead's social psychology and with his intersubjectivist reading of the young Hegel. As Danielle Petherbridge points out, in his later work, Mead tends to drop out while Winnicott remains central to the story. See Petherbridge, *The Critical Theory of Axel Honneth* (Lanham, MD: Lexington, 2013), 149.

17. See Honneth, *Struggle for Recognition*, 99. The claim that infants begin their psychic lives in a state of symbiotic fusion with their primary caregivers is a version of Freud's theory of primary narcissism, which I will discuss more fully in chapter 1. For discussion of the concept of symbiosis in Honneth, see Petherbridge,

Critical Theory of Axel Honneth, 147–64. For a critique of Honneth's reading of Winnicott that centers on the notion of symbiosis, see Noelle McAfee, *Fear of Breakdown: Politics and Psychoanalysis* (New York: Columbia University Press, 2019), 34–41. In his early work, Honneth tends to refer to the primary caregiver as the "mother," even as he acknowledges that the person who fulfills this function for the infant need not be the biological mother. For the sake of simplicity, I will follow Honneth's usage when quoting him, but will endeavor to use the more neutral term "caregiver" when speaking in my own voice. On this point, see Honneth, *Struggle for Recognition* 192n12.

18. The locus classicus here is Daniel Stern, *The Interpersonal World of the Infant: A View from Psychoanalysis and Developmental Psychology* (New York: Basic Books, 1985). Stern's research has generated a spirited methodological debate among psychoanalysts. For an overview, see André Green and Daniel Stern, *Clinical and Observational Psychoanalytic Research: Roots of a Controversy*, ed. Joseph Sandler, Anne-Marie Sandler, and Rosemary Davies (London: Karnac, 2000). Although I share some of Green's methodological concerns about Stern's approach, I set this issue aside here.
19. Axel Honneth, "Facets of the Presocial Self: Rejoinder to Joel Whitebook," in *The I in We: Studies in the Theory of Recognition* (Cambridge: Polity, 2012), 217–31.
20. Honneth, "Facets of the Presocial Self," 226.
21. Honneth, 226.
22. Joel Whitebook, "Mutual Recognition and the Work of the Negative," in *Pluralism and the Pragmatic Turn: Essays in Honor of Thomas McCarthy*, ed. James Bohman and William Rehg (Cambridge, MA: MIT Press, 2001). See also Petherbridge, *Critical Theory of Axel Honneth*, 147–64.
23. Whitebook, "Mutual Recognition," 278.
24. Indeed, in his debate with Whitebook, Honneth makes it clear that this is why he prefers not to use the term "omnipotence." See Honneth and Whitebook, "Omnipotence or Fusion?," 178.
25. Whitebook, "Mutual Recognition," 279; quoting Honneth, *Struggle for Recognition*, 98. For his later retraction of this claim, see Honneth, "Facets of the Presocial Self," 227.
26. Honneth, "Facets of the Presocial Self," 227.
27. Honneth, 229.
28. For further discussion, see Amy Allen, "Recognizing Ambivalence: Honneth, Butler, and Philosophical Anthropology," in *Recognition, Ambivalence, and Conflict: Axel Honneth, Judith Butler, and Beyond*, ed. Heikki Ikaheimo, Kristina Lepold, and Titus Stahl (New York: Columbia University Press, forthcoming).
29. For Honneth's claims about the pervasiveness and source of aggression, see "Work of Negativity," and "Facets of the Presocial Self." For further critical discussion, see Allen, "Are We Driven?" Zurn has suggested that Honneth ought to settle for a more modest moral anthropology, so as to avoid becoming embroiled in contentious debates in empirical psychology, while acknowledging that this is not the

route that Honneth has chosen. See Christopher Zurn, *Axel Honneth* (Cambridge: Polity, 2015), 48–49.
30. Honneth, "Work of Negativity," 134. For variations on this charge, see the responses to Honneth's Tanner Lectures by Raymond Geuss, Judith Butler, and Jonathan Lear in Axel Honneth, *Reification: A New Look at an Old Idea*, ed. Martin Jay (New York: Oxford University Press, 2008). See also Petherbridge, *Critical Theory of Axel Honneth*.
31. Honneth, "Work of Negativity," 134, 135.
32. Honneth, "Facets of the Presocial Self," 228.
33. Honneth, "Work of Negativity," 135.
34. See Freud's definition of Eros as the drive to "preserve living substance and to join it into ever larger units" (*Civilization and Its Discontents*, in *The Standard Edition of the Complete Psychological Works of Sigmund Freud*, vol. 21 (1927–31), ed. James Strachey (London: Vintage, 2001), 118).
35. Many have argued against this rather common interpretation of Freud's drive theory. For discussion of this issue in relation to critical theory, see Whitebook, *Perversion and Utopia*.
36. Freud, *Civilization and Its Discontents*, 114.
37. For a discussion of the importance of this idea in Freud's work, see Whitebook, *Freud: An Intellectual Biography* (Cambridge: Cambridge University Press, 2017), 343–76.
38. Benjamin Fong, *Death and Mastery: Psychoanalytic Drive Theory and the Subject of Late Capitalism* (New York: Columbia University Press, 2016), 17.
39. Fong, *Death and Mastery*, 17.
40. For further discussion, see Amy Allen, "Foucault, Psychoanalysis, and Critique: Two Aspects of Problematization," *Angelaki: Journal of the Theoretical Humanities* 23, no. 2 (April 2018): 170–86.
41. Whitebook, *Freud*, 391.
42. Although Klein herself tends to speak of the drives as rooted in innate, constitutional, bodily forces, I will argue in chapter 1 that, given the social and relational character of her conception of drives, her work is particularly amenable to being interpreted in the nonreductive, historically conditioned way articulated by Fong.
43. For critical discussion of this aspect of Habermas's work, see Amy Allen, *The Politics of Our Selves: Power, Autonomy, and Gender in Contemporary Critical Theory* (New York: Columbia University Press, 2008), 96–122.
44. See Jürgen Habermas, *The Theory of Communicative Action, Volume 1: Reason and the Rationalization of Society*, trans. Thomas McCarthy (Boston: Beacon, 1985), 43–74.
45. Amy Allen, *The End of Progress: Decolonizing the Normative Foundations of Critical Theory* (New York: Columbia University Press, 2016), 37-79.
46. Sanjay Seth, *Beyond Reason? Postcolonial Theory and the Social Sciences*, chapter 2, page 20 (unpublished manuscript).

47. Indeed, Seth contends that Habermas's theory of social evolution rests on his account of individual cognitive and moral development, rather than vice versa, which suggests that we could still accept the latter even if we reject the former and the link between the two. Even if the relationship between the two accounts is more reciprocal, with each providing support for the other and both offering falsifiable but empirically grounded support for Habermas's overall position, independent arguments for criticizing developmental models of the self would still be required.
48. See Theodor Adorno and Max Horkheimer, *Dialectic of Enlightenment: Philosophical Fragments*, trans. Edmund Jephcott (Stanford, CA: Stanford University Press, 2002).
49. Whitebook, *Perversion and Utopia*. Whitebook's reading of Lacan is admittedly quite unsympathetic. Still.
50. Lacan, *The Seminar of Jacques Lacan: Book II: The Ego in Freud's Theory and in the Technique of Psychoanalysis* (1954–55), ed. Jacques-Alain Miller, trans. Sylvana Tomaselli (New York: Norton, 1991), 148.
51. Lacan, *Ego in Freud's Theory*, 246.
52. Whitebook, *Perversion and Utopia*, 14.
53. See Theodor Adorno, *Negative Dialectics*, trans. E. B. Ashton (New York: Continuum, 1973), 150.
54. For insightful discussion see Whitebook, *Perversion and Utopia*, 1–18.
55. Marcuse, *Eros and Civilization*. I discuss Marcuse's work in more detail in chapter 4.
56. On this point, see Whitebook, *Perversion and Utopia*, 85–86. See also Albrecht Wellmer, "Truth, Semblance, and Reconciliation: Adorno's Aesthetic Redemption of Modernity," trans. Maeve Cooke, *Telos* 62 (Winter 1984–85): 89–94; and Seyla Benhabib, *Critique, Norm, and Utopia: A Study of the Foundations of Critical Theory* (New York: Columbia University Press, 1986), 213ff.
57. Whitebook, *Perversion and Utopia*, 75–90.
58. Whitebook, *Perversion and Utopia*, 179–96.
59. Jürgen Habermas, *Knowledge and Human Interests*, trans. Jeremy Shapiro (Boston: Beacon, 1971), 241; cited in Whitebook, *Perversion and Utopia*, 184. Habermas infers this claim from the fact that psychoanalysis is a talking cure; the passage quoted in the text continues as follows: "Otherwise it would not be possible to reverse the defensive process hermeneutically, via the analysis of language." As Whitebook argues, it isn't at all clear that this is a valid inference. Moreover, it rests on a highly selective and incomplete understanding of how analysis works, leaving aside the affective, economic, and dynamic aspects of working through the transference. See Whitebook, *Perversion and Utopia*, 195 and 305n67. I discuss the problems with Habermas's understanding of analytic method more fully later in this introduction and in chapter 5.
60. Whitebook contends that this move not only generates a problem for Habermas's account of subject-object relationships; it also causes trouble at the core of Habermas's theory of intersubjectivity. See Whitebook, *Perversion and Utopia*, 193–94.

61. Whitebook, 87.
62. See Freud, "Inhibitions, Symptoms, and Anxiety," in *The Standard Edition of the Complete Psychological Works of Sigmund Freud*, vol. 20 (1925–26), ed. James Strachey (London: Vintage, 2001), 98.
63. Habermas argues for the necessity of stage seven in Jürgen Habermas, "Moral Development and Ego Identity," in *Communication and the Evolution of Society*, trans. Thomas McCarthy (Boston: Beacon, 1979), 69–94. He later retreats from this position in Jürgen Habermas, "Moral Consciousness and Communicative Action," in *Moral Consciousness and Communicative Action*, trans. Christian Lenhardt and Shierry Weber Nicholsen (Cambridge, MA: MIT Press, 1990), 116–94.
64. This is not to suggest that psychoanalysis can, by itself, provide a complete analysis of colonial racism. For such a project, structural economic, historical, political, cultural, and social analyses would also be required. It is to stake the claim, however, that one cannot provide a fully satisfactory analysis of colonial racism—or of other contemporary forms of domination and oppression, including gender subordination and heterosexism—*without* psychoanalysis, for psychoanalysis helps us to understand how racialized subjects become attached to their own subjection, and this is crucial for understanding how those attachments might be renegotiated and transformed.
65. Whitebook, *Perversion and Utopia*, 78.
66. Whitebook, 79.
67. Inara Luisa Marin, "The Bi-Dimensionality of Marcuse's Critical Psychoanalytical Model of Emancipation: Between Negativity and Normativity," *Radical Philosophy Review* 19, no. 1 (2016): 229–40.
68. Whitebook, *Perversion and Utopia*, 89; citing Jürgen Habermas, "Walter Benjamin: Consciousness Raising or Rescuing Critique," in Habermas, *Philosophical-Political Profiles*, trans. Frederick G. Lawrence (Cambridge, MA: MIT Press, 1983), 157.
69. See Amy Allen, "Emancipation without Utopia: Subjection, Modernity, and the Normative Claims of Feminist Critical Theory," *Hypatia* 30, no. 3 (Summer 2015): 513–29, 524–25. For a related argument, see Allen, *End of Progress*, 187–89.
70. Whitebook, "Marriage of Marx and Freud," 89.
71. See, for example, the discussion of progress in Theodor Adorno, *History and Freedom: Lectures 1964–1965*, ed. Rolf Tiedemann, trans. Rodney Livingstone (Cambridge: Polity, 2006), 146.
72. Theodor Adorno, *Problems of Moral Philosophy*, ed. Thomas Schröder, trans. Rodney Livingstone (Stanford, CA: Stanford University Press, 2001), 79.
73. Adorno, *Negative Dialectics*, 150.
74. Adorno, *Minima Moralia*, 247.
75. Adorno, 247.
76. For a compelling exploration of the relationship between Adorno and Lacan from the perspective of feminist theory, see Claudia Leeb, *Power and Feminist Agency: Toward a New Theory of the Political Subject* (New York: Oxford University Press, 2017).

77. See, especially, Jacques Lacan, *The Seminar of Jacques Lacan: Book VII: The Ethics of Psychoanalysis* (1959–60), ed. Jacques-Alain Miller, trans. Dennis Porter (New York: Norton, 1992).
78. Mari Ruti, The *Ethics of Opting Out: Queer Theory's Defiant Subjects* (New York: Columbia University Press, 2017), 46.
79. Ruti, *Ethics of Opting Out*, 51.
80. By far the most prominent and eloquent representative of this aspect of Lacan's work is Lee Edelman, *No Future: Queer Theory and the Death Drive* (Durham, NC: Duke University Press, 2004). For a compelling critique of the one-sidedness of Edelman's reading of Lacan, see Ruti, *Ethics of Opting Out*, 87–129.
81. Ruti, 79. For a fascinating comparison of Marcuse and Lacan, see Ruti, 59–67.
82. Ruti, 113.
83. Ruti, 113.
84. Ruti, 114.
85. Ruti, 118.
86. Ruti, 129.
87. Thomas McCarthy, *The Critical Theory of Jürgen Habermas* (Cambridge MA: MIT Press, 1978), 194–95.
88. McCarthy, *Critical Theory of Jürgen Habermas*, 195.
89. Note: this list is NOT intended to be exhaustive.

1. Kleinian Realism

1. For a related critique of Honneth's overly optimistic philosophical anthropology, see Danielle Petherbridge, *The Critical Theory of Axel Honneth* (Lanham, MD: Lexington, 2013).
2. See, especially, Jessica Benjamin, *Like Subjects, Love Objects: Essays on Recognition and Sexual Difference* (New Haven, CT: Yale University Press, 1995) and *The Shadow of the Other: Intersubjectivity and Gender in Psychoanalysis* (New York: Routledge, 1998). Benjamin, like Honneth, turns to Winnicott to theorize the intersubjective dimension, which she finds lacking in Klein's work. Unlike Honneth, she puts greater emphasis on primary aggression and infantile omnipotence, and she is more open to the language of drives. For reasons that I will discuss further on, I see more resources for theorizing intersubjectivity in Klein than Benjamin does.
3. For a related reading of Klein in relation to critical theory, see David McIvor, "Pressing the Subject: Critical Theory and the Death Drive," *Constellations* 22, no. 3 (2015): 405–19; and *Mourning in America: Race and the Politics of Loss* (Ithaca, NY: Cornell University Press, 2016). I'm quite sympathetic not only with McIvor's critique of Habermas and Honneth's unsatisfactory engagement with psychoanalysis but also with his fascinating and productive reading of Klein's relevance for contemporary political theory. However, in what follows I'm less interested in situating my reading of Klein within a Honneth-inspired recognition

framework or a Habermasian account of intersubjective autonomy. As I'll explore further in the next chapter, I prefer to read Klein's conception of the subject in relation to an Adornian conception of critique.

4. For a succinct account of the different stages of Klein's work, see Jay R. Greenberg and Stephen Mitchell, *Object Relations in Psychoanalytic Theory* (Cambridge, MA: Harvard University Press, 1983), 121–30.
5. Jan Abram and R. D. Hinshelwood, *The Clinical Paradigms of Melanie Klein and Donald Winnicott* (New York: Routledge, 2018), 16.
6. To be sure, this aspect of Klein's view raises worries about biological and gender essentialism. Although Klein herself tended toward a literal interpretation according to which the breast refers to the physical body part of the child's biological mother, there are also moments where she acknowledges that what is most important is the nourishment, love, and gratification provided to the infant, and that this can also come from a bottle. Klein makes this point explicit when she notes that the infant's ability to develop a sense of security "depends on the infant's capacity to cathect sufficiently the breast or its symbolic representative, the bottle" ("Envy and Gratitude," in *Envy and Gratitude and Other Works, 1946–1963* [New York: Free Press, 1975], 178–79). By extension, one could argue that the nourishment, love, and gratification that come from the "breast" can also come from someone who is neither the child's biological mother, nor a woman or a female. In what follows, I will thus refer to the primary caregiver when discussing Klein's view; when quoting her I will leave her references to the mother as they are, but the reader should bear these qualifications in mind. I discuss the issue of gender essentialism in Klein more fully in Amy Allen and Mari Ruti, *Critical Theory Between Klein and Lacan: A Dialogue* (New York: Bloomsbury Academic, 2019), 52–53.
7. Melanie Klein, "The Origins of Transference," in *Envy and Gratitude*, 53.
8. Hanna Segal, *Introduction to the Work of Melanie Klein* (London: Karnac, 1988), 24.
9. On this point I disagree with Michael Rustin, who reads Klein as endorsing primary narcissism in the sense of fusion or undifferentiation. See, for example, Rustin, *The Good Society and the Inner World: Psychoanalysis, Politics, and Culture* (London: Verso, 1991), 186. Whereas Rustin conflates Klein and Winnicott on this point, Abram and Hinshelwood emphasize that Klein's rejection of primary narcissism and Winnicott's acceptance of it was one of their main points of disagreement. See Abram and Hinshelwood, *Clinical Paradigms of Melanie Klein and Donald Winnicott*, 29–38.
10. Sigmund Freud, *Civilization and Its Discontents*, in *The Standard Edition of the Complete Psychological Works of Sigmund Freud*, vol. 21 (1927–31), ed. James Strachey (London: Vintage, 2001), 68.
11. I discuss the implications of her rejection of primary narcissism for critical theory more fully later in this chapter, and in Allen and Ruti, *Critical Theory Between Klein and Lacan*, 33–62. Klein's rejection of primary narcissism played a crucial

role in her contentious debate with Anna Freud. For a helpful discussion, see Meira Likierman, *Melanie Klein: Her Work in Context* (New York: Continuum, 2002), 55; and Phyllis Grosskurth, *Melanie Klein: Her World and Her Work* (New York: Knopf, 1986), 285, 321.

12. In a related vein, Jessica Benjamin rejects primary narcissism while emphasizing the importance of infantile omnipotence and the ongoing challenge that it poses for intersubjectivity. For Benjamin, "mental omnipotence is a complex intrapsychic condition, not an immediate, originary state," one that takes the place occupied by primary narcissism in Freudian theory (*Like Subjects*, 88).
13. Segal, *Introduction*, ix.
14. Klein, "Notes on Some Schizoid Mechanisms," in *Envy and Gratitude*, 1.
15. For discussion of this point, see Likierman, *Melanie Klein*, 144–55. Although Klein did not claim that every child is psychotic, she did maintain that "every child will periodically exhibit psychotic phenomena" (Klein, *The Psychoanalysis of Children*, trans. Alix Strachey [New York: Free Press, 1975], 155). As any parent who has ever experienced a toddler meltdown knows, this is not such an outrageous claim.
16. Compare Joel Whitebook, *Freud: An Intellectual Biography* (Cambridge: Cambridge University Press, 2017), 5.
17. Klein, "Notes on Some Schizoid Mechanisms," 10.
18. Klein, 2.
19. Klein, "On the Development of Mental Functioning," in *Envy and Gratitude*, 239.
20. Klein, "Notes on Some Schizoid Mechanisms," 6.
21. Klein, 11.
22. Klein, 10.
23. As Hinshelwood explains, there are two fundamental anxieties for Klein: "An anxiety about the fate of the object, and an anxiety about the survival of the self. These she called the 'depressive position' and the 'paranoid-schizoid position,' respectively" (in Abram and Hinshelwood, *Clinical Paradigms of Melanie Klein and Donald Winnicott*, 16).
24. Klein, "Notes on Some Schizoid Mechanisms," 14.
25. This general tendency is evident in Eve Sedgwick's groundbreaking and massively influential essay, "Paranoid Reading and Reparative Reading, Or, You're So Paranoid, You Probably Think this Essay Is About You," in *Touching/Feeling: Affect, Pedagogy, Performativity* (Durham, NC: Duke University Press, 2003). Arguably, it has been imported from Sedgwick into the broader reception of Klein in affect theory. For discussion, see Allen and Ruti, *Critical Theory Between Klein and Lacan*, 95–128.
26. Klein, "Some Theoretical Conclusions Regarding the Emotional Life of the Infant," in *Envy and Gratitude*, 80.
27. Klein, "Some Theoretical Conclusions," 87.
28. Klein, "A Contribution to the Psychogenesis of Manic-Depressive States," in *Love, Guilt, and Reparation and Other Works, 1921–1945* (New York: Free Press, 1975), 285–86.

29. I first developed this account of Kleinian drives as relational passions in Allen, "Are We Driven? Critical Theory and Psychoanalysis Reconsidered," *Critical Horizons* 16, no. 4 (2015): 311–28, 9–13. This section draws on that earlier account, although in the intervening years I have greatly complicated and reformulated my understanding of Freudian drive theory, in large part thanks to the work of Benjamin Fong.
30. Klein, "On the Development of Mental Functioning," 236.
31. For discussion, see Grosskurth, *Melanie Klein*, 317. The other major post-Freudian psychoanalytic theorist to take the death drive as seriously as Klein was Jacques Lacan. For comparison of Klein and Lacan's understandings of the death drive, see Allen and Ruti, *Critical Theory Between Klein and Lacan*, 57–61.
32. Klein, "On the Development of Mental Functioning," 236.
33. Klein, 245.
34. This distinction is unfortunately obscured by the Strachey translation of Freud's *Standard Edition*, which renders both German terms as "instinct." For an elegant interpretation and defense of the contemporary relevance of Freud's drive theory, see Teresa de Lauretis, *Freud's Drive: Psychoanalysis, Literature, and Film* (New York: Palgrave MacMillan, 2010).
35. Freud, "Instincts and Their Vicissitudes," in *The Standard Edition of the Complete Psychological Works of Sigmund Freud*, vol. 14 (1914–16), ed. James Strachey (London: Vintage, 2001), 121–22.
36. Freud, "Instincts and Their Vicissitudes," 123.
37. Freud, 122.
38. Freud, 122–23.
39. Freud, *Beyond the Pleasure Principle* in *The Standard Edition of the Complete Psychological Works of Sigmund Freud*, vol. 18 (1920–22), ed. James Strachey, (London: Vintage, 2001), 34.
40. Benjamin Fong, *Death and Mastery: Psychoanalytic Drive Theory and the Subject of Late Capitalism* (New York: Columbia University Press, 2016), 1–20.
41. For the definition of drives as internal stimuli that produce psychical representations, see Freud, "Instincts and Their Vicissitudes," 118; for the definition of drives as psychical representations of those stimuli, see 122.
42. Fong, *Death and Mastery*, 8, 9.
43. Fong, 10.
44. Fong, 11.
45. Fong, 17.
46. Greenberg and Mitchell, *Object Relations in Psychoanalytic Theory*, 136.
47. Greenberg and Mitchell, 145.
48. Klein, "Origins of Transference," 51.
49. Klein, 53.
50. Greenberg and Mitchell, *Object Relations in Psychoanalytic Theory*, 143, 144. For a related characterization of the drive in Klein as referring to "a specific potentiality

for one or another kind of object-relating, loving or hating an object (or the self),"
see Hinshelwood, "Who Wants to Be a Scientist? The Historical and Psychoanalytic
Context at the Start of Klein's Career, circa 1918–1921," in *Other Banalities: Melanie
Klein Revisited*, ed. Jon Mills (New York: Routledge, 2006), 20. However, in my
view, Hinshelwood goes too far in suggesting that because she rejects a biologically
based conception of somatically rooted instinctual drives that Klein is "not really a
drive theorist" (Abram and Hinshelwood, *Clinical Paradigms of Melanie Klein and
Donald Winnicott*, 2).

51. To be sure, Klein's notion of the internal object complicates this picture, as I will discuss further in the next section.
52. Freud, *Civilization and Its Discontents*. As I discuss further in chapter 3, the situation is a bit more complicated, as Freud conceives of Eros as basically prosocial and locates the source of antisociality in the death drive.
53. Moreover, for Freud, the ego is the psychical agency tasked with mediating this conflict between the drives and the demands of social reality. As I'll discuss further in the next chapter, Klein reconceptualizes the ego by identifying it with the integrating forces of the life instinct, and thus with love. On this point, see Greenberg and Mitchell, *Object Relations in Psychoanalytic Theory*, 142.
54. Greenberg and Mitchell, 142–43.
55. To be sure, it is possible to find the outlines of a more object-relational perspective in Freud's late work. On this point, see Axel Honneth, *Pathologies of Reason: On the Legacy of Critical Theory*, trans. James Ingram (New York: Columbia University Press, 2009), 126–45. Although I wouldn't deny this interpretation, it is worth noting that Klein's biographer suggests that Freud may have gone in this direction in response to Klein, whose views were being discussed widely in the psychoanalytic community at the time. See Grosskurth, *Melanie Klein*, 173.
56. Grosskurth notes that Klein's first explicit discussion of the duality of life and death drives occurs in her watershed 1932 book, *The Psychoanalysis of Children*. See Grosskurth, *Melanie Klein*, 192.
57. Freud, *Beyond the Pleasure Principle*, 36.
58. Freud, 37.
59. For insightful discussion of how Freud gets from the postulate of the repetition compulsion to his conception of the death drive, and the problems with this move, see Jonathan Lear, *Freud*, 2nd ed. (New York: Routledge, 2015), 156–63.
60. Freud, *Beyond the Pleasure Principle*, 38.
61. Freud, 39.
62. Freud, 50.
63. Freud, 55–56.
64. Freud, 62.
65. Freud, 63.
66. Freud acknowledges this problem and attempts to solve it by claiming that the pleasure principle is the modified form that the Nirvana principle takes in human

beings. See Freud, "The Economic Problem of Masochism," in *The Standard Edition of the Complete Psychological Works of Sigmund Freud*, vol. 19 (1923–25), ed. James Strachey (London: Vintage, 2001), 159–70.
67. See Fong, *Death and Mastery*, 29–38.
68. Lear, *Freud*, 163.
69. Lear, 163. Lear also suggests turning to the work of Klein and her followers to develop such a theory of aggression (165–66).
70. On this point, see Grosskurth, *Melanie Klein*, 192.
71. Fong, *Death and Mastery*, 27.
72. Freud, *Beyond the Pleasure Principle*, 53. For Klein's account of her departure from Freud on this point, see Klein, "On the Development of Mental Functioning," 237.
73. Klein, "Love, Guilt, and Reparation," in *Love, Guilt, and Reparation and Other Works*, 307–8.
74. Klein, "On the Development of Mental Functioning," 243.
75. Klein, 238–39.
76. This understanding of Eros makes it much broader than libido or sexual gratification, which become particular expressions of love/Eros. On this point, see Hinshelwood, "Who Wants to Be a Scientist?"; and C. Fred Alford, *Melanie Klein and Critical Social Theory: An Account of Politics, Art, and Reason Based on Her Psychoanalytic Theory* (New Haven, CT: Yale University Press, 2001). I will return to this point in chapter 4, when I discuss Klein in relation to Marcuse.
77. Susan Isaacs, "The Nature and Function of Phantasy," *International Journal of Psychoanalysis* 29 (1948): 73–97.
78. Isaacs, "Nature and Function of Phantasy," 81.
79. Freud, "Instincts and Their Vicissitudes," 122.
80. Isaacs, "Nature and Function of Phantasy," 82.
81. Isaacs, 82.
82. Isaacs, 82.
83. Isaacs, 84.
84. Isaacs, 85.
85. Isaacs, 93.
86. Isaacs, 93.
87. Isaacs, 86.
88. Isaacs, 88. For related discussion focusing on the relation of drives to the body, see Greenberg and Mitchell, *Object Relations in Psychoanalytic Theory*, 138–39.
89. Klein, "Envy and Gratitude," 180.
90. Isaacs, "Nature and Function of Phantasy," 89.
91. Isaacs, 90.
92. Isaacs, 89.
93. Isaacs, 92.
94. Isaacs, 83.
95. Isaacs, 83.
96. Freud, "Instincts and Their Vicissitudes," 135–36.

1. Kleinian Realism ✳ 213

97. Greenberg and Mitchell, *Object Relations in Psychoanalytic Theory*, 137.
98. In this sense, as Hinshelwood contends, Klein's depressive position is aligned with the reality principle, insofar as it enables the subject to narrow the gap between internal and external objects and relations. See Hinshelwood in Abram and Hinshelwood, *Clinical Paradigms of Melanie Klein and Donald Winnicott*, 89.
99. See Greenberg and Mitchell, *Object Relations in Psychoanalytic Theory*, 136.
100. As Greenberg and Mitchell explain, Klein "replaced Freud's distinction between narcissistic libido and object libido with the distinction between relations with internal versus external objects" (137).
101. Segal, *Introduction*, 14.
102. Hinshelwood in Abram and Hinshelwood, *Clinical Paradigms of Melanie Klein and Donald Winnicott*, 75.
103. Indeed, Klein's alleged neglect of environmental factors was a major point of contention in her famous and consequential debate with Anna Freud, and also in Winnicott's critique of her work. For helpful discussion of the former, see Grosskurth, *Melanie Klein*, 279–362; and Likierman, *Melanie Klein*, 44–64. For discussion of the latter, see Abram and Hinshelwood, *Clinical Paradigms of Melanie Klein and Donald Winnicott*, 67–94.
104. Greenberg and Mitchell, *Object Relations in Psychoanalytic Theory*, 147, 148, 150.
105. For discussion of this concern, see Allen and Ruti, *Critical Theory Between Klein and Lacan*, 24ff.
106. Likierman, *Melanie Klein*, 25.
107. Benjamin, *Shadow of the Other Subject*, 90. For a related critique, see Alford, *Melanie Klein and Critical Social Theory*, 46–50.
108. Benjamin, *Shadow of the Other Subject*, 90.
109. As Grosskurth notes, Hanna Segal referred to Klein's alleged neglect of external reality as an "old chestnut" (*Melanie Klein*, 450).
110. Klein, "Origins of Transference," 49.
111. Klein, 51.
112. Klein, "Notes on Some Schizoid Mechanisms," 10. For helpful discussion of this point, see Rustin, "Klein on Human Nature," in *Other Banalities*, 34.
113. See Freud, *Civilization and Its Discontents*, 130.
114. Klein, "Notes on Some Schizoid Mechanisms," 14.
115. Grosskurth, *Melanie Klein*, 338.
116. Segal, *Introduction*, 15.
117. Abram in Abram and Hinshelwood, *Clinical Paradigms of Melanie Klein and Donald Winnicott*, 64.
118. Benjamin is a welcome exception to this trend in the object-relations tradition, inasmuch as she views aggression as "a necessary moment of psychic life" and cautions against the "idealism that otherwise afflicts relational theories—the tendency to throw out with the drives the fundamental psychic place of aggression" (*Like Subjects*, 45, 46).
119. Klein, "Origins of Transference," 53.

120. Klein, 54.
121. In connection with this idea, see Klein's fascinating discussion of two types of anxiety—the one arising intersubjectively, from the infant's perception of their radical dependence on their mother, and the other arising intrapsychically—in her essay "On the Theory of Anxiety and Guilt," in *Envy and Gratitude and Other Works*. For discussion, see Allen and Ruti, *Critical Theory Between Klein and Lacan*, 63–94.
122. Benjamin, *Shadow of the Other Subject*, 90.
123. Jacques Lacan, *The Seminar of Jacques Lacan, Book II: The Ego in Freud's Theory and in the Technique of Psychoanalysis, 1954–55*, ed. Jacques Alain-Miller, trans. Sylvana Tomaselli (New York: W. W. Norton, 1991), 241. Although Lacan does not mention Klein by name, and although most of his critique in this seminar concerns the reception of the object-relations tradition in France, his description of ego integration in this passage seems implicitly aimed at a Kleinian account. Thanks to Inara Marin for pushing me to clarify this point.

2. A System of Scars

1. Joel Whitebook, *Perversion and Utopia: A Study in Psychoanalysis and Critical Theory* (Cambridge, MA: MIT Press, 1995), 91–118.
2. For the first quote, see Sigmund Freud, *New Introductory Lectures on Psychoanalysis*, in *The Standard Edition of the Complete Psychological Works of Sigmund Freud*, vol. 22 (1932–36), ed. James Strachey (London: Vintage, 2001), 80. For the second, see Freud, "A Difficulty in the Path of Psycho-analysis," in *The Standard Edition of the Complete Psychological Works of Sigmund Freud*, vol. 17 (1917–19), ed. James Strachey (London: Vintage, 2001), 143. For discussion, see Whitebook, *Perversion and Utopia*, 91–92.
3. For a similar argument about how post-Freudian psychoanalysis failed to maintain the complex ambiguities—perhaps even contradictions—of Freud's thinking, see Peter Dews, *Logics of Disintegration: Poststructuralist Thought and the Claims of Critical Theory* (London: Verso, 1987), 55–106.
4. See Whitebook, *Perversion and Utopia*, 92–99.
5. Freud, *Inhibitions, Symptoms, and Anxiety*, in *The Standard Edition of the Complete Psychological Works of Sigmund Freud*, vol. 20 (1925–26), ed. James Strachey (London: Vintage, 2001), 97.
6. See Whitebook, *Perversion and Utopia*, 111–13.
7. Freud, *Inhibitions, Symptoms, and Anxiety*, 97ff.
8. Whitebook, *Perversion and Utopia*, 117.
9. Whitebook, 117.
10. As I discuss further in the next chapter, Whitebook later refers to this strand of Freud's thinking as his unofficial position on the psyche. See Whitebook, *Freud: An Intellectual Biography* (Cambridge: Cambridge University Press, 2017), 1–16.

11. For discussion of the similarities between Adorno's and Lacan's critique of the ego, see Whitebook, *Perversion and Utopia*, 133. For an account of the relationship between Lacan and Adorno that is more sympathetic to Lacan, see Claudia Leeb, *Power and Feminist Agency in Capitalism* (Oxford: Oxford University Press, 2017).
12. For a related argument that does not reference Klein, see Whitebook, *Perversion and Utopia*, 152–64.
13. Peter Dews, "Adorno, Post-Structuralism and the Critique of Identity," *New Left Review* 1, no. 157 (May–June 1986): 28–44, 43.
14. Dews, "Adorno, Post-Structuralism, and the Critique of Identity," 43.
15. Theodor Adorno, "Revisionist Psychoanalysis," trans. Nan-Nan Lee, *Philosophy and Social Criticism* 40, no. 3 (2014): 326–38, 328.
16. For Adorno and Horkheimer, the domination of inner nature goes hand in hand with the domination of outer nature, including the domination of other human beings. Since my focus here is on the ego as a structure of internalized domination, I set aside this aspect of their critique.
17. Theodor Adorno and Max Horkheimer, *Dialectic of Enlightenment: Philosophical Fragments*, trans. Edmund Jephcott (Stanford, CA: Stanford University Press, 2002), 26.
18. Adorno and Horkheimer, *Dialectic of Enlightenment*, 43.
19. Adorno and Horkheimer, 35.
20. Adorno and Horkheimer, 47–48.
21. Adorno and Horkheimer, 53.
22. Adorno, *Negative Dialectics*, trans. E. B. Ashton (London: Continuum, 1973), 272.
23. Adorno, *Negative Dialectics*, 272.
24. Adorno, 272.
25. Adorno, 271, translation modified.
26. Adorno, 272–73.
27. Joel Whitebook, "The Marriage of Marx and Freud: Critical Theory and Psychoanalysis," in *The Cambridge Companion to Critical Theory*, ed. Fred Rush (Cambridge: Cambridge University Press, 2004), 78.
28. Whitebook, "Marriage of Marx and Freud," 78.
29. Whitebook, 79.
30. Whitebook, 79.
31. Whitebook, 81.
32. Joel Whitebook, "Weighty Objects: Adorno's Kant-Freud Interpretation," in *The Cambridge Companion to Adorno*, ed. Thomas Huhn (Cambridge: Cambridge University Press, 2004), 70.
33. Whitebook, "Marriage of Marx and Freud," 80.
34. Whitebook, "Weighty Objects," 71.
35. Whitebook, 71.
36. Adorno and Horkheimer, *Dialectic of Enlightenment*, 26.
37. Whitebook, "Weighty Objects," 72–73.
38. Whitebook, 69.

39. For further elaboration of this reading, see Amy Allen, *The End of Progress: Decolonizing the Normative Foundations of Critical Theory* (New York: Columbia University Press, 2016), 166–76. For a related reading that also connects the argument of *Dialectic of Enlightenment* to Freudian psychoanalytic concepts, see Natalia Baeza, "Adorno's 'Wicked Queen of Snow White': Paranoia, Fascism, and the Fate of Modernity," *European Journal of Psychoanalysis*, https://www.journal-psychoanalysis.eu/adornos-wicked-queen-of-snow-white/ (accessed February 20, 2020).
40. Adorno, *Negative Dialectics*, 281.
41. See Whitebook, *Perversion and Utopia*, 138.
42. Jessica Benjamin, "The End of Internalization: Adorno's Social Psychology," *Telos* 32 (June 1977): 42–64, 42.
43. Benjamin, "End of Internalization," 44. On this point, see also Whitebook, *Perversion and Utopia*, 135–40; Whitebook, "Marriage of Marx and Freud," 79; and Susan Buck-Morss, *The Origin of Negative Dialectics: Theodor W. Adorno, Walter Benjamin, and the Frankfurt Institute* (New York: Free Press, 1977), 82.
44. See Lars Rensmann, *The Politics of Unreason: The Frankfurt School and the Origins of Modern Antisemitism* (Albany, NY: SUNY Press, 2017).
45. See Theodor Adorno, Else Frenkel-Brunswik, Daniel J. Levinson, and R. Nevitt Sanford, *The Authoritarian Personality*, ed. Max Horkheimer and Samuel Flowerman (New York: Norton, 1982).
46. Rensmann, *Politics of Unreason*, 83–84.
47. For insightful and elegant discussion of these issues, see Peter Gordon, "The Authoritarian Personality Revisited: Reading Adorno in the Age of Trump," in Wendy Brown, Peter Gordon, and Max Pensky, *Authoritarianism: Three Inquiries in Critical Theory* (Chicago: University of Chicago Press, 2018), 45–84.
48. Theodor Adorno, "Freudian Theory and the Pattern of Fascist Propaganda," in *The Essential Frankfurt School Reader*, ed. Andrew Arato and Eike Gephardt (London: Bloomsbury Academic, 1982), 120.
49. Adorno, "Freudian Theory," 136.
50. For an argument to this effect, see C. Fred Alford, *Melanie Klein and Critical Social Theory: An Account of Politics, Art, and Reason Based on Her Psychoanalytic Theory* (New Haven, CT: Yale University Press, 2001), 143–45.
51. Theodor Adorno, *Lectures on Negative Dialectics: Fragments of a Lecture Course 1965/1966*, ed. Rolf Tiedemann, trans. Rodney Livingstone (Cambridge: Polity, 2008), 8–9.
52. See Adorno, *Lectures on Negative Dialectics*, 7.
53. See Michel Foucault, "Preface," in Gilles Deleuze and Félix Guattari, *Anti-Oedipus: Capitalism and Schizophrenia*, trans. Robert Hurley, Mark Seem, and Helen R. Lane (London: Continuum, 2004), xiv–xv.
54. For a trenchant feminist critique of this move, see Robyn Marasco, "'Already the Effect of the Whip': Critical Theory and the Feminine Ideal," *differences* 17, no. 1 (2006): 88–115, 101–6. Although Marasco's discussion of this point focuses on Marcuse and Horkheimer, the point can easily be extended to Adorno.

2. A System of Scars ※ 217

55. Adorno, "Revisionist Psychoanalysis," 332.
56. Benjamin, "End of Internalization," 42–43.
57. For a related diagnosis of the paradox of the ego in the early Frankfurt School, and a similar turn to Klein to "successfully address problems the Frankfurt School took seriously but could not solve," see Alford, *Melanie Klein and Critical Social Theory*, 13. My disagreements with Alford's reading will be made clear in the last section of the chapter.
58. Adorno's critique of revisionism focuses on the work of Karen Horney, but the former member of the Frankfurt School, Erich Fromm, is also clearly a target.
59. Theodor Adorno, "Sociology and Psychology (Part 1)," trans. Irving Wohlfarth, *New Left Review* 1, no. 46 (November–December 1967): 67–80, 69.
60. Adorno, "Sociology and Psychology (Part 1)," 70.
61. Adorno, "Sociology and Psychology (Part 1)," 74.
62. Adorno, "Revisionist Psychoanalysis," 326.
63. Adorno, 327.
64. Adorno, 328.
65. Adorno, 329.
66. Adorno, 329.
67. Adorno, 331.
68. Adorno, 332.
69. Adorno, 333.
70. Adorno, 332–33.
71. Adorno, 334.
72. Adorno, 335.
73. Adorno, 336.
74. Adorno, 336.
75. Adorno, 336.
76. Adorno, 336.
77. Adorno, 337.
78. Adorno, 337. See also Adorno, "Sociology and Psychology (Part 1)," 68.
79. Adorno, "Revisionist Psychoanalysis," 337.
80. Adorno, 337.
81. Adorno, "Sociology and Psychology (Part 1)," 75.
82. Alford, *Melanie Klein and Critical Social Theory*, 8.
83. Alford, 10.
84. Whitebook, "Marriage of Marx and Freud," 99n12.
85. See Melanie Klein, "Envy and Gratitude," in *Envy and Gratitude and Other Works 1946–1963* (New York: Free Press, 1975), 220–21.
86. Klein, "Envy and Gratitude," 235.
87. Klein, 183–84.
88. For a related discussion, see Whitebook, "Marriage of Marx and Freud," 82. Whitebook turns not to Klein but to Hans Loewald for the kind of differentiated and expansive account of ego integration that I explore in this section. Without

denying the importance of Loewald's work, I find related resources in Klein along with a strong emphasis on an ambivalent but thoroughly relational conception of the drives and thus a compelling and original way of preserving the moment of nonidentity and negativity within the self.

89. For discussion, see Susan Buck-Morss, *Origin of Negative Dialectics*, 63–64.
90. Adorno and Horkheimer, *Dialectic of Enlightenment*, 94–136.
91. Adorno and Horkheimer, 100.
92. Adorno and Horkheimer, 124.
93. Theodor Adorno, *Negative Dialectics*, 362.
94. Theodor Adorno, "Sociology and Psychology (Part 2)," trans. Irving Wohlfarth, *New Left Review* 1, no. 47 (January–February 1968): 79–97, 83.
95. Klein, "Envy and Gratitude," 231.
96. Klein, "Notes on Some Schizoid Mechanisms," in *Envy and Gratitude and Other Works*, 4.
97. Klein, "Notes on Some Schizoid Mechanisms," 6.
98. Klein, "On the Development of Mental Functioning," in *Envy and Gratitude and Other Works*, 245.
99. Klein, "Notes on Some Schizoid Mechanisms," 14.
100. Klein, "Some Theoretical Conclusions Regarding the Emotional Life of the Infant," in *Envy and Gratitude and Other Works*, 72–73.
101. See discussion of this point in chapter 1.
102. Klein, "A Contribution to the Psychogenesis of Manic-Depressive States," in *Love, Guilt, and Reparation and Other Works, 1921–1945* (New York: Free Press, 1975), 285–86.
103. Klein, "Envy and Gratitude," 225.
104. Klein, "Notes on Some Schizoid Mechanisms," 10.
105. See Klein, "On the Development of Mental Functioning," 238–39.
106. Klein, "Mourning and Its Relation to Manic-Depressive States," in *Love, Guilt and Reparation and Other Works, 1921–1945* (New York: Free Press, 1975), 353.
107. Klein, "Envy and Gratitude," 221–22.
108. Jacques Lacan, *The Seminar of Jacques Lacan, Book II: The Ego in Freud's Theory and in the Technique of Psychoanalysis, 1954–55*, ed. Jacques Alain-Miller, trans. Sylvana Tomaselli (New York: Norton, 1991), 241.
109. Klein, "Envy and Gratitude," 233.
110. Klein, 193.
111. See Klein, "Some Theoretical Conclusions," 75.
112. Dews, "Adorno, Post-Structuralism, and the Critique of Identity," 42.
113. Adorno, "Revisionist Psychoanalysis," 328.
114. Adorno, *Lectures on Negative Dialectics*, 80. See also Adorno, *Against Epistemology: A Metacritique*, trans. Willis Domingo (Cambridge: Polity, 2013).
115. Adorno, *Lectures on Negative Dialectics*, 80.
116. Adorno, 84.
117. Adorno, 80.

118. Adorno, 84. On this point, see Susan Buck-Morss, *Origin of Negative Dialectics*, 123.
119. Theodor Adorno, "On Subject and Object," in *Critical Models: Interventions and Catchwords*, trans. Henry Pickford (New York: Columbia University Press, 2005), 246.
120. Adorno, "On Subject and Object," 246.
121. Adorno, 246.
122. Adorno, 247.
123. Adorno, 249–50.
124. Adorno, *Negative Dialectics*, 56.
125. "The primacy of the object is the *intentio obliqua* [reflective act] of the *intentio obliqua* [reflective act], not the warmed over *intentio recta* [thing in itself]; the corrective to the subjective reduction, not the denial of a subjective share" (Adorno, "On Subject and Object," 250)
126. Whitebook, "Weighty Objects," 63.
127. Whitebook, 64. Whitebook links this expansive conception of psychic integration to an account of sublimation, which enables him to sketch the possibility of "less violent, increasingly flexible, and more spontaneous forms of postconventional psychic integration" (59).
128. Adorno, *Negative Dialectics*, 281.
129. Benjamin, "End of Internalization."
130. On this point, see Teresa Brennan, *History After Lacan* (New York: Routledge, 1993), 93–100.
131. Alford, *Melanie Klein and Critical Social Theory*, 105–6.
132. Alford, 115.
133. Alford, 115.
134. Alford, 116.
135. Hanna Segal, "A Psychoanalytic Approach to Aesthetics," in *Reading Melanie Klein*, ed. Lyndsey Stonebridge and John Phillips (New York: Routledge, 1998), 203–22, 219. For further discussion of this passage in the context of a comparison of Klein's and Lacan's conceptions of creativity, see Amy Allen and Mari Ruti, *Critical Theory between Klein and Lacan: A Dialogue* (New York: Bloomsbury Academic, 2019), 175–77.
136. Alford, *Melanie Klein and Critical Social Theory*, 138.
137. Alford, 152.
138. Adorno, *Negative Dialectics*, 150.
139. For a helpful discussion of this point in Adorno, see Deborah Cook, *Adorno on Nature* (New York: Routledge, 2011), 34–61.

3. Beyond Developmentalism

1. Joel Whitebook, *Freud: An Intellectual Biography* (Cambridge: Cambridge University Press, 2017), 11.
2. Whitebook, *Freud*, 146.

3. Whitebook, 310.
4. On this point, see Whitebook's critique of *Moses and Monotheism*, in which, he argues, "the concept of Geistigkeit is too uncritical and affirmative—indeed, too un-analytic—and contains more than a whiff of sanctimony and self-satisfaction. . . . The 'third ear' of every self-respecting analyst should perk up at the mention of Fortschritt, for, as Freud taught us, there is no unambiguous progress in psychic life or in cultural history. Every advance exacts its price" (*Freud*, 445–46). For a more positive assessment of Freud's argument in *Moses and Monotheism*, see Eli Zaretsky, *Political Freud: A History* (New York: Columbia University Press, 2015), 80–118.
5. Freud, "Formulations on the Two Principles of Mental Functioning," in *The Standard Edition of the Complete Psychological Works of Sigmund Freud*, vol. 12 (1911–13), ed. James Strachey (London: Vintage, 2001).
6. Freud, "Two Principles," 219.
7. Freud, 219.
8. This is a significant caveat that I will discuss further on.
9. Freud, "Two Principles," 220.
10. Freud, 219.
11. See Whitebook, *Freud*, 160.
12. Whitebook, 162.
13. Corneulius Castoriadis, *The Imaginary Institution of Society*, trans. Kathleen Blamey (Cambridge, MA: MIT Press, 1987), 104.
14. See Whitebook, *Freud*, 298; and Jean Laplanche, *New Foundations for Psychoanalysis*, trans. David Macey (New York: Basil Blackwell, 1989), 75.
15. Freud, *New Introductory Lectures on Psychoanalysis*, in *The Standard Edition of the Complete Psychological Works of Sigmund Freud*, vol. 22 (1932–36), ed. James Strachey (London: Vintage, 2001), 80.
16. Whitebook, *Freud*, 163.
17. Freud, "Why War?" in *The Standard Edition of the Complete Psychological Works of Sigmund Freud*, vol. 22 (1932–36), ed. James Strachey (London: Vintage, 2001), 213.
18. Whitebook, *Freud*, 163.
19. Whitebook tends to refer to the primary caregiver, somewhat problematically, in my view, as "the archaic mother." I discuss the problems with Whitebook's account of the archaic mother more fully later in the chapter. For now I note that in order to avoid the potentially essentializing implications of this term, and in recognition of the fact that the maternal function may be filled by a person who is neither a biological parent nor a woman or a female, I will strive to use the term "primary caregiver" when speaking in my own voice, though I will leave the terminology unchanged when quoting Whitebook and others.
20. Whitebook, *Freud*, 163–64.
21. Whitebook, 164.
22. Whitebook, 154.

3. Beyond Developmentalism ✳ 221

23. Whitebook, 154.
24. See Whitebook, 1–16.
25. Whitebook, 310.
26. For a related critique, see Jonathan Lear, *Freud*, 2nd ed. (New York: Routledge, 2015), 200–207.
27. Whitebook, *Freud*, 400–401.
28. Whitebook, 401.
29. Whitebook, 310–11.
30. Whitebook, 394.
31. Whitebook, 398.
32. Whitebook, 419.
33. Whitebook, 420.
34. This brings Whitebook, perhaps surprisingly, quite close to Habermas's recent work on postsecularism. For a critical discussion of Habermas's postsecular turn, see *Habermas and Religion*, ed. Craig Calhoun, Eduardo Mendieta, and Jonathan Van Antwerpen (Cambridge: Polity, 2013).
35. Whitebook, *Freud*, 166; citing Hans Loewald, "Defense and Reality," in *The Essential Loewald: Collected Papers and Monographs* (Hagerstown, MD: University Publishing Group, 2000), 30.
36. Whitebook, *Freud*, 30.
37. Whitebook, 30.
38. Whitebook, 170.
39. Celia Brickman, *Aboriginal Populations in the Mind: Race and Primitivity in Psychoanalysis* (New York: Columbia University Press, 2003), 1–2.
40. Élisabeth Roudinesco notes the irony that Freud turned to evolutionary anthropology at the very same time that anthropologists were starting to abandon "the old theses about the opposition between the primitive and the civilized, the animal and the human, and especially . . . the colonial thematics of the hierarchy of the races" (*Freud: In His Time and Ours*, trans. Catherine Porter (Cambridge, MA: Harvard University Press, 2016), 165).
41. Brickman, *Aboriginal Populations*, 4–5.
42. Brickman, 16.
43. Brickman, 16.
44. Brickman, 76–77.
45. Brickman, 4.
46. Brickman focuses on the impact of colonial encounters on the emergence of the discipline of anthropology. For a related account that details the impact of such encounters on the development of sociology, see Gurminder Bhambra, *Rethinking Modernity: Postcolonialism and the Sociological Imagination* (Basingstoke: Palgrave Macmillan, 2007).
47. Dipesh Chakrabarty, *Provincializing Europe: Postcolonial Thought and Historical Difference* (Princeton, NJ: Princeton University Press, 2007), 238.
48. Brickman, *Aboriginal Populations*, 50.

49. Brickman, 45.
50. Brickman, 69.
51. Freud, *Totem and Taboo*, in *The Standard Edition of the Complete Psychological Works of Sigmund Freud*, vol. 13 (1914–16), ed. James Strachey (London: Vintage, 2001), 1.
52. Freud, *Totem and Taboo*, 1.
53. Freud, 4. For a related methodological caution, see 102–3n1.
54. Freud, 1.
55. Freud, 17.
56. Freud, 26.
57. Freud, 26.
58. Freud, 77.
59. Freud, 83.
60. Freud, 88.
61. Freud, 90.
62. Freud bases his account of the primal horde on his reading of Darwin, but the idea seems to be much more Freud's than Darwin's. See Richard Smith, "Darwin, Freud, and the Continuing Misrepresentation of the Primal Horde," *Current Anthropology* 57, no. 6 (December 2016): 838–43.
63. Freud, *Totem and Taboo*, 131.
64. Freud, 132.
65. Freud, 141–43. While acknowledging that the Freud of *Totem and Taboo* remains "attached to the frameworks of evolutionism from which early twentieth century ethnology was freeing itself," Roudinesco nonetheless insists that "he denied all theories predicated on the 'inferiority' of the primitive state" and even suggests (though without argument or even explanation) that his account of the murder of the primal father constitutes "a radical break. . . . with all forms of colonialism" (*Freud*, 166–67). Although Roudinesco is no doubt correct to insist on the universalizing aspects of Freud's argument in *Totem and Taboo*, she does not, in my view, take seriously enough how that argument is entangled with his social evolutionist commitments.
66. Freud, *Group Psychology and the Analysis of the Ego*, in *The Standard Edition of the Complete Psychological Works of Sigmund Freud*, vol. 18 (1920–22), ed. James Strachey (London: Vintage, 2001), 77–79.
67. Freud, *Group Psychology*, 80.
68. Freud, 117.
69. Freud, 123.
70. Freud, *The Future of an Illusion*, in *The Standard Edition of the Complete Psychological Works of Sigmund Freud*, vol. 21 (1927–31), ed. James Strachey (London: Vintage, 2001), 7.
71. Freud, *Future of an Illusion*, 21.
72. Freud, 31.
73. Freud, 43.

3. Beyond Developmentalism ✵ 223

74. Freud, 49.
75. Freud, 56.
76. Freud, 53.
77. See Brickman, *Aboriginal Populations*, 80.
78. Brickman, 52.
79. Brickman, 5.
80. Freud, *Civilization and Its Discontents*, in *The Standard Edition of the Complete Psychological Works of Sigmund Freud*, vol. 21, ed. James Strachey (1927–31) (London: Vintage, 2001), 76.
81. Freud, *Civilization and Its Discontents*, 86.
82. Freud, 86.
83. Freud, 89.
84. Freud, 79.
85. Freud, 79.
86. Freud, 118.
87. Freud, 111.
88. Freud, 111.
89. Freud, 112.
90. Freud, 121.
91. Freud, 122.
92. See Freud, 123.
93. Freud, 123–24.
94. Freud, 134.
95. Freud, 142–43.
96. Freud, 143.
97. See my discussion of this issue in the introduction and chapter 1.
98. Freud, *Civilization and Its Discontents*, 144.
99. Freud, 144.
100. Freud, 144.
101. Friedrich Nietzsche, *On the Genealogy of Morals and Ecce Homo* (New York: Vintage, 1989), 65.
102. Freud, *Civilization and Its Discontents*, 96.
103. See also Roudinesco, *Freud*, 215–32.
104. By emphasizing the problematizing nature of Freud's genealogy of morality, I offer an alternative to Lear's claim that Freud's genealogy aims to delegitimate (or subvert) morality and open up a potential line of response to his critique of Freud on this point. See Lear, *Freud*, 191–92. For an insightful discussion of problematization as a distinctive mode of genealogy, see Colin Koopman, *Genealogy as Critique: Foucault and the Problems of Modernity* (Bloomington: Indiana University Press, 2013).
105. The apparently paradoxical conjunction of Freud's own embrace of developmental racism and the productivity of his theory for critical work on race is noted repeatedly in the literature on psychoanalysis and race/colonialism. See Brickman,

Aboriginal Populations; Ranjana Khanna, *Dark Continents: Psychoanalysis and Colonialism* (Durham, NC: Duke University Press, 2003); and Christopher Lane, "Introduction," in *The Psychoanalysis of Race*, ed. Christopher Lane (New York: Columbia University Press, 1998), 1–40.

106. For example, Whitebook contends that *Civilization and Its Discontents* "poses a seemingly insurmountable challenge to any progressivist desire to substantially transform modern society and ameliorate humanity's situation in modernity" because its primary lesson is that "the *telos* of modernity is a dead-end" (*Freud*, 252).
107. See Whitebook, 160.
108. One could also read Freud's official position in historicized terms, as offering an account of the psyche as formed under conditions of bourgeois capitalism. Interpreted in this way, his adherence to the official position with regard to the psyche would not necessarily be at odds with a radical critique of notions of civilizational progress—indeed, the two could well go hand in hand.
109. Jacques Lacan, *The Seminar of Jacques Lacan, Book I: Freud's Papers on Technique, 1953–54*, ed. Jacques-Alain Miller, trans. John Forrester (New York: Norton, 1991), 217. For a discussion of Lacan's and Klein's distinct but in some ways overlapping critiques of primary fusion/narcissism, see Amy Allen and Mari Ruti, *Critical Theory between Klein and Lacan* (New York: Bloomsbury, 2019), 33–62.
110. On the degree of ego organization presupposed by Klein's account of the infant, see Hanna Segal, *Introduction to the Work of Melanie Klein* (New York: Routledge, 1988), 13–14.
111. See Brickman, *Aboriginal Populations*, 118.
112. Brickman, 207.
113. Brickman, 207.
114. I discuss this issue in more detail in the conclusion to this chapter.
115. On this point, see Meira Likierman, *Melanie Klein: Her Work in Context* (London: Continuum, 2002), 71–77.
116. See Likierman, *Melanie Klein*, 71.
117. Klein, "Criminal Tendencies in Normal Children," in *Love, Guilt, and Reparation and Other Works, 1921–1945* (New York: Free Press, 1975), 170.
118. See Likierman, *Melanie Klein*, 77.
119. On this point, see Segal, *Introduction*, ix.
120. Likierman, *Melanie Klein*, 115. Indeed, Likierman insists that overcoming the depressive position is essential to Klein's view and that this point distinguishes her work from that of later Kleinians (*Melanie Klein*, 112–33). By contrast, Segal contends that the depressive position "is never fully worked through" and thus that its characteristic anxieties and experiences are always with us (*Introduction*, 80). For reasons I will discuss later on, these two positions are not as contradictory as they might at first seem.
121. Likierman, *Melanie Klein*, 118.
122. Likierman, 119.

123. Likierman, 120.
124. Likierman, 120.
125. Likierman, 124.
126. Likierman, 124.
127. On this point, see also Eve Sedgwick, "Melanie Klein and the Difference Affect Makes," *South Atlantic Quarterly* 106, no. 3 (Summer 2007): 625–42, 636.
128. Jacqueline Rose, "Negativity in the Work of Melanie Klein," in *Why War? Psychoanalysis, Politics, and the Return to Melanie Klein* (Oxford: Blackwell, 1993), 167.
129. Rose, "Negativity," 167.
130. Rose, 168.
131. For an interesting discussion of indigenous notions of relationality that links them to Kleinian conceptions of love and reparation, see Allison Weir, *Decolonizing Freedom* (New York: Oxford University Press, forthcoming).
132. David Eng, "Colonial Object Relations," *Social Text* 126 34, no. 1 (March 2016): 1–19, 5.
133. Eng, "Colonial Object Relations," 6.
134. Eng, 6.
135. See Judith Butler, "Moral Sadism and Doubting One's Own Love," in *Reading Melanie Klein*, ed. Lyndsey Stonebridge and John Phillips (London: Routledge, 1998), 179–89.
136. Eng, "Colonial Object Relations," 9.
137. Klein, "Love, Guilt, and Reparation," in *Love, Guilt, and Reparation and Other Works*, 311.
138. Eng, "Colonial Object Relations," 5.
139. Klein, "Love, Guilt, and Reparation," 329; cited in Eng, "Colonial Object Relations," 10.
140. Klein, 330; cited in Eng, 11.
141. Klein, 333; cited in Eng, 11.
142. Klein, 334.
143. Eng, "Colonial Object Relations," 15.
144. Eng, 14.

4. The Cure Is That There Is No Cure

1. For the distinction between backward-looking and forward-looking claims about progress—progress as a "fact" versus progress as a moral-political imperative—and an argument for the self-congratulatory and potentially Eurocentric nature of the former, see Amy Allen, *The End of Progress: Decolonizing the Normative Foundations of Critical Theory* (New York: Columbia University Press, 2016).
2. For helpful discussion of the emergence of the medical model, see Élisabeth Roudinesco, *Freud: In His Time and Ours*, trans. Catherine Porter (Cambridge, MA: Harvard University Press, 2016), 223ff.

3. For Adorno's critique of this tendency, see "Revisionist Psychoanalysis," trans. Nan-Nan Lee, *Philosophy and Social Criticism* 40, no. 3 (2014): 326–38; and my discussion in the previous chapter. Lacan also criticizes the normalizing implications of American ego psychology throughout his work; for a representative text, see *The Seminar of Jacques Lacan, Book II: The Ego in Freud's Theory and in the Technique of Psychoanalysis* (1954–55), ed. Jacques Alain Miller, trans. Sylvana Tomaselli (New York: Norton, 1991).
4. Melanie Klein, "The Early Development of Conscience in the Child," in *Love, Guilt, and Reparation and Other Works, 1921–1945* (New York: Free Press, 1975), 257.
5. Erich Fromm, *The Crisis of Psychoanalysis: Essays on Freud, Marx, and Social Psychology* (Boston: Holt, Rinehart, Winston, 1970), 45. Fromm rejected the death drive because he thought that it was incompatible with the political vision of universal peace and harmony that he took from the Hebrew prophets. On this point, see Martin Jay, *The Dialectical Imagination: A History of the Frankfurt School and the Institute of Social Research, 1923–1950* (Berkeley: University of California Press, 1963), 100. Thus, the presumed incompatibility of the death drive and historical progress is also at the heart of what Adorno called revisionist psychoanalysis.
6. Karen Horney, *New Ways in Psychoanalysis* (New York: Norton, 1939), 132; quoted in Herbert Marcuse, *Eros and Civilization: A Philosophical Inquiry into Freud* (Boston: Beacon, 1966), 272.
7. As in previous chapters, my primary focus is on the death drive in a Kleinian sense, where this refers to primary aggression, rather than in the Freudian sense of the speculative biological Nirvana principle, the drive to return to inorganic nature. This is partly because, as I argued in chapter 1, I find Klein's conception of the death drive and of the fundamental ambivalence of the drives more convincing and well-worked-out than Freud's account, and partly because I suspect that it is primary aggression more so than entropy that is viewed by critical theorists as the real stumbling block to the idea of progress.
8. Marcuse, *Eros and Civilization*, 11. On this point, see Inara Luisa Marin, "The Bi-Dimensionality of Marcuse's Critical Psychoanalytical Model of Emancipation: Between Negativity and Normativity," *Radical Philosophy Review* 19, no. 1 (2016): 229–40, 240.
9. Marcuse, 3.
10. Marcuse, 4.
11. Marcuse, 4–5.
12. I am grateful to Eva von Redecker for pushing me to clarify this point.
13. Marcuse, *Eros and Civilization*, 6.
14. Marcuse, 20.
15. Marcuse, 15.
16. Marcuse, 17.
17. Marcuse, 34.
18. Marcuse, xiv.

19. Marcuse, 40.
20. Compare, for example, Freud's claim that "on the one hand, love comes into opposition to the interests of civilization; on the other, civilization threatens love with substantial restrictions" with his claim that "civilization is a process in the service of Eros, whose purpose is to combine single human individuals, and after that families, then races, peoples and nations, into one great unity, the unity of mankind." *Civilization and Its Discontents, The Standard Edition of the Complete Psychological Works of Sigmund Freud*, vol. 21 (1927–31), ed. James Strachey (London: Vintage, 2001), 103, 122.
21. Marcuse, *Eros and Civilization*, 43.
22. Marcuse, 49.
23. Marcuse, 49.
24. Marcuse, 50.
25. Marcuse, xiv–xv.
26. For more detailed discussion of the relationship between repressive desublimation and capitalism, see Herbert Marcuse, *One-Dimensional Man*, 2nd ed. (Boston: Beacon, 1991), 71–79.
27. Marcuse, *Eros and Civilization*, 95.
28. Marcuse, 19.
29. Marcuse, 19.
30. See Marcuse, *One-Dimensional Man*, 73.
31. Marcuse, 75.
32. Inara Marin refers to this as Marcuse's "libidinal utopia." Marin, "Bi-Dimensionality," 233–37.
33. Marcuse, *Eros and Civilization*, 134.
34. Marcuse, 132.
35. Marcuse, 132.
36. Marcuse, 151.
37. Marcuse, 138–39.
38. Marcuse, 234.
39. Marcuse, 235.
40. Marcuse, 153–54.
41. Marcuse, 235.
42. Marcuse, 143.
43. Marcuse, 142.
44. Marcuse, 141, 146.
45. Marcuse, 143.
46. Marcuse, 149.
47. Marcuse, 149–50.
48. Marcuse, 198.
49. See, for example, Eva von Redecker, "Marx's Concept of Radical Needs in the Guise of Queer Desire," in *Global Justice and Desire: Queering Economy*, ed. Nikita Dhawan, Antke Engel, Christoph F. E. Holzhey, and Volker Woltersdorff (London:

Routledge, 2015), 33. For a contrasting defense of Marcuse's ambivalent reading of psychoanalysis, see Marin, "Bi-Dimensionality."

50. Whitebook, "The Marriage of Marx and Freud," in *The Cambridge Companion to Critical Theory*, ed. Fred Rush (Cambridge: Cambridge University Press, 2004), 88; quoting Freud, *The Future of an Illusion*, in *The Standard Edition of the Complete Psychological Works of Sigmund Freud*, vol. 21 (1927–31), ed. James Strachey (London: Vintage, 2001), 16.
51. For Marcuse's own acknowledgment of the difficulties involved in such a project, see *Eros and Civilization*, 151–53.
52. See Marcuse, *Eros and Civilization*, 21–54.
53. Michel Foucault, *History of Sexuality, Volume 1: An Introduction*, trans. Robert Hurley (New York: Vintage, 1978).
54. Marcuse, *Eros and Civilization*, 160.
55. C. Fred Alford, *Melanie Klein and Critical Social Theory: An Account of Politics, Arts, and Reason Based on Her Psychoanalytic Theory* (New Haven, CT: Yale University Press, 2001), 8.
56. See the discussion of Narcissus in Marcuse, *Eros and Civilization*, 159–71.
57. In this respect, my reading parts company with Alford, who, in my view, downplays the strong notion of reconciliation in Marcuse and attributes to Klein an overly ambitious idea of reconciliation.
58. Melanie Klein, "Love, Guilt, and Reparation," in *Love, Guilt, and Reparation and Other Works 1921–1945* (New York: Free Press, 1975), 308.
59. Melanie Klein, "The Oedipus Complex in the Light of Early Anxieties," in *Love, Guilt, and Reparation and Other Works 1921–1945* (New York: Free Press, 1975), 410.
60. Melanie Klein, "On the Theory of Anxiety and Guilt," in *Envy and Gratitude and Other Works, 1946–1963* (New York: Free Press, 1975), 35–36.
61. Klein, "On the Theory of Anxiety and Guilt," 36.
62. Klein, 36.
63. Klein, "Love, Guilt, and Reparation," 316.
64. For further discussion of this point also in relation to Lacan's critique of Klein, see Amy Allen and Mari Ruti, *Critical Theory Between Klein and Lacan: A Dialogue* (New York: Bloomsbury Academic, 2019), 8–10.
65. Melanie Klein, "Some Theoretical Conclusions Regarding the Emotional Life of the Infant," in *Envy and Gratitude and Other Works, 1946–1963* (New York: Free Press, 1975), 75.
66. Hanna Segal, *Introduction to the Work of Melanie Klein* (London: Karnac, 1988), 93.
67. Segal, *Introduction*, 95. On this point, see Klein: "Omnipotence decreases as the infant gradually gains a greater confidence both in his objects and in his reparative powers. He feels that all steps in development, all new achievements are giving pleasure to the people around him and that in this way he expresses his love, counter-balances or undoes the harm done by his aggressive impulses and makes reparation to his injured love objects" ("Some Theoretical Conclusions," 75).

68. Melanie Klein, "Mourning and Its Relation to Manic-Depressive States," in *Love, Guilt, and Reparation and Other Works, 1921–1945* (New York: Free Press, 1975), 353.
69. Klein, "Some Theoretical Conclusions," 75.
70. Klein, 75.
71. Klein, 75.
72. Melanie Klein, "The Early Development of Conscience in the Child," *Love, Guilt, and Reparation and Other Works, 1921–1945* (New York: Free Press, 1975), 257.
73. Judith Butler, "To Preserve the Life of the Other," in *The Force of Non-Violence* (London: Verso, 2020), 86.
74. Butler, "To Preserve the Life of the Other," 92.
75. Butler, 95.
76. David McIvor, *Mourning in America: Race and the Politics of Loss* (Ithaca, NY: Cornell University Press, 2016). For related, though less detailed, discussions of the connection between Klein and theories of reparative justice, see Michael Rustin, "Klein on Human Nature," in *Other Banalities: Melanie Klein Revisited*, ed. Jon Mills (New York: Routledge, 2006), 25–44; and David Eng, "Reparations and the Human," *Columbia Journal of Gender and Law* 21, no. 2 (2011): 561–83.
77. McIvor, *Mourning in America*, 143.
78. McIvor, 149.
79. Sigmund Freud, "On Narcissism: An Introduction," in *The Standard Edition of the Complete Psychological Works of Sigmund Freud*, vol. 14 (1914–16), ed. James Strachey (London: Vintage, 2001), 94.
80. For helpful discussion of this point, see Ken Gemes, "Freud and Nietzsche on Sublimation," *Journal of Nietzsche Studies* 38 (2009): 38–59.
81. Jacques Lacan, *The Seminar of Jacques Lacan, Book VII: The Ethics of Psychoanalysis, 1959–1960*, ed. Jacques-Alain Miller and trans. Dennis Porter (New York: Norton, 1992), 142–43.
82. Marcuse, *One-Dimensional Man*, 76.
83. Marcuse, 76.
84. For this reason, as I'll explore more fully in the conclusion to this book, I'm skeptical of Wendy Brown's turn to Marcuse's analysis of repressive desublimation as a model for theorizing the rise of right-wing authoritarian populism. Wendy Brown, "Neoliberalism's Frankenstein," in Brown, Peter Gordon, and Max Pensky, *Authoritarianism: Three Inquiries in Critical Theory* (Chicago: University of Chicago Press, 2018).
85. On this point, see Eve Sedgwick, "Melanie Klein and the Difference Affect Makes," *South Atlantic Quarterly* 106, no. 3 (2007): 625–42.
86. Jan Abram and R. D. Hinshelwood, *The Clinical Paradigms of Melanie Klein and Donald Winnicott* (New York: Routledge, 2018), 16.
87. Segal, *Introduction*, 93.
88. Sigmund Freud, "Mourning and Melancholia," in *The Standard Edition of the Complete Psychological Works of Sigmund Freud*, vol. 16 (1916–17), ed. James Strachey (London: Vintage, 2001), 245–49.

89. Sigmund Freud, "The Ego and the Id," in *The Standard Edition of the Complete Psychological Works of Sigmund Freud*, vol. 19 (1923–1925), ed. James Strachey (London: Vintage, 2001), 28.
90. Freud, "Ego and the Id," 29.
91. Freud, 29.
92. See Klein, "Mourning and Its Relation to Manic-Depressive States," in *Love, Guilt, and Reparation and Other Works*, 345.
93. Here is Klein: "The good breast, introjected in situations of gratification and happiness, becomes in my view a vital part of the ego and strengthens its capacity for integration. For this internal good breast—forming also the helpful and benign aspect of the early super-ego—strengthens the infant's capacity to love and trust his objects, heightens the stimulus for introjection of good objects and situations, and is therefore an essential source of reassurance against anxiety; it becomes the representative of the life instinct within" ("Some Theoretical Conclusions," 67).
94. Melanie Klein, "Envy and Gratitude," in *Envy and Gratitude and Other Works, 1946–1963* (New York: Free Press, 1975), 201.
95. Melanie Klein, "On the Development of Mental Functioning," in *Envy and Gratitude and Other Works, 1946–1963* (New York: Free Press, 1975), 245.
96. For example, Klein describes the "omnipotent reassurance derived from the idealization of the object" as one of the key features of the paranoid-schizoid position ("Some Theoretical Conclusions," 71).
97. Thomas Ogden, *The Primitive Edge of Experience* (Lanham, MD: Rowman & Littlefield, 2004), 29.
98. Ogden, *Primitive Edge of Experience*, 30.
99. Ogden, 30.
100. Klein, "Love, Guilt, and Reparation," 311–12n1.
101. Hanna Segal, "A Psychoanalytic Approach to Aesthetics," in *Reading Melanie Klein*, ed. Lyndsey Stonebridge and John Phillips (New York: Routledge, 1998). For further discussion of this essay in the context of Klein and Lacan's overlapping and diverging accounts of creativity, see Allen and Ruti, *Critical Theory Between Klein and Lacan*, 157–86.
102. Segal, "Psychoanalytic Approach to Aesthetics," 208–9.
103. See Segal, 219, and my discussion of this passage in chapter 2.
104. Marcuse, *Eros and Civilization*, 143.
105. Although I agree with much of Alford's argument, I worry that he wrongly attributes a strong notion of reconciliation to Klein and thus has an insufficient appreciation for the crucial role of ambivalence in her understanding of ego integration, reparation, and creativity. See, for example, his claim that Klein stresses "the achievement of wholeness, restoration, unity, and completeness. . . . to such an extent that the idea of art telling us the truth about a broken, fragmented reality, except by complete contrast, tends to be lost" (*Melanie Klein and Critical Social Theory*, 116).

106. See Klein, "Early Development of Conscience in the Child," 257.
107. By aligning Klein with (the unofficial) Freud on this point, I part company with Rustin, who contends that Klein's work is less pessimistic than Freud's because of her stress on reparation and creativity; see *The Good Society and the Inner World: Psychoanalysis, Politics and Culture* (London: Verso Press, 1991), 21–22 and 46. As I argued in chapter 3, I read the late Freud as a skeptic about progress rather than a cultural pessimist.
108. See, for example, Lacan, *Ethics of Psychoanalysis*, 183–84.
109. So much so that it may seem as if there is no such thing in Freud's work as the official position—indeed, that the latter is instead no more than the gross misinterpretation of Freud put forward by ego psychology. Although I would readily agree that Freud's unofficial position provides a much richer, more complicated, and more productive starting point for psychoanalysis, I would not go so far as to say that the official Freud doesn't exist. In other words, I think there is a reason that both ego psychology and Lacan can trace their roots to Freud's work.
110. On this point, see Jacques Alain Miller: "Without a doubt, psychoanalysis has therapeutic effects.... However these effects may only be obtained on the condition that you question the very notion of cure, because for the human condition, there is no cure." "Response to the Anti-Freudians," *Le Point*, August 22, 2005, http://www.lacan.com/antimill.htm.
111. Whitebook, "Marriage of Marx and Freud," 89. With respect to Klein's views on utopianism, see Rustin, "Klein on Human Nature," 33.
112. Sigmund Freud, "The Psychotherapy of Hysteria," in Josef Breuer and Sigmund Freud, *Studies on Hysteria*, in *The Standard Edition of the Complete Psychological Works of Sigmund Freud*, vol. 2 (1893–95), ed. James Strachey (London: Vintage, 2001), 305.
113. See Sigmund Freud, *Introductory Lectures on Psychoanalysis* (Part 3), in *The Standard Edition of the Complete Psychological Works of Sigmund Freud*, vol. 16 (1916–17), ed. James Strachey (London: Vintage, 2001), 444–45.
114. Sigmund Freud, "Analysis Terminable and Interminable," in *The Standard Edition of the Complete Psychological Works of Sigmund Freud*, volume 23 (1937–39) ed. James Strachey (London: Vintage, 2001), 242.
115. Freud, "Analysis Terminable and Interminable," 243.
116. Lacan, *Ethics of Psychoanalysis*, 230.
117. Lacan, 237.
118. Lacan, 240.
119. Lacan, 300.
120. Lacan, 313.
121. See Lacan, 314 and 319 On the importance of accepting the idiosyncratic nature of one's desire, see Mari Ruti, *The Singularity of Being: Lacan and the Immortal Within* (New York: Fordham University Press, 2012).
122. For a beautiful exploration of this Lacanian idea, see Mari Ruti, *A World of Fragile Things: Psychoanalysis and the Art of Living* (Albany: SUNY Press, 2009).

123. For discussion of this point, see Allen and Ruti, *Critical Theory Between Klein and Lacan*, 1-32.
124. For an influential "antirelational" reading of Lacan, see Lee Edelman, *No Future: Queer Theory and the Death Drive* (Durham, NC: Duke University Press, 2004). For a compelling critique of Edelman, see Mari Ruti, *The Ethics of Opting Out: Queer Theory's Defiant Subjects* (New York: Columbia University Press, 2017).
125. For an insightful reading of Lacan's antiprogressivism that also makes interesting connections to Adorno and Benjamin's critique of progress, see Jamieson Webster, "On the Question of the Future of Psychoanalysis: Some Reflections on Jacques Lacan," *European Journal of Psychoanalysis*, http://www.journal-psychoanalysis.eu/on-the-question-of-the-future-of-psychoanalysis-some-reflections-on-jacques-lacan/ (accessed March 28, 2019).
126. "In neurosis, there is generally a whole series of master signifiers that manifest themselves in the course of treatment and that catch our attention as being stopping points or dead ends of some kind. It is those dead ends that analysis sets out to make into through streets." Bruce Fink, *The Lacanian Subject: Between Language and Jouissance* (Princeton: Princeton University Press, 1996), 78. For a related argument, see Jonathan Lear, *Wisdom Won from Illness: Essays in Philosophy and Psychoanalysis* (Cambridge, MA: Harvard University Press, 2017), 150.
127. Alford, *Melanie Klein and Critical Social Theory*, 136.
128. For insightful discussion of the connection between the paranoid-schizoid position and the dynamics of domination, see Teresa Brennan, *History After Lacan* (New York: Routledge, 1993), 93–100; and Noelle McAfee, *Fear of Breakdown: Politics and Psychoanalysis* (New York: Columbia University Press, 2019), 167–88.
129. For a more detailed account of such a conception of progress, though without reference to Klein, see Amy Allen, "Emancipation Without Utopia: Subjection, Modernity, and the Normative Claims of Feminist Critical Theory," *Hypatia* 30, no. 3 (Summer 2015): 513–29.
130. Adorno, "Revisionist Psychoanalysis," 335.

5. Transference

1. Susan Buck-Morss, *The Origin of Negative Dialectics: Theodor W. Adorno, Walter Benjamin, and the Frankfurt Institute* (New York: Free Press, 1977), 18.
2. Theodor Adorno, *Negative Dialectics*, trans. E. B. Ashton (New York: Continuum, 1973), 5.
3. Buck-Morss, *Origin of Negative Dialectics*, 77.
4. Theodor Adorno, *Minima Moralia: Reflections from a Damaged Life*, trans. E. F. N. Jephcott (London: Verso, 2006), 50.
5. Theodor Adorno, *Lectures on Negative Dialectics* (Cambridge: Polity, 2008), 63. Adorno is referencing the following passage from Freud: "It is true that

psychoanalysis cannot boast that it has never concerned itself with trivialities. On the contrary, the material for its observations is usually provided by the inconsiderable events which have been put aside by the other sciences as being too unimportant—the dregs, one might say, of the world of phenomena." *Introductory Lectures on Psychoanalysis* (Parts 1 and 2), in *The Standard Edition of the Complete Psychological Works of Sigmund Freud*, vol. 15 (1915–16), ed. James Strachey (London: Vintage, 2001), 26–27.

6. Buck-Morss, *Origin of Negative Dialectics*, 277–78n86.
7. Adorno, *Lectures on Negative Dialectics*, 63. See similar references to this passage in Theodor Adorno, "The Actuality of Philosophy," *Telos* 31 (1977): 120–33, 128; Adorno, *Minima Moralia*, 240 Adorno, *Negative Dialectics*, 170.
8. Adorno, *Lectures on Negative Dialectics*, 69–70.
9. Jürgen Habermas, *Knowledge and Human Interests*, trans. Jeremy J. Shapiro (Boston: Beacon, 1971), 214.
10. Sigmund Freud, *New Introductory Lectures on Psychoanalysis*, in *The Standard Edition of the Complete Psychological Works of Sigmund Freud*, vol. 22 (1932–36), ed. James Strachey (London: Vintage, 2001), 57.
11. Habermas, *Knowledge and Human Interests*, 224.
12. Habermas, 227.
13. Habermas, 227.
14. Indeed, as I discussed in the introduction, he famously—and controversially—rejects Freud's distinction between thing-presentations and word-presentations and argues that all unconscious contents can be translated into linguistic terms (*Knowledge and Human Interests*, 241–42). For a trenchant critique of this aspect of Habermas's interpretation of psychoanalysis, see Joel Whitebook, *Perversion and Utopia: A Study in Psychoanalysis and Critical Theory* (Cambridge, MA: MIT Press, 1995).
15. Habermas, *Knowledge and Human Interests*, 234.
16. Habermas, 235.
17. Habermas, 288.
18. For critical discussion of this development in Habermas's work, see Whitebook, *Perversion and Utopia*.
19. Rahel Jaeggi also draws parallels between psychoanalysis and critical theory in articulating her conception of immanent critique. However, unlike Habermas, Honneth, and Celikates, she does not suggest that psychoanalysis should be taken as a *model* of critique; rather, she contends that it constitutes a compelling *example* or *version* of immanent criticism. See Jaeggi, *Critique of Forms of Life*, trans. Ciaran Cronin (Cambridge, MA: Harvard University Press, 2018), 197.
20. Axel Honneth, "A Social Pathology of Reason: On the Intellectual Legacy of Critical Theory," in Honneth, *Pathologies of Reason: On the Legacy of Critical Theory*, trans. James Ingram (New York: Columbia University Press, 2009), 22.
21. Honneth, "Social Pathology of Reason," 33.
22. Honneth, 36.

23. Honneth, 36.
24. Honneth, 37.
25. Honneth, 39.
26. Honneth, 38.
27. Honneth, 39–40.
28. See Axel Honneth, "Appropriating Freedom: Freud's Conception of Individual Self-Relation," in Honneth, *Pathologies of Reason: On the Legacy of Critical Theory*, trans. James Ingram (New York: Columbia University Press, 2009). To be sure, although Honneth acknowledges that the process of appropriating these previously split off contents is both cognitive and affective, he, like Habermas, tends to give conceptual priority to the rational aspects of this process insofar as he understands rational insight to be a precondition for affective transformation. For critical discussion of this aspect of Honneth's reading of Freud, see Amy Allen, "Psychoanalysis and the Methodology of Critique," *Constellations* 23, no. 2 (June 2016): 244–54.
29. See Axel Honneth, "Is There an Emancipatory Interest? An Attempt to Answer Critical Theory's Most Fundamental Question," *European Journal of Philosophy* 25, no. 4 (December 2017): 908–20, 911.
30. Honneth, "Is There an Emancipatory Interest?," 912.
31. Honneth, 915–19.
32. Honneth, 911.
33. Honneth, 912.
34. Robin Celikates, *Critique as Social Practice: Critical Theory and Social Self-Understanding*, trans. Naomi van Steenbergen (London: Rowman & Littlefield International, 2018), 157.
35. Celikates, *Critique as Social Practice*, 145.
36. Celikates, 146.
37. Celikates, 146.
38. Celikates, 147.
39. Celikates, 148.
40. Celikates, 148–49.
41. Celikates, 151.
42. Celikates, 152.
43. Celikates, 157.
44. To be sure, Celikates emphasizes that the work of analysis is necessarily ongoing and open-ended. In this respect, his view coheres with my argument in the previous chapter, which emphasized the open-ended yet progressive nature of the transformation that psychoanalysis aims to bring about.
45. Primarily ego psychology, but perhaps also certain interpersonal or intersubjective approaches to psychoanalysis as well. For a helpful overview of the dizzying variety of post-Freudian psychoanalytic approaches, see Stephen A. Mitchell and Margaret J. Black, *Freud and Beyond: A History of Modern Psychoanalytic Thought* (New York: Basic Books, 1995).

46. Habermas discusses these papers on analytic technique at length but without acknowledging their potential to undermine his rationalist interpretation of psychoanalysis. See Habermas, *Knowledge and Human Interests*, 228–45.
47. Freud, "'Wild' Psychoanalysis," in *The Standard Edition of the Complete Psychological Works of Sigmund Freud*, vol. 11 (1910), ed. James Strachey (London: Vintage, 2001), 225.
48. Freud, "'Wild' Psychoanalysis," 225.
49. Freud, 225.
50. Freud, 226.
51. Freud, "Remembering, Repeating, and Working Through," in *The Standard Edition of the Complete Psychological Works of Sigmund Freud*, vol. 12 (1911–13), ed. James Strachey (London: Vintage, 2001), 150; emphasis added.
52. Freud, "The Dynamics of Transference," in *The Standard Edition of the Complete Psychological Works of Sigmund Freud*, vol. 12 (1911–13), ed. James Strachey (London: Vintage, 2001), 106.
53. Freud, "Remembering, Repeating, and Working Through," 154.
54. Freud, 155.
55. Freud, 155.
56. Jonathan Lear, *Freud*, 2nd ed. (New York: Routledge, 2015), 5.
57. Lear, *Freud*, 5.
58. Lear, 7.
59. More radically still, Lear contends, perhaps "the conception of rationality as reflective distance becomes inappropriate" (7).
60. Lear, 53.
61. Lear, 54–55.
62. Lear, 9.
63. Lear, 55.
64. Lear, 55.
65. Lear, 106.
66. For helpful discussion of the role of analytic technique in general and transference in particular in the debate between Melanie Klein and Anna Freud, see Phyllis Grosskurth, *Melanie Klein: Her World and Her Work* (New York: Knopf, 1986), 337–38.
67. Melanie Klein, "Memorandum on Her Technique: 25th October 1943," in *The Freud-Klein Controversies, 1941–45*, ed. Pearl King and Riccardo Steiner (New York: Routledge, 1991), 635.
68. Klein, "Memorandum on Her Technique," 635.
69. Klein, 636.
70. Klein, 636.
71. Klein, 637.
72. Klein, 637.
73. Hanna Segal, *Introduction to the Work of Melanie Klein* (New York: Routledge, 1989), 117–18.

74. Segal, *Introduction*, 120.
75. Segal, 123.
76. Segal, 123.
77. Jacques Lacan, *The Seminar of Jacques Lacan, Book VIII: Transference 1960–61*, ed. Jacques-Alain Miller, trans. Bruce Fink (Cambridge: Polity, 2015), 173.
78. Lacan, *Transference*, 207–8.
79. Lacan, 51–52. As I will discuss further on, the fundamentally asymmetrical nature of both love and transference is crucial for Lacan's critique of countertransference. See Lacan, 180–95.
80. Lacan, 65.
81. Bruce Fink, *Lacan on Love: An Exploration of Lacan's Seminar VIII, Transference* (Cambridge: Polity, 2016), 46–47.
82. Fink, *Lacan on Love*, 48.
83. Mari Ruti, *The Ethics of Opting Out: Queer Theory's Defiant Subjects* (New York: Columbia University Press, 2017), 69.
84. Lacan, *Transference*, 65.
85. Lacan, 117.
86. Lacan, 34–35.
87. Lacan, 34.
88. Lacan, 117.
89. Lacan, 207–8.
90. For an account of critical theory as engaged in partisan if not uncritical dialogue with emancipatory social movements, see Nancy Fraser, *Unruly Practices: Power, Discourse, and Gender in Contemporary Social Theory* (Minneapolis: University of Minnesota Press, 1989).
91. Lear, *Freud*, 139.
92. Lear, 128.
93. Lear, 129.
94. Lear, 143.
95. Lacan, 188.
96. This is where Lacan, unfairly, in my view, situates object relations. See Lacan, *Transference*, 179.
97. Lacan, 172.
98. Lacan, 175.
99. Lacan, 193.
100. See Amy Allen, *The End of Progress: Decolonizing the Normative Foundations of Critical Theory* (New York: Columbia University Press, 2016); drawing on Colin Koopman, *Genealogy as Critique: Foucault and the Problems of Modernity* (Bloomington: Indiana University Press, 2013).
101. Michel Foucault, "What Is Enlightenment?," in *Ethics, Subjectivity, and Truth: Essential Works of Michel Foucault*, vol. 1, ed. Paul Rabinow (New York: New Press, 1997), 315–16.

102. The claim that Foucault's critical genealogical method can be understood as analogous to psychoanalysis might seem surprising and implausible in light of Foucault's well-known critique of the normalizing implications of psychoanalysis especially with respect to sexuality. However, as I have argued in more detail elsewhere, Foucault's relationship to psychoanalysis is more complicated than is often supposed. See Amy Allen, "Foucault, Psychoanalysis, and Critique: Two Aspects of Problematization," *Angelaki: Journal of Theoretical Humanities* 23, no. 2 (April 2018): 170–86.
103. See Michel Foucault, "Truth and Juridical Forms," in *Power: Essential Works of Michel Foucault*, vol. 3, ed. James Faubion (New York: New Press, 2000), 3.
104. I argue for this claim in more detail in Amy Allen, *The Politics of Our Selves: Power, Autonomy, and Gender in Contemporary Critical Theory* (New York: Columbia University Press, 2008), 22–44.
105. Michel Foucault, *History of Madness*, ed. Jean Khalfa, trans. Jonathan Murphy and Jean Khalfa (New York: Routledge, 2006), 510.
106. Foucault, 339.
107. Although Foucault doesn't use the term "normalization" here to characterize the analyst-analysand relationship—perhaps because the term hadn't yet entered his lexicon—something like the concept of disciplinary normalization is very much at work even in Foucault's early critique of psychoanalytic method. For a brilliant discussion of this point, see Lynne Huffer, *Mad for Foucault: Rethinking the Foundations of Queer Theory* (New York: Columbia University Press, 2010), 127–86,
108. Sigmund Freud, "The Future Prospects of Psychoanalytic Therapy," in *The Standard Edition of the Complete Psychological Works of Sigmund Freud*, vol. 11 (1910), ed. James Strachey (London: Vintage, 2001), 144–45. Lacan famously took Freud to task for failing to see how countertransference was operative in his failed analysis of Dora. See Jacques Lacan, "Intervention on Transference," in *In Dora's Case: Freud-Hysteria-Feminism*, 2nd ed., ed. Charles Bernheimer and Claire Kahane (New York: Columbia University Press, 1990).
109. See R. D. Hinshelwood, "Melanie Klein and Countertransference: A Note on Some Archival Material," *Psychoanalysis and History* 10, no. 1 (2008): 95–113.
110. Joel Whitebook, "Against Interiority: Foucault's Struggle with Psychoanalysis," in *The Cambridge Companion to Foucault*, 2nd ed., ed. Gary Gutting (Cambridge: Cambridge University Press, 2005), 330.
111. Indeed, Lacan explicitly connects this to a critique of the Kleinian school (though not of Klein herself). See Lacan, *Transference*, 188.
112. Lacan, 188.
113. Lacan, 192–93.
114. Lacan, 196.
115. Lacan, 173.
116. Lacan, *Ethics of Psychoanalysis*, 300. For insightful discussion of this point in Lacan, see Ruti, *Ethics of Opting Out*, 69.

117. Lacan, *Transference*, 182.
118. For an extended and compelling argument to this effect, see Celikates, *Critique as Social Practice*.
119. Lear, *Freud*, 9.
120. Adorno, "The Actuality of Philosophy," *Telos* 31 (1977): 120–33, 120.
121. As Buck-Morss points out, Adorno's underlying assumption that social reality is itself contradictory connects to Marx's account of social contradictions and to Freud's concept of ambivalence. See Buck-Morss, *Origin of Negative Dialectics*, 100.
122. Adorno, "Actuality of Philosophy," 127.
123. Adorno, 127.
124. Adorno, 127.
125. Adorno, 127.
126. Adorno, 128.
127. Adorno, 128.
128. Buck-Morss, *Origin of Negative Dialectics*, 277–78n86.
129. Martin Saar, "Rethinking Resistance: Critical Theory Before and After Deleuze," *Coils of the Serpent*, forthcoming 2020, 2. Note that although Saar himself does not discuss the psychoanalytic valences of Adorno's conception of philosophy as interpretation, my reading fits well with his contention that, for Adorno, philosophical intelligibility "is the outcome of a construction that is in itself figural or imaginal, the formal construction of a totality out of many elements, an act of making us see a coherent whole, a Zusammenhang, where empirical reality until now just gives the impression of an incoherent ensemble of many different, plural, non-cohering phenomena" ("Rethinking Resistance," 3).
130. Lear, *Freud*, 104.
131. Lear, 55.
132. On this point, see Buck-Morss, *Origin of Negative Dialectics*, 76.
133. Adorno, *Negative Dialectics*, 28.
134. Adorno, "Sociology and Psychology, Part I," *New Left Review* 1, no. 46 (November–December 1967): 67–80, 77.
135. Adorno, "Sociology and Psychology," 77.
136. Adorno, 75.
137. Adorno, "Actuality of Philosophy," 126.
138. Adorno, *History and Freedom*, 120–21.
139. Theodor Adorno, "Education after Auschwitz," in *Critical Models: Interventions and Catchwords*, trans. Henry Pickford (New York: Columbia University Press, 1998), 200.
140. I discuss these points of convergence in more detail in Amy Allen, "Critique as Melancholy Science," forthcoming in *Critique in German Philosophy*, ed. María del Rosario Acosta Lopez and Colin McQuillan (Albany: SUNY Press, 2020).
141. Sigmund Freud, "Analysis Terminable and Interminable," in *The Standard Edition of the Complete Psychological Works of Sigmund Freud*, vol. 23 (1937–39) ed. James Strachey (London: Vintage, 2001), 219.

142. Freud, "Analysis Terminable and Interminable," 223.
143. Adorno, "Actuality of Philosophy," 131.
144. Max Horkheimer, "Traditional and Critical Theory," in Horkheimer, *Critical Theory: Selected Essays* (New York: Continuum, 1972), 242.
145. Horkheimer, "Traditional and Critical Theory," 242.
146. Horkheimer, 220.
147. Once again, for insightful discussion of this aspect of critique, see Celikates, *Critique as Social Practice*.
148. Foucault, "What Is Enlightenment?" 316–17.

Conclusion

1. Nancy Fraser has been making this argument for quite some time, at least since her work on recognition and redistribution in the 1990s. See Nancy Fraser, *Justice Interruptus: Critical Reflections on the "Postsocialist" Condition* (New York: Routledge, 1997); Nancy Fraser and Axel Honneth, *Redistribution or Recognition? A Political-Philosophical Exchange* (London: Verso, 2003); and Nancy Fraser, *Fortunes of Feminism: From State-Managed Capitalism to Neoliberal Crisis* (London: Verso, 2013). For a more recent take, see Albena Azmanova, *Capitalism on Edge: How Fighting Precarity can Achieve Radical Change without Crisis or Utopia* (New York: Columbia University Press, 2020).
2. See, for example, Wendy Brown, "Neoliberalism's Frankenstein: Authoritarian Freedom in Twenty-First Century 'Democracies,'" in Brown, Peter Gordon, and Max Pensky, *Authoritarianism: Three Inquiries in Critical Theory* (Chicago: University of Chicago Press, 2018), 7–43; Samir Gandesha, "'Identifying with the Aggressor': From the Authoritarian to Neoliberal Personality," *Constellations* 25, no. 1 (March 2018): 147–64; Claudia Leeb, "Mass Hypnoses: The Rise of the Far Right from an Adornian and Freudian Perspective," *Berlin Journal of Critical Theory* 2, no. 3 (2018): 59–81; Leeb, "Mystified Consciousness: Rethinking the Rise of the Far Right with Marx and Lacan," *Open Cultural Studies* 2 (2018): 236–48; Noelle McAfee, *Fear of Breakdown: Politics and Psychoanalysis* (New York: Columbia University Press, 2019); Samuel Moyn, "Freud's Discontents," *Nation*, November 2, 2016, https://www.thenation.com/article/archive/freuds-discontents/; and Joel Whitebook, "Trump's Method, Our Madness," *New York Times*, 3/20/2017, https://www.nytimes.com/2017/03/20/opinion/trumps-method-our-madness.html.
3. Peter Gordon, "The Authoritarian Personality Revisited: Reading Adorno in the Age of Trump," in Brown, Gordon, and Pensky, *Authoritarianism*, 47.
4. Gordon, "Authoritarian Personality Revisited," 56.
5. Gordon, 57.
6. Gordon, 62.
7. Gordon, 63.
8. Gordon, 67.

9. Gordon, 67–68.
10. Gordon, 69.
11. Gordon, 75.
12. Gordon, 77.
13. Gordon, 56.
14. See Brown, "Neoliberalism's Frankenstein," and Brown, *In the Ruins of Neoliberalism: The Rise of Anti-Democratic Politics in the West* (New York: Columbia University Press, 2019), chapter 5.
15. Brown, "Neoliberalism's Frankenstein," 35.
16. Brown, 32.
17. To her credit, Brown acknowledges the question of whether or not we need to analyze left-wing movements using the same terms. However, this question is literally the last sentence of her essay.
18. Nancy Fraser and Rahel Jaeggi, *Capitalism: A Conversation in Critical Theory* (Cambridge: Polity, 2018), 199.
19. Fraser and Jaeggi, *Capitalism*, 217.
20. For an argument to this effect, see Asad Haider, "Four Concepts in Depoliticized Politics," forthcoming.
21. Brown, "Neoliberalism's Frankenstein," and *In the Ruins of Neoliberalism*, 161–88.
22. Note: the claim here is not that society is some sort of macrosubject but rather that psychoanalysis offers us a vocabulary that enables us to illuminate certain persistent features and logics of our politics.
23. On mass incarceration, see Michelle Alexander, *The New Jim Crow: Mass Incarceration in the Age of Colorblindness*, rev. ed. (New York: New Press, 2012); on the criminalization of immigration, see Natalie Cisneros, *The Illegal Alien* (New York: Oxford University Press, forthcoming).
24. See the Pew survey from 2014 that shows that rates of political polarization in the United States are at a two-decade high: Pew Research Center, "Political Polarization and the American Public," June 2014, https://www.people-press.org/2014/06/12/political-polarization-in-the-american-public/ (accessed October 2, 2019).
25. McAfee, *Fear of Breakdown*, 205.
26. McAfee, 9.
27. Indeed, recent empirical literature in political science bears this out. See Joseph Uscinski and Joseph Parent, *American Conspiracy Theories* (New York: Oxford University Press, 2014), 130–53.
28. Brown, *In the Ruins of Neoliberalism*, 175.
29. Robyn Marasco, "Toward a Critique of Conspiratorial Reason," *Constellations* 23, no. 2 (2016): 236–43.
30. Theodor Adorno, "The Meaning of Working Through the Past," in *Critical Models: Interventions and Catchwords*, trans. Henry Pickford (New York: Columbia University Press, 2005), 100.
31. Adorno, "Meaning of Working Through the Past," 101.

32. Theodor Adorno, "Education After Auschwitz," in *Critical Models: Interventions and Catchwords*, trans. Henry Pickford (New York: Columbia University Press, 2005), 192.
33. David McIvor, *Mourning in America: Race and the Politics of Loss* (Ithaca: Cornell University Press, 2016). See my discussion of this point in chapter 4.
34. McIvor, *Mourning in America*, 149.
35. McAfee, *Fear of Breakdown*, 149.
36. See McAfee, 167–88.
37. McAfee, 164.
38. McAfee, 186.
39. On this point, see Bonnie Honig, *Public Things: Democracy in Disrepair* (New York: Fordham University Press, 2017), 37–57.
40. However, there is at least some experimental evidence that democratic deliberation can change participant's minds, moving them toward more centrist, less polarizing, political positions. See James Fishkin and Larry Diamond, "This Experiment Has Some Great News for Our Democracy," *New York Times*, October 2, 2019, https://www.nytimes.com/2019/10/02/opinion/america-one-room-experiment.html.
41. See Alessandro Ferrara, *The Democratic Horizon: Hyperpluralism and the Renewal of Political Liberalism* (Cambridge: Cambridge University Press, 2014).
42. See Jodi Dean, *Democracy and Other Neoliberal Fantasies: Communicative Capitalism and Left Politics* (Durham, NC: Duke University Press, 2009).

Bibliography

Abram, Jan, and R. D. Hinshelwood, *The Clinical Paradigms of Melanie Klein and Donald Winnicott*. New York: Routledge, 2018.

Adorno, Theodor. "The Actuality of Philosophy." *Telos* 31 (1977): 120–33.

———. *Against Epistemology: A Metacritique*. Translated by Willis Domingo. Cambridge: Polity, 2013.

———. "Education After Auschwitz." In *Critical Models: Interventions and Catchwords*, translated by Henry Pickford, 191–204. New York: Columbia University Press, 1998.

———. "Freudian Theory and the Pattern of Fascist Propaganda." In *The Essential Frankfurt School Reader*, edited by Andrew Arato and Eike Gephardt, 118–37. London: Bloomsbury Academic, 1982.

———. *History and Freedom: Lectures 1964–1965*. Edited by Rolf Tiedemann. Translated by Rodney Livingstone. Cambridge: Polity, 2006.

———. *Lectures on Negative Dialectics: Fragments of a Lecture Course 1965/1966*. Edited by Rolf Tiedemann. Translated by Rodney Livingstone. Cambridge: Polity, 2008.

———. "The Meaning of Working Through the Past." In *Critical Models*, 89–104.

———. *Minima Moralia: Reflections from a Damaged Life*. Translated by E. F. N. Jephcott. London: Verso, 2006.

———. *Negative Dialectics*. Translated by E. B. Ashton. London: Continuum, 1973.

———. "On Subject and Object." In *Critical Models*, 245–58.

———. *Problems of Moral Philosophy*. Edited by Thomas Schröder. Translated by Rodney Livingstone. Stanford, CA: Stanford University Press, 2001.

———. "Revisionist Psychoanalysis." Translated by Nan-Nan Lee. *Philosophy and Social Criticism* 40, no. 3 (2014): 326–38.

———. "Sociology and Psychology (Part I)." Translated by Irving Wohlfarth. *New Left Review* 1, no. 46 (November–December 1967): 67–80.

———. "Sociology and Psychology (Part 2)." Translated by Irving Wohlfarth. *New Left Review* 1, no. 47 (January–February 1968): 79–97.

———, Else Frenkel-Brunswik, Daniel J. Levinson, and R. Nevitt Sanford. *The Authoritarian Personality*. Edited by Max Horkheimer and Samuel Flowerman. New York: Norton, 1982.

———, and Max Horkheimer. *Dialectic of Enlightenment: Philosophical Fragments*. Translated by Edmund Jephcott. Stanford, CA: Stanford University Press, 2002.

Alford, C. Fred. *Melanie Klein and Critical Social Theory: An Account of Politics, Art, and Reason Based on Her Psychoanalytic Theory*. New Haven, CT: Yale University Press, 2001.

Alexander, Michelle. *The New Jim Crow: Mass Incarceration in the Age of Colorblindness*. Rev. ed. New York: New Press, 2012.

Allen, Amy. "Are We Driven? Critical Theory and Psychoanalysis Reconsidered." *Critical Horizons* 16, no. 4 (2015): 311–28.

———. "Critique as Melancholy Science." In *Critique in German Philosophy*, edited by María del Rosario Acosta Lopez and Colin McQuillan. Albany: SUNY Press, forthcoming.

———. "Emancipation without Utopia: Subjection, Modernity, and the Normative Claims of Feminist Critical Theory." *Hypatia* 30, no. 3 (Summer 2015): 513–29.

———. *The End of Progress: Decolonizing the Normative Foundations of Critical Theory*. New York: Columbia University Press, 2016.

———. "Foucault, Psychoanalysis, and Critique: Two Aspects of Problematization." *Angelaki: Journal of Theoretical Humanities* 23, no. 2 (April 2018): 170–86.

———. *The Politics of Our Selves: Power, Autonomy, and Gender in Contemporary Critical Theory*. New York: Columbia University Press, 2008.

———. "Psychoanalysis and the Methodology of Critique." *Constellations* 23, no. 2 (June 2016): 244–54.

———. "Recognizing Ambivalence: Honneth, Butler, and Philosophical Anthropology." In *Recognition, Ambivalence, and Conflict: Axel Honneth, Judith Butler, and Beyond*, edited by Heiki Ikaheimo, Kristina Lepold, and Titus Stahl. New York: Columbia University Press, forthcoming.

———, and Mari Ruti, *Critical Theory Between Klein and Lacan: A Dialogue*. New York: Bloomsbury Academic, 2019.

Anderson, Joel. "Situating Axel Honneth in the Frankfurt School Tradition." In *Axel Honneth: Critical Essays*, edited by Danielle Petherbridge, 31–57. Leiden: Brill, 2011.

Azmanova, Albena. *Capitalism on Edge: How Fighting Precarity can Achieve Radical Change without Crisis or Utopia*. New York: Columbia University Press, 2020.

Baeza, Natalia. "Adorno's 'Wicked Queen of Snow White': Paranoia, Fascism, and the Fate of Modernity." *European Journal of Psychoanalysis*, https://www.journal-psychoanalysis.eu/adornos-wicked-queen-of-snow-white/ (accessed February 20, 2020).

Benhabib, Seyla. *Critique, Norm, and Utopia: A Study of the Foundations of Critical Theory*. New York: Columbia University Press, 1986.

Benjamin, Jessica. "The End of Internalization: Adorno's Social Psychology." *Telos* 32 (June 1977): 42–64.

——. *Like Subjects, Love Objects: Essays on Recognition and Sexual Difference*. New Haven, CT: Yale University Press, 1995.

——. *The Shadow of the Other: Intersubjectivity and Gender in Psychoanalysis*. New York: Routledge, 1998.

Bhambra, Gurminder. *Rethinking Modernity: Postcolonialism and the Sociological Imagination*. Basingstoke: Palgrave Macmillan, 2007.

Brennan, Teresa. *History after Lacan*. New York: Routledge, 1993.

Brickman, Celia. *Aboriginal Populations in the Mind: Race and Primitivity in Psychoanalysis*. New York: Columbia University Press, 2003.

Brown, Wendy. *In the Ruins of Neoliberalism: The Rise of Anti-Democratic Politics in the West*. New York: Columbia University Press, 2019.

——. "Neoliberalism's Frankenstein." In *Authoritarianism: Three Inquiries in Critical Theory*, by Brown, Peter Gordon, and Max Pensky, 7–44. Chicago: University of Chicago Press, 2018.

Buck-Morss, Susan. *The Origin of Negative Dialectics: Theodor W. Adorno, Walter Benjamin, and the Frankfurt Institute*. New York: Free Press, 1977.

Butler, Judith. "Moral Sadism and Doubting One's Own Love." In *Reading Melanie Klein*, edited by Lyndsey Stonebridge and John Phillips, 179–89. London: Routledge, 1998.

——. "To Preserve the Life of the Other." In *Force of Non-Violence*, 67–102. London: Verso, 2020.

Calhoun, Craig, Eduardo Mendieta, and Jonathan van Antwerpen, eds. *Habermas and Religion*. Cambridge: Polity, 2013.

Castoriadis, Cornelius. *The Imaginary Institution of Society*. Translated by Kathleen Blamey. Cambridge, MA: MIT Press, 1987.

Celikates, Robin. *Critique as Social Practice: Critical Theory and Social Self-Understanding*. Translated by Naomi van Steenbergen. London: Rowman & Littlefield International, 2018.

Cisneros, Natalie. *The Illegal Alien*. New York: Oxford University Press, forthcoming.

Chakrabarty, Dipesh. *Provincializing Europe: Postcolonial Thought and Historical Difference*. Princeton, NJ: Princeton University Press, 2007.

Cook, Deborah. *Adorno on Nature*. New York: Routledge, 2011.

Dean, Jodi. *Democracy and Other Neoliberal Fantasies: Communicative Capitalism and Left Politics*. Durham, NC: Duke University Press, 2009.

Dews, Peter. "Adorno, Post-Structuralism, and the Critique of Identity," *New Left Review* 1, no. 157 (May–June 1986): 28–44.

——. *Logics of Disintegration: Poststructuralist Thought and the Claims of Critical Theory*. London: Verso, 1987.

Edelman, Lee. *No Future: Queer Theory and the Death Drive*. Durham, NC: Duke University Press, 2004.

Eng, David. "Colonial Object Relations," *Social Text* 34, no. 1 (March 2016): 1–19.

——. "Reparations and the Human." *Columbia Journal of Gender and Law* 21, no. 2 (2011): 561–83.

Ferrara, Alessandro. *The Democratic Horizon: Hyperpluralism and the Renewal of Political Liberalism*. Cambridge: Cambridge University Press, 2014.

Fink, Bruce. *The Lacanian Subject: Between Language and Jouissance*. Princeton, NJ: Princeton University Press, 1996.

——. *Lacan on Love: An Exploration of Lacan's Seminar VIII, Transference*. Cambridge: Polity, 2016.

Fishkin, James, and Larry Diamond. "This Experiment Has Some Great News for Our Democracy." *New York Times*, October 2, 2019, https://www.nytimes.com/2019/10/02/opinion/america-one-room-experiment.html.

Fong, Benjamin. *Death and Mastery: Psychoanalytic Drive Theory and the Subject of Late Capitalism*. New York: Columbia University Press, 2016.

Foucault, Michel. *History of Madness*. Edited by Jean Khalfa. Translated by Jonathan Murphy and Jean Khalfa. New York: Routledge, 2006.

——. *The History of Sexuality, Volume 1: An Introduction*. Translated by Robert Hurley. New York: Vintage, 1978.

——. "Preface." In Gilles Deleuze and Félix Guattari, *Anti-Oedipus: Capitalism and Schizophrenia*, translated by Robert Hurley, Mark Seem, and Helen R. Lane, xi–xiv. London: Continuum, 2004.

——. "Truth and Juridical Forms." In *Power: Essential Works of Michel Foucault, 1954–1984 (Vol. 3)*. Edited by James Faubion. New York: New Press, 2000.

——. "What Is Enlightenment?" In *Ethics, Subjectivity, and Truth: Essential Works of Michel Foucault, 1954–1984 (Vol. 1)*. Edited by Paul Rabinow. New York: New Press, 1997.

Fraser, Nancy. *Fortunes of Feminism: From State-Managed Capitalism to Neoliberal Crisis*. London: Verso, 2013.

——. *Justice Interruptus: Critical Reflections on the "Postsocialist" Condition*. New York: Routledge, 1997.

——. *Unruly Practices: Power, Discourse, and Gender in Contemporary Social Theory*. Minneapolis: University of Minnesota Press, 1989.

——, and Axel Honneth. *Redistribution or Recognition? A Political-Philosophical Exchange*. London: Verso, 2003.

——, and Rahel Jaeggi. *Capitalism: A Conversation in Critical Theory*. Cambridge: Polity, 2018.

Freud, Sigmund. "Analysis Terminable and Interminable." In *The Standard Edition of the Complete Psychological Works of Sigmund Freud*, vol. 23 (1937–39), edited by James Strachey, 209–53. London: Vintage, 2001.

——. *Beyond the Pleasure Principle*. In *The Standard Edition of the Complete Psychological Works of Sigmund Freud*, vol. 18 (1920–22), edited by James Strachey, 7–64. London: Vintage, 2001.

——. *Civilization and Its Discontents*. In *The Standard Edition of the Complete Psychological Works of Sigmund Freud*, vol. 21 (1927–31), edited by James Strachey, 64–145. London: Vintage, 2001.

———. "A Difficulty in the Path of Psycho-analysis." In *The Standard Edition of the Complete Psychological Works of Sigmund Freud*, vol. 17 (1917–19), edited by James Strachey, 135–44. London: Vintage, 2001.

———. "The Dynamics of Transference." In *The Standard Edition of the Complete Psychological Works of Sigmund Freud*, vol. 12 (1911–13), edited by James Strachey, 97–108. London: Vintage, 2001.

———. "The Economic Problem of Masochism." In *The Standard Edition of the Complete Psychological Works of Sigmund Freud*, vol. 19 (1923–25), edited by James Strachey, 159–70. London: Vintage, 2001.

———. "The Ego and the Id." In *Standard Edition*, vol. 19, 1–66.

———. "Formulations on the Two Principles of Mental Functioning." In *The Standard Edition*, vol. 12, 213–26.

———. *The Future of an Illusion*. In *Standard Edition*, vol. 21, 1–56.

———. "The Future Prospects of Psychoanalytic Therapy." In *The Standard Edition of the Complete Psychological Works of Sigmund Freud*, vol. 11 (1910), edited by James Strachey, 139–51. London: Vintage, 2001.

———. *Group Psychology and the Analysis of the Ego*. In *Standard Edition*, vol. 18, 65–143.

———. *Inhibitions, Symptoms, and Anxiety*. In *The Standard Edition of the Complete Psychological Works of Sigmund Freud*, vol. 20 (1925–26), edited by James Strachey, 75–175. London: Vintage, 2001.

———. "Instincts and Their Vicissitudes." In *The Standard Edition of the Complete Psychological Works of Sigmund Freud*, vol. 14 (1914–16), edited by James Strachey, 117–40. London: Vintage Press, 2001.

———. *Introductory Lectures on Psychoanalysis* (parts 1 and 2). In *The Standard Edition of the Complete Psychological Works of Sigmund Freud*, vol. 15 (1915–16), edited by James Strachey. London: Vintage, 2001.

———. *Introductory Lectures on Psychoanalysis* (part 3). In *The Standard Edition of the Complete Psychological Works of Sigmund Freud*, vol. 16 (1916–17), edited by James Strachey. London: Vintage, 2001.

———. "Mourning and Melancholia." In *Standard Edition*, vol. 16, 237–58.

———. "On Narcissism: An Introduction." In *Standard Edition*, vol. 14, 57–102.

———. *New Introductory Lectures on Psycho-analysis*. In *The Standard Edition of the Complete Psychological Works of Sigmund Freud*, vol. 22 (1932–36), edited by James Strachey, 1–182. London: Vintage, 2001.

———. "The Psychotherapy of Hysteria." In Josef Breuer and Sigmund Freud, *Studies on Hysteria*. In *The Standard Edition of the Complete Psychological Works of Sigmund Freud*, vol. 2 (1893–95), edited by James Strachey, 253–305. London: Vintage, 2001.

———. "Remembering, Repeating, and Working Through." In *Standard Edition*, vol. 12, 145–56.

———. *Totem and Taboo*. In *The Standard Edition of the Complete Psychological Works of Sigmund Freud*, vol. 13 (1914–16), edited by James Strachey, 1–162. London: Vintage, 2001.

———. "Why War?" In *Standard Edition*, vol. 22, 197–215.

———. "'Wild' Psychoanalysis." In *Standard Edition*, vol. 11, 219–27.

Fromm, Erich. *The Crisis of Psychoanalysis: Essays on Freud, Marx, and Social Psychology*. Boston: Holt, Rinehart, Winston, 1970.

Gandesha, Samir. "'Identifying with the Aggressor': From the Authoritarian to Neoliberal Personality." *Constellations* 25, no. 1 (March 2018): 147–64.

Gemes, Ken. "Freud and Nietzsche on Sublimation," *Journal of Nietzsche Studies* 38 (2009): 38–59.

Geuss, Raymond. *Philosophy and Real Politics*. Princeton, NJ: Princeton University Press, 2008.

Gordon, Peter. "The Authoritarian Personality Revisited: Reading Adorno in the Age of Trump." In Wendy Brown, Peter Gordon, and Max Pensky, *Authoritarianism: Three Inquiries in Critical Theory*, 45–84. Chicago: University of Chicago Press, 2018.

Green, André, and Daniel Stern. *Clinical and Observational Psychoanalytic Research: Roots of a Controversy*. Edited by Joseph Sandler, Anne-Marie Sandler, and Rosemary Davies. London: Karnac, 2000.

Greenberg, Jay R., and Stephen Mitchell. *Object Relations in Psychoanalytic Theory*. Cambridge, MA: Harvard University Press, 1983.

Grosskurth, Phyllis. *Melanie Klein: Her World and Her Work*. New York: Alfred A. Knopf, 1986.

Habermas, Jürgen. *Knowledge and Human Interests*. Translated by Jeremy J. Shapiro. Boston: Beacon, 1971.

———. "Moral Consciousness and Communicative Action." In *Moral Consciousness and Communicative Action*. Translated by Christian Lenhardt and Shierry Weber Nicholsen, 116–94. Cambridge, MA: MIT Press, 1990.

———. "Moral Development and Ego Identity." In *Communication and the Evolution of Society*, translated by Thomas McCarthy, 69–94. Boston: Beacon, 1979.

———. *The Theory of Communicative Action, Volume 1: Reason and the Rationalization of Society*. Translated by Thomas McCarthy. Boston: Beacon, 1985.

———. "Walter Benjamin: Consciousness Raising or Rescuing Critique." In *Philosophical-Political Profiles*, translated by Frederick G. Lawrence, 129–64. Cambridge, MA: MIT Press, 1983.

Haider, Asad. "Four Concepts in Depoliticized Politics." In *Power, Neoliberalism, and the Reinvention of Politics: The Feminist Critical Theory of Wendy Brown*, edited by Amy Allen and Eduardo Mendieta. University Park, PA: Penn State University Press, forthcoming.

Hinshelwood, R. D. "Melanie Klein and Countertransference: A Note on Some Archival Material." *Psychoanalysis and History* 10, no. 1 (2008): 95–113.

———. "Who Wants to be a Scientist? The Historical and Psychoanalytic Context at the Start of Klein's Career, circa 1918–1921." In *Other Banalities: Melanie Klein Revisited*, edited by Jon Mills, 8–24. New York: Routledge, 2006.

Honig, Bonnie. *Public Things: Democracy in Disrepair*. New York: Fordham University Press, 2017.

Honneth, Axel. "Facets of the Presocial Self: Rejoinder to Joel Whitebook." In *The I in We: Studies in the Theory of Recognition*, 217–31. Cambridge: Polity, 2012.

———. "Is There an Emancipatory Interest? An Attempt to Answer Critical Theory's Most Fundamental Question." *European Journal of Philosophy* 25, no. 4 (December 2017): 908–20.

———. *Pathologies of Reason: On the Legacy of Critical Theory*. Translated by James Ingram. New York: Columbia University Press, 2009.

———. *Reification: A New Look at an Old Idea*. Edited by Martin Jay. New York: Oxford University Press, 2008.

———. *The Struggle for Recognition: The Moral Grammar of Social Conflict*. Translated by Joel Anderson. Cambridge, MA: MIT Press, 1995.

———. "The Work of Negativity: A Psychoanalytical Revision of the Theory of Recognition." In *Recognition, Work, Politics: New Directions in French Critical Theory*, edited by Jean-Philippe Deranty, Danielle Petherbridge, John Rundell, and Robert Sinnerbrink, 127–36. Leiden: Brill, 2007.

———, and Joel Whitebook. "Omnipotence or Fusion? A Conversation between Axel Honneth and Joel Whitebook." *Constellations* 23, no. 2 (June 2016): 170–79.

Horkheimer, Max. "Traditional and Critical Theory." In *Critical Theory: Selected Essays*, 188-243. New York: Continuum, 1972.

Horney, Karen. *New Ways in Psychoanalysis*. New York: Norton, 1939.

Huffer, Lynne. *Mad for Foucault: Rethinking the Foundations of Queer Theory*. New York: Columbia University Press, 2010.

Isaacs, Susan. "The Nature and Function of Phantasy." *International Journal of Psychoanalysis* 29 (1948): 73–97.

Jaeggi, Rahel. *Critique of Forms of Life*. Translated by Ciaran Cronin. Cambridge, MA: Harvard University Press, 2018.

Jay, Martin. *The Dialectical Imagination: A History of the Frankfurt School and the Institute of Social Research, 1923–1950*. Berkeley: University of California Press, 1963.

Khanna, Ranjana. *Dark Continents: Psychoanalysis and Colonialism*. Durham, NC: Duke University Press, 2003.

Klein, Melanie. "A Contribution to the Psychogenesis of Manic-Depressive States." In *Love, Guilt, and Reparation and Other Works, 1921–1945*, 262–89. New York: Free Press, 1975.

———. "Criminal Tendencies in Normal Children." In *Love, Guilt, and Reparation*, 170–85.

———. "The Early Development of Conscience in the Child." In *Love, Guilt, and Reparation*, 248–57.

———. "Envy and Gratitude." In *Envy and Gratitude and Other Works, 1946–1963*, 176–235. New York: Free Press, 1975.

———. "Love, Guilt, and Reparation." In *Love, Guilt, and Reparation*, 306–43.

———. "Memorandum on Her Technique 25th October 1943." In *The Freud-Klein Controversies: 1941–1945*, edited by Pearl King and Riccardo Steiner, 476–78. New York: Routledge, 1991.

———. "Mourning and Its Relation to Manic-Depressive States." In *Love, Guilt, and Reparation*, 344–69.

———. "Notes on Some Schizoid Mechanisms." In *Envy and Gratitude*, 1–24.

———. "The Oedipus Complex in the Light of Early Anxieties." In *Love, Guilt, and Reparation*, 370–419.

———. "On the Development of Mental Functioning," in *Envy and Gratitude*, 236–46.

———. "On the Theory of Anxiety and Guilt," in *Envy and Gratitude*, 25–42.

———. "Some Theoretical Conclusions Regarding the Emotional Life of the Infant." In *Envy and Gratitude*, 61–93.

———. "The Origins of Transference." In *Envy and Gratitude*, 48–56.

———. *The Psychoanalysis of Children*. Translated by Alix Strachey. New York: Free Press, 1975.

Koopman, Colin. *Genealogy as Critique: Foucault and the Problems of Modernity*. Bloomington: Indiana University Press, 2013.

Lacan, Jacques. "Intervention on Transference." In *In Dora's Case: Freud-Hysteria-Feminism*, 2nd ed., edited by Charles Bernheimer and Claire Kahane, 92–104. New York: Columbia University Press, 1990.

———. *The Seminar of Jacques Lacan, Book I: Freud's Papers on Technique, 1953–54*. Edited by Jacques-Alain Miller. Translated by John Forrester. New York: Norton, 1991.

———. *The Seminar of Jacques Lacan, Book II: The Ego in Freud's Theory and in the Technique of Psychoanalysis, 1954–55*. Edited by Jacques Alain-Miller. Translated by Sylvana Tomaselli. New York: Norton, 1991.

———. *The Seminar of Jacques Lacan, Book VII: The Ethics of Psychoanalysis, 1959–1960*. Edited by Jacques-Alain Miller. Translated by Dennis Porter. New York: Norton, 1992.

———. *The Seminar of Jacques Lacan, Book VIII: Transference 1960–61*. Edited by Jacques-Alain Miller. Translated by Bruce Fink. Cambridge: Polity, 2015.

Lane, Christopher, ed. *The Psychoanalysis of Race*. New York: Columbia University Press, 1998.

Laplanche, Jean. *New Foundations for Psychoanalysis*. Translated by David Macey. New York: Basil Blackwell, 1989.

de Lauretis, Teresa. *Freud's Drive: Psychoanalysis, Literature, and Film*. New York: Palgrave MacMillan, 2010.

Lear, Jonathan. *Freud*. 2nd ed. New York: Routledge, 2015.

———. *Wisdom Won from Illness: Essays in Philosophy and Psychoanalysis*. Cambridge, MA: Harvard University Press, 2017.

Leeb, Claudia. "Mass Hypnoses: The Rise of the Far Right from an Adornian and Freudian Perspective." *Berlin Journal of Critical Theory* 2, no. 3 (2018): 59–81.

———. "Mystified Consciousness: Rethinking the Rise of the Far Right with Marx and Lacan." *Open Cultural Studies* 2 (2018): 236–48.

———. *Power and Feminist Agency in Capitalism*. Oxford: Oxford University Press, 2017.

Likierman, Meira. *Melanie Klein: Her Work in Context*. New York: Continuum, 2002.

Loewald, Hans. "Defense and Reality." In *The Essential Loewald: Collected Papers and Monographs*, 3–21. Hagerstown, MD: University Publishing Group, 2000.

Marasco, Robyn. "'Already the Effect of the Whip': Critical Theory and the Feminine Ideal." *differences* 17, no. 1 (2006): 88–115.

———. "Toward a Critique of Conspiratorial Reason," *Constellations* 23, no. 2 (2016): 236–43.

Marcuse, Herbert. *Eros and Civilization: A Philosophical Inquiry into Freud*. Boston: Beacon, 1966.

———. *One-Dimensional Man*. 2nd ed. Boston: Beacon, 1991.

———, Jürgen Habermas, Heinz Lubasc, and Telman Spenglar. "Theory and Politics: A Discussion." *Telos* 38 (1978–79): 124–53.

Marin, Inara Luisa. "The Bi-Dimensionality of Marcuse's Critical Psychoanalytical Model of Emancipation: Between Negativity and Normativity." *Radical Philosophy Review* 19, no. 1 (2016): 229–40.

McAfee, Noelle. *Fear of Breakdown: Politics and Psychoanalysis*. New York: Columbia University Press, 2019.

McCarthy, Thomas. *The Critical Theory of Jürgen Habermas*. Cambridge, MA: MIT Press, 1978.

McIvor, David. "Pressing the Subject: Critical Theory and the Death Drive." *Constellations* 22, no. 3 (2015): 405–19.

———. *Mourning in America: Race and the Politics of Loss*. Ithaca, NY: Cornell University Press, 2016.

Miller, Jacques Alain. "Response to the Anti-Freudians." *Le Point*, September 22, 2005, http://www.lacan.com/antimill.htm.

Mitchell, Stephen A., and Margaret J. Black, *Freud and Beyond: A History of Modern Psychoanalytic Thought*. New York: Basic Books, 1995.

Moyn, Samuel. "Freud's Discontents." *Nation*, November 2, 2016, https://www.thenation.com/article/archive/freuds-discontents/.

Nietzsche, Friedrich. *On the Genealogy of Morals and Ecce Homo*. New York: Vintage, 1989.

Ogden, Thomas. *The Primitive Edge of Experience*. Lanham, MD: Rowman & Littlefield, 2004.

Petherbridge, Danielle. *The Critical Theory of Axel Honneth*. Lanham, MD: Lexington, 2013.

Pew Research Center. "Political Polarization and the American Public." June 2014, https://www.people-press.org/2014/06/12/political-polarization-in-the-american-public/ (accessed October 2, 2019).

Redecker, Eva von. "Marx's Concept of Radical Needs in the Guise of Queer Desire." In *Global Justice and Desire: Queering Economy*, edited by Nikita Dhawan, Antke Engel, Christoph F. E. Holzhey, and Volker Wolterrsdorff, 31–46. London: Routledge, 2015.

Rensmann, Lars. *The Politics of Unreason: The Frankfurt School and the Origins of Modern Antisemitism*. Albany: SUNY Press, 2017.

Rickert, John. "The Fromm-Marcuse Debate Revisited." *Theory and Society* 15 (1986): 351–400.

Rose, Jacqueline. "Negativity in the Work of Melanie Klein." In *Why War? Psychoanalysis, Politics, and the Return to Melanie Klein*, 137–90. Oxford: Blackwell, 1993.

Roudinesco, Élisabeth. *Freud: In His Time and Ours*. Translated by Catherine Porter. Cambridge, MA: Harvard University Press, 2016.

Rustin, Michael. *The Good Society and the Inner World: Psychoanalysis, Politics, and Culture*. London: Verso, 1991.

———. "Klein on Human Nature." In *Other Banalities: Melanie Klein Revisited*, edited by Jon Mills, 25–44. New York: Routledge, 2006.

Ruti, Mari. *The Ethics of Opting Out: Queer Theory's Defiant Subjects*. New York: Columbia University Press, 2017.

———. *The Singularity of Being: Lacan and the Immortal Within*. New York: Fordham University Press, 2012.

———. *A World of Fragile Things: Psychoanalysis and the Art of Living*. Albany: SUNY Press, 2009.

Saar, Martin. "Rethinking Resistance: Critical Theory Before and After Deleuze." In *Coils of the Serpent*, forthcoming.

Sedgwick, Eve. "Melanie Klein and the Difference Affect Makes." *South Atlantic Quarterly* 106, no. 3 (Summer 2007): 625–42.

———. "Paranoid Reading and Reparative Reading, Or, You're So Paranoid, You Probably Think This Essay Is About You." In *Touching/Feeling: Affect, Pedagogy, Performativity*, 123–51. Durham, NC: Duke University Press, 2003.

Segal, Hanna. *Introduction to the Work of Melanie Klein*. London: Karnac, 1988.

———. "A Psychoanalytic Approach to Aesthetics." In *Reading Melanie Klein*, edited by Lyndsey Stonebridge and John Phillips, 203–22. New York: Routledge, 1998.

Seth, Sanjay. *Beyond Reason? Postcolonial Theory and the Social Sciences*, forthcoming.

Smith, Richard. "Darwin, Freud, and the Continuing Misrepresentation of the Primal Horde." *Current Anthropology* 57, no. 6 (December 2016): 838–43.

Stern, Daniel. *The Interpersonal World of the Infant: A View from Psychoanalysis and Developmental Psychology*. New York: Basic Books, 1985.

Uscinski, Joseph, and Joseph Parent. *American Conspiracy Theories*. New York: Oxford University Press, 2014.

Webster, Jamieson, "On the Question of the Future of Psychoanalysis: Some Reflections on Jacques Lacan." *European Journal of Psychoanalysis*, http://www.journal-psychoanalysis.eu/on-the-question-of-the-future-of-psychoanalysis-some-reflections-on-jacques-lacan/ (accessed March 28, 2019).

Wellmer, Albrecht. "Truth, Semblance, and Reconciliation: Adorno's Aesthetic Redemption of Modernity." Translated by Maeve Cooke. *Telos* 62 (Winter 1984–85): 89–94.

Weir, Allison. *Decolonizing Freedom*. New York: Oxford University Press, forthcoming.

Whitebook, Joel. "Against Interiority: Foucault's Struggle with Psychoanalysis." In *The Cambridge Companion to Foucault*, 2nd ed., edited by Gary Gutting, 312–47. Cambridge: Cambridge University Press, 2005.

———. *Freud: An Intellectual Biography*. Cambridge: Cambridge University Press, 2017.

———. "The Marriage of Marx and Freud: Critical Theory and Psychoanalysis." In *The Cambridge Companion to Critical Theory*, edited by Fred Rush, 74–102. Cambridge: Cambridge University Press, 2004.

———. "Mutual Recognition and the Work of the Negative." In *Pluralism and the Pragmatic Turn: Essays in Honor of Thomas McCarthy*, edited by James Bohman and William Rehg, 257–92. Cambridge, MA: MIT Press, 2001.

———. *Perversion and Utopia: A Study in Psychoanalysis and Critical Theory*. Cambridge, MA: MIT Press, 1995.

———. "Trump's Method, Our Madness." *New York Times*, March 20, 2017, https://www.nytimes.com/2017/03/20/opinion/trumps-method-our-madness.html.

———. "Weighty Objects: Adorno's Kant-Freud Interpretation." In *The Cambridge Companion to Adorno*, edited by Thomas Huhn, 51–78. Cambridge: Cambridge University Press, 2004.

Zaretsky, Eli. *Political Freud: A History*. New York: Columbia University Press, 2015.

Zurn, Christopher. *Axel Honneth*. Cambridge: Polity, 2015.

Index

Abram, Jan, 52
"Actuality of Philosophy, The" (Adorno), 177
Adorno, Theodor: authoritarianism and, 188, 194–95; on bourgeois society, 12; on constellations, 177; on the criteria of successful critique, 182; critique of identity thinking of, 84; critique of the ego of, 59, 60, 60–68; on dialectical thinking, 20; drive theory of, 72; genealogy and, 180–81; on integration, 74–75; on Kantian morality, 61; Klein and, 71–72, 75, 84–85, 150; Lacan and, 20; Oedipalization and, 189–90; on philosophy, 177, 238n129; psychoanalysis and, 1, 151–52, 180; on revisionist psychoanalysis, 68–74, 217n58; on social reality, 238n121; stereotypical thinking and, 188; utopia and, 19
aesthetic theory, 62–63, 86, 87. *See also* art; work of art, the
affect theory, 118
aggression: anxiety and, 193; Benjamin, J. on, 213n118; civilization and, 109; creativity and, 143–44; death drive and, 41; democracy and, 198; desire and, 44; disintegration and, 78; Freud and, 41; intractability of, 54; love and, 119, 143; Marcuse on, 131; role of environmental factors in, 52; the superego and, 108, 136. *See also* primary aggression
Alford, Fred, 72, 86, 132, 149, 228n57, 230n105
alterity, 49. *See also* intersubjectivity
"alternative facts," 193, 197
alt-right, the, 190–91
ambivalence: the death drive and, 134, 143; depressive position and, 84, 115; ego integration and, 141–42; integration and, 77, 94; love and, 73–74, 78, 134; overcoming and, 117; politics and, 195, 196; primary aggression and, 79; reparation and, 86, 120; wholeness and, 87
analysand, the: analyst and, 152, 162, 170, 175; autonomy and, 159; countertransference and, 173–74; cure of, 157; demands of, 168; desire and, 166; integration and, 73; interpretation and, 178; love and, 167; progress and, 121–22; repression and, 162–63; transference and, 162, 165, 170, 178; transformation of, 146–47; the unconscious and, 164
analysis. *See* psychoanalysis
"Analysis Terminable and Interminable" (Freud), 146
analyst, the: analysand and, 152, 162, 170, 175; love and, 167; superego and, 51; transference and, 51, 170

Ananke, 95, 128, 130. *See also* necessity
animism, 101–2
Antigone (Sophocles), 147
anti-Semitism, 65
anxiety: aggression and, 7, 193; disintegration and, 75; ego integration and, 142; the good and bad breast and, 33, 230n93; the Great Refusal and, 129; idealization and, 80, 143; in the infant, 31; Klein on, 209n23; power and, 194; reparation and, 133; role of environmental factors in, 52
archaic mother, the, 113, 114, 220n19
Arendt, Hannah, 9
art, 86, 87. *See also* aesthetic theory; work of art, the
Auschwitz, 195
authoritarianism, 70, 74, 88, 188, 198
authoritarian personality, 66
authority, 65–67
autonomy: aims of critical theory and, 160; of the analysand, 159; communicative action and, 14; defined, 161; domination and, 192; heteronomy and, 64; in postliberal societies, 65; rationalism and, 12; socialization and, 67; sublimation and, 139

bad breast, the, 32, 42, 80, 133, 134
Balint, Michael, 113
Benjamin, Jessica: on aggression, 213n118; critique of Klein of, 49; on intersubjectivity, 60, 67, 84; on the paradox of authoritarianism, 65; on primary narcissism, 209n12; on relation to the other, 54; on the self, 28; Winnicott and, 207n2
Beyond the Pleasure Principle (Freud), 36, 39
Big Other, the, 21, 148
Brickman, Celia, 98, 104, 114, 221n46
Brown, Wendy, 190, 229n84, 240n17
Buck-Morss, Susan, 151, 152, 178
Butler, Judith, 118, 136, 138

capitalism: domination and, 65; Freud and, 224n108; individual and society in, 68; integration and, 74; libido and, 127; pathology of reason and, 156; repressive desublimation and, 190; surplus repression and, 125
Castoriadis, Cornelius, 93
castration, 70
catharsis, 162
Celikates, Robin, 153, 156, 159–61, 234n44
Chakrabarty, Dipesh, 99
character, 69
civilization: Eros and, 126, 227n20; human nature and, 124; instinct and, 128; progress and, 90, 105–11
Civilization and Its Discontents (Freud), 39, 106–8; oceanic feeling and, 30
cognition, 82
colonialism, 98, 99, 114, 117–20
"Colonial Object Relations" (Eng), 117–18
communicative action, 14
communism, 1
comparative method, the, 100–3, 115
concepts, 151–52
consciousness, 83–84
conspiracy theories, 194
constellations, 177, 179
contradiction, 67
Counter-Enlightenment, the, 89
countertransference, 173–74, 236n79, 237n108
creativity, 25, 138–45, 199
critical theory: aims of, 160; autonomy and, 160; on capitalism, 65; criteria of success of, 182; the depressive position and, 192; drive theory and, 2, 53–54; formation of, 1; intersubjectivity and, 84; primary narcissism and, 208–9n11; psychoanalysis and, 152–53, 159–60, 169, 175; rational insight and, 175–76; social transformation and, 23; theory and praxis and, 187; transference and, 153; the unconscious and, 18–19
critique: aims of, 22, 186; false consciousness and, 155; Habermas on, 176; methodology of, 186; possibility of, 65; psychoanalysis and, 17, 154–55; rational insight and, 176; social change and, 155; transference and, 169–75
culture industry, the, 67, 74

dark enlightenment, the, 89, 110, 150
Darwin, Charles, 90
death drive, the: aggression and, 54; ambivalence and, 134, 143; civilization and, 106, 108, 110; creativity and, 123; drive to mastery and, 41; Eros and, 129; ethics and, 136; the Frankfurt School and, 123; Freud on, 8; Freud's "unofficial" position and, 94; Honneth on, 7; Klein on, 8, 34, 39, 88; Lacan on, 21; love and, 132; Marcuse and, 128–31; the Nirvana principle and, 128; omnipotence and, 108; paranoid-schizoid position and, 42–43; pleasure principle and, 40; primacy of, 40; primary aggression and, 35, 226n7; progress and, 106–7, 122, 123, 128, 143; psychoanalysis and, 136; reparation and, 132, 135; revisionist psychoanalysis and, 68; the superego and, 110 *See also* Thanatos
deliberation, 196–97, 241n40
democracy, 198
depressive position, the: ambivalence and, 77, 115; anxiety and, 133; creativity and, 122; critical theory and, 192; as developmental achievement, 32; guilt and, 133; identity thinking and, 84; the infant and, 133; integration and, 76; loss and, 79, 141, 197; love and, 43; moral strand of, 116; nonreified thinking and, 88; overcoming of, 33, 115–17, 224n120; paranoid-schizoid position and, 29, 31, 42, 75–76, 115, 143; politics and, 195, 197; primary caregiver and, 28, 50, 137; primary object and, 34; the reality principle and, 243n98; reparation and, 33, 135; sublimation and, 144; tragic strand of, 116; the work of art and, 86
depth hermeneutics, 154
desire, 44, 166, 171, 174, 175
despair, 20, 24, 74
Dews, Peter, 59, 80
Dialectical Imagination, The (Jay), 1
dialectical thinking, 20
Dialectic of Enlightenment (Adorno and Horkheimer), 60, 61, 63–64
dictatorship of reason, 93

discursive rationality, 11–12
disintegration, 74, 75, 78
domination: autonomy and, 192; bourgeois enlightenment ideals and, 64; bourgeois society and, 61; of drives, 93; independence and, 82–83; of inner and outer nature, 215n15; maturity as, 97; paradox of authoritarianism and, 65, 67; primary aggression and, 150; progress and, 112, 124–25, 127; racism and, 99
drive: defined, 35; human conflict and, 39; instinct and, 44; interpersonal psychoanalysis and, 2; mechanistic and organic views of, 36–37; metapsychology and, 36; object and, 36, 38; phantasy and, 44–45; relationality of, 38; revisionist psychoanalysis and, 2
drive theory: of Adorno and Horkheimer, 72; critical theory and, 53–54; Freud's late version of, 39; Honneth and, 4, 7; infancy and, 9; intersubjectivity and, 4; Klein on, 8, 24, 28, 204n42; revisionist psychoanalysis and, 2, 68; sociality and, 53
drive to mastery, 41

Edelman, Lee, 22
"Education After Auschwitz" (Adorno), 194
ego, the: Adorno on, 15, 60–68; Freud on, 57, 211n53; the id and, 57–59; individuation and, 14; the infant and, 114; integration and, 33–34; intersubjectivity and, 60; Klein on, 15, 30, 75, 186, 211n53; Lacan's critique of, 13; libido and, 62; loss and, 140; love and, 43; as master, 90, 94; melancholia and, 141; mourning and, 140; omnipotence and, 58; paranoid-schizoid position and, 42; phantasy and, 46; pleasure principle and, 46–47; in postliberal societies, 66; the psyche and, 140; reason and, 94; violence and, 61; wholeness of, 55
Ego and the Id, The (Freud), 141
ego development, 96
ego identity, 10
ego integration: ambivalence and, 141–42; ego strength and, 75, 78; Freud's "unofficial"

ego integration (*cont.*)
position and, 94; intersubjectivity and, 68; Klein on, 59, 60, 74–81, 112–13, 186; loss and, 88; love and, 43, 78; negative dialectics and, 85; nondominating modes of, 64; phantasy and, 142; reparative reason and, 87–88; violence and, 62, 63. *See also* integration
ego loss, 140
ego psychology, 57, 122, 202n8, 231n109
ego strength, 58–59, 75, 78, 186
ego weakness, 66
emancipation, 67, 176
emancipatory interest, 155, 157–58
"End of Internalization, The" (Benjamin), 65
Eng, David, 16–17, 117–18
Enlightenment, the: Freud and, 57, 89, 110, 124; progress and, 90, 110
envy, 73
Epicharmus, 81
episteme, 168
epistemic interests, 158
Eros: aggression and, 7; civilization and, 107, 126; the death drive and, 129; defined, 126, 204n34; the depressive position and, 43; liberation of, 129; libido and, 212n76; Marcuse on, 18, 126; nonrepressive sublimation and, 128; the performance principle and, 127; phantasy and, 126–27; Thanatos and, 108. *See also* erotic drive; love
Eros and Civilization (Marcuse), 25, 123
erotic drive, 7. *See also* Eros; love
essentialism, 208n6
ethics, 109, 136, 148
Ethics of Psychoanalysis, The (Lacan), 145
Eurocentrism, 97, 98, 111, 186
evolutionary anthropology, 90, 98, 104, 221n40
evolutionary biology, 90
external object, 50. *See also* object, the

false consciousness, 68, 155
fascism, 65–67, 74, 188, 194, 198
father, the, 92
fear, 118, 136, 148
feminism, 67

Fink, Bruce, 149, 167
Fong, Benjamin, 8–9, 36–37, 40–41, 210n29
"Formulation on the Two Principles of Mental Functioning" (Freud), 91
Foucault, Michel: Adorno and, 67; on critique, 183; on emancipation, 131; Marcuse and, 192; normalization and, 237n107; psychoanalysis and, 237n102; transference and, 171–74
Frankfurt School, the: aims of, 123; on authoritarianism, 198; the death drive and, 123; Honneth and, 156; psychoanalysis and, 1, 151, 198; revisionist psychoanalysis and, 2; the unconscious and, 17
Fraser, Nancy, 191
freedom, 107, 190
Freud, Anna, 165, 209n11
Freud, Sigmund: Adorno on, 70–71; aggression and, 41; capitalism and, 224n108; on civilization, 105–11; coldness of, 70–71; on the criteria of successful analysis, 182; Darwin and, 90; on the death drive, 8; drive theory of, 35–38; on the ego, 57–59, 211n53; the Enlightenment and, 57, 89, 110, 124; on Eros, 204n34, 211n52; on ethics, 109; evolutionary anthropology and, 104; Foucault on, 173; genealogy of morality of, 223n104; historicized reading of, 224n108; Honneth and, 156–57; on the id, 57–59; Klein and, 30, 38, 44, 211n55; Lacan and, 145, 237n108; Marcuse and, 127; on morality, 110; pessimism of, 111–12; on the pleasure principle, 211–12n66; on the primal horde, 222n62; on progress, 95–96, 105–11, 145–46; racism and, 223–24n105; on sublimation, 138–39; on trivialities, 232–33n5; Whitebook on, 89–98
"Freudian Theory and the Pattern of Fascist Propaganda" (Adorno), 66
Fromm, Erich: Adorno and, 217n58; on the death drive, 226n5; drive theory and, 2; drive theory of, 201n5; on Freud, 123; on Piaget, 202n8
future, the, 22
Future of an Illusion, The (Freud), 103

genealogy, 180
genealogy of morality, 223n104
genocide, 75
good breast, the, 45, 141, 230n93
good-enough mother, the, 4
good object, the, 73, 78, 79, 143, 166
Gordon, Peter, 188–90, 192
Great Refusal, the, 129, 131, 139
Greenberg, Jay R., 38, 39, 48
Grosskurth, Phyllis, 51, 211n56
Group Psychology and the Analysis of the Ego (Freud), 102
groups, 102–3
guilt, 109, 118, 120, 133

Habermas, Jürgen: on analytic technique, 235n46; cognitive psychology and, 10; on critique, 176; on the ego, 14; Foucault and, 172; Honneth and, 158, 234n28; on intersubjectivity, 205n60; on moral development, 15; on postsecularism, 221n34; psychoanalysis and, 2, 151, 152–53, 161, 181, 205n59; on social evolution, 10–11, 205n47; on transference, 154; on validity claims, 10–11; Whitebook and, 221n34; Whitebook on, 18, 205n59, 205n60
Haeckel, Ernst, 99
happiness, 106, 109
hatred, 119, 132, 136, 137, 148
hermeneutics, 177
heteronomy, 64
Hinshelwood, R. D., 29, 210–11n50, 212n76
historicism, 8–9
History of Madness (Foucault), 173
History of Sexuality, The (Foucault), 192
Holocaust, the, 1, 75
Honneth, Axel: on critical theory, 156; on the death drive, 7; drive theory and, 4, 7; early work of, 202n16; the Frankfurt School and, 156; Freud and, 156–57; on the good-enough mother, 4; Habermas and 158, 234n28; moral anthropology and, 203–4n29; object-relations theory and, 4; philosophical anthropology and, 4, 6, 27; on primary fusion, 5–6, 7, 27; on psychoanalysis, 3, 153, 158–59; psychoanalysis and, 2–3; Whitebook and, 203n24; Winnicott and, 4, 27
hope, 149
Horkheimer, Max, 12, 72, 182
Horney, Karen, 123, 217n58
human condition, the, 9, 111, 122, 130, 143
hypostasization, 82

id, the, 46, 57–59, 141
idealism, 109, 177, 180
idealization, 80, 143
identity thinking, 84, 151
ideology, 178
id psychology, 72
imagination, 129. *See also* phantasy
immortality, 81–82, 142
incest, 107
individual, the, 68
individual transformation, 24
individuation: the ego and, 14; Honneth on, 6; phantasy and, 129; reason and, 129; repression and, 129; socialization and, 10, 186; sublimation and, 139
infancy: anxiety and, 31; drive theory and, 9; primary object and, 32
infant, the: the depressive position and, 133; the ego and, 114; Freud on, 92–93; loss and, 141; object relations and, 49, 114; the other and, 52; phantasy and, 114; precarious life of, 118; primary caregiver and, 202n17; primary fusion and, 113, 114; primary narcissism and, 114; psyche and, 113; reality and, 47
Inhibitions, Symptoms, and Anxiety (Freud), 58
insight, 155, 163, 166. *See also* rational insight
instinct: civilization and, 90, 128; defined, 39–40; drive and, 44; object and, 36; phantasy and, 44
"Instincts and Their Vicissitudes" (Freud), 35, 36, 44, 46
Institute for Social Research, the, 2, 198
instrumental reason, 87
integration: Adorno's view of, 74, 83; ambivalence and, 77, 94; capitalism and, 74; defined, 33–34, 94, 112; depressive position and, 76; as developmental goal,

integration (*cont.*)
34, 73; fascism and, 74; genocide and, 75; the Holocaust and, 74–75; incompleteness of, 79; introjection and, 76; paranoid-schizoid position and, 80; politics and, 195; sublimation and, 140, 219n127; trust and, 79. *See also* ego integration; political integration

internal object, 50. *See also* object, the

interpersonal psychoanalysis, 2

interpretation, 73, 175–181, 238n129

intersubjectivity: autonomy and, 68; drive theory and, 4; the ego and, 60; emancipation and, 67; ethics of, 148; Habermas on, 205n60; intrapsychic experience and, 48–54; Klein on, 16, 47; love and, 166; phantasy and, 53; primary fusion and, 113; projection and, 53; reparative reason and, 87; subjectivity and, 53, 54. *See also* alterity

intrapsychic experience, 48–54

introjection: the good breast and, 230n93; integration and, 76; phantasy and, 45–46; primary narcissism and, 46; primary object and, 32; the superego and, 108

Isaacs, Susan, 44

Jaeggi, Rahel, 191, 233n19

Jay, Martin, 1

Kantian morality, 61

Klein, Melanie: Adorno and, 71–72, 75, 84–85, 150; Anna Freud and, 165; on anxiety, 209n23, 214n121; on art, 86; Butler and, 136, 138; the comparative method and, 115; on countertransference, 173; on the death drive, 8, 34, 39, 131–132; on drive theory, 8, 24, 28, 204n42; on the ego, 15–16, 211n53; on ego integration, 59, 60; on ego strength, 59; essentialism and, 208n6; ethics and, 136; Freud and, 30, 38, 44, 211n55; on intersubjectivity, 16, 47; Lacan and, 148, 214n123; on libido, 213n100; Marcuse and, 149; McIvor and, 138; metapsychology and, 16–17, 29–34; on negativity, 117; neglect of environmental factors of, 213n103; on omnipotence, 228n67; on overcoming, 115–17; philosophical anthropology and, 24, 27; politics and, 26; on primary aggression, 24, 28, 41–42, 114; on primary fusion, 113; on primary narcissism, 30, 87, 208n9; on progress, 131–32; on psychosis in children, 209n15; on the reality principle, 72; reconceptualization of drives of, 38; reconciliation and, 228n57; on the self, 16; on subjectivity, 28; on sublimation, 138–40; on transference, 165, 166, 170; Winnicott and, 52. *See also* phantasy

Knowledge and Human Interests (Habermas): methodology and, 22–23; psychoanalysis and, 2, 151, 154

Kohlberg, Lawrence, 15, 156

Koopman, Colin, 171

Lacan, Jacques: Adorno and, 20; on *Antigone*, 147; on countertransference, 174, 237n108; critique of the ego of, 59; on the death drive, 21, 210n31; on the ego, 13; Fink on, 149; on Freud, 145, 237n108; on the future, 22; Klein and, 148, 214n123; on love, 167–68; on primary fusion, 113; on sublimation, 139; on transference, 166, 170, 174–75; utopia and, 20, 21

language, 154

Lear, Jonathan: on aggression, 41; on the aims of psychoanalysis, 163, 178; on Freud's genealogy, 223n104; on rational insight, 168; on reflective distance, 176; on transference, 25, 154, 169

liberty, 107

libidinal utopia, 18

libido, 41, 62, 127

Likierman, Meira, 49, 114–16, 117, 224n120

Loewald, Hans, 217n88

loss: acceptance of, 132; the depressive position and, 116, 197; ego growth and, 140; ego integration and, 88; as foundational for Kleinian subject, 148; subject formation and, 79

love: aggression and, 119, 143; ambivalence of, 73–74, 78, 134; the analysand and, 167; the

analyst and, 167; civilization and, 107, 227n20; countertransference and, 236n79; the death drive and, 132; the depressive position and, 43, 73; the ego and, 43; ego integration and, 78; hatred and, 132, 143; integration and, 78; intersubjectivity and, 166; Lacan on, 167–68; melancholia and, 140; necessity and, 107; primary aggression and, 78, 132; recognition and, 7; reparation and, 118, 132–33; revisionist psychoanalysis and, 70–71; transference and, 166–67, 236n79; transference of, 119. *See also* Eros; erotic drive
"Love, Guilt, and Reparation" (Klein), 113, 143

magical thinking, 95, 96, 104
Marasco, Robyn, 194, 216n54
Marcuse, Herbert: on aggression, 131; Brown on, 190; Butler and, 136; the death drive and, 128–31, 186; on Eros, 126; Foucault and, 131, 192; Freud and, 127; on Fromm, 201n5; Klein and, 149; progress and, 123, 125, 131, 186; reconciliation and, 228n57; on repression, 18, 229n84; on revisionist psychoanalysis, 2; on sublimation, 138–40; utopia and, 17–18
Marin, Inara, 18
Marxism, 123, 198
mass culture, 188, 189
masses, 103
mass society, 65
master signifiers, 232n126
maturity, 97
McAfee, Noelle, 193, 196, 198
McCarthy, Thomas, 22
McIvor, David, 137–38, 195, 207n3
Mead, George Herbert, 202n16
"Meaning of Working Through the Past, The" (Adorno), 194
melancholia, 140–41
method, 22, 25
mind, 82
misrecognition, 13
Mitchell, Stephen, 38, 39, 48
modernity, 11–12
modern philosophy, 74

modern worldviews, 11
monogamy, 107
moral anthropology, 203–4n29
moral development, 15
moralistic idealism, 4
morality, 110, 118
mortals, 81
Moses and Monotheism (Freud), 220n4
mourning, 25, 132, 137, 138–144, 186
"Mourning and Its Relation to Manic-Depressive States" (Klein), 141
"Mourning and Melancholia" (Freud), 140
Mourning in America (McIvor), 137–38
mythical worldviews, 11

narcissism, 80, 81. *See also* primary narcissism
necessity, 107. *See also* Ananke
negative dialectics, 67, 74, 84–85, 85, 151–52
Negative Dialectics (Adorno), 61, 64, 179
negativity, 6, 117, 156
neoliberalism, 190, 191, 194
neurosis, 232n126
Nietzsche, Friedrich, 110
Nirvana principle, the, 40, 128, 211–12n66, 226n7
nonconceptual, the, 152–53
nondomination, 148
nonidentity, 151
nonreified cognition, 84, 87, 88
nonrepressive sublimation, 127–28
nonviolence, 136
normalization, 237n107
normative idealism, Honneth and, 27

object, the: defined, 36, 38; drive and, 36, 38; phantasy and, 85; primacy of, 83; relation and, 49; subject and, 82
object relations: the infant and, 49; in Klein's metapsychology, 29–30; object and, 49; phantasy and, 54; the primary caregiver and, 49; primary narcissism and, 50
object-relations theory, 4
oceanic feeling, 30
Odysseus, 61
Oedipal conflict, the, 92, 102, 189–90

Oedipus, 102
Ogden, Thomas, 143
omnipotence: anxiety and, 133; Benjamin, J. on, 207n2; the death drive and, 108; development and, 97, 101; the ego and, 58; guilt and, 133; immortality and, 142; Klein on, 228n67; phantasy and, 30, 46; primary fusion and, 5–6; reality and, 92; recognition and, 5; reparation and, 135; science and, 95; Whitebook on, 5
"On Narcissism" (Freud), 94
"On Subject and Object" (Adorno), 82
ontogeny, 90, 99
"Origins of Transference, The" (Klein), 38
other, the, 52
overcoming, 115–17

paradox of authoritarianism, 65
paradox of self-defeat, the, 62
paranoid-schizoid position: death drive and, 42–43; depressive position and, 29, 31, 42, 75–76, 115, 143; disintegration and, 78; the ego and, 42, 75; in the infant, 31; integration and, 80; metapsychology and, 31; politics and, 193, 197; primary object and, 31, 42
paranoid-schizoid reason, 87
parenting, 52
pathology, 157, 176
pathology of reason, 156
performance principle, the, 123, 125, 127
personality, 113, 140, 142
Perversion and Utopia (Whitebook), 57
Petherbridge, Danielle, 202n16
phantasy: the breast and, 44–45, 76; defined, 44; drive and, 44–45; ego integration and, 142; Eros and, 126–27; the Great Refusal and, 131; id and ego and, 46; individuation and, 129; the infant and, 114; instinct and, 44; as internal object, 43–48; intersubjectivity and, 53; introjection and, 45–46; Klein on, 28; object relations and, 54; omnipotence and, 30, 46; primacy of the object and, 85; primary process and, 44; projection and, 45–46; reality and, 47–48, 51–52, 72; reason and, 131; reconciliation and, 129; sensation and, 45; the unconscious and, 43. *See also* imagination
philosophical anthropology: Freud and, 121, 124; Habermas and, 2; Honneth and, 4, 6, 7, 27; Klein and, 24, 27, 121; methodology and, 8, 22; psychoanalysis and, 3
philosophical hermeneutics, 177
philosophy, 82, 175–81, 238n129
philosophy of history, 64, 95
phylogeny, 90, 99, 114
Piaget, Jean, 156, 202n8
pleasure principle: aim of, 40; civilization and, 107; death drive and, 40; development of the subject and, 91; the ego and, 46–47; happiness and, 106; the Nirvana principle and, 211–12n66; reality principle and, 91–92, 106, 125; reconciliation and, 186
polarization, 193, 194
political integration, 138. *See also* integration
political realism, 4
politics, 26, 193, 195, 196, 197
Polyphemus, 61
position, 30–31
postconventional identity, 63
postconventional subjects, 11
postliberal society, 65–66
postsecularism, 221n34
power, 7, 9, 194
power grab, 93, 97
primary aggression: analysis and, 148; anxiety and, 7; Benjamin, J. on, 207n2; death drive and, 8, 35, 41–42, 226n7; domination and, 150; as ineliminable, 79; intersubjectivity and, 87; Klein on, 24, 28, 41–42, 114; love and, 78, 132; reparation and, 137. *See also* aggression
primary caregiver: depressive position and, 28, 137; object relations and, 49; primary narcissism and, 202–3n17; primary process and, 92; transference and, 163; as whole object, 32, 34, 133
primary fusion: Honneth on, 5, 7, 27; the infant and, 113; intersubjectivity and, 113; Klein on, 113; Lacan on, 113; negativity

and, 6–7; object relations and, 114; omnipotence and, 5–6; primary narcissism and, 202n17; the primitive and, 114; recognition and, 6, 27; Stern on, 4–5; Whitebook on, 5, 113

primary narcissism: animism and, 102; Benjamin, J. on, 209n12; critical theory and, 208–9n11; introjection and, 46; Klein on, 30, 87, 208n9; object relations and, 50, 114; primary fusion and, 202n17; projection and, 46; the psyche and, 93. *See also* narcissism

primary object: depressive position and, 34; as good and bad breast, 32, 132; paranoid-schizoid position and, 31, 42

primary process: phantasy and, 44; secondary process and, 91–92

"primitive, the," 90, 91, 96–105, 106, 114, 186

progress: ambiguity of, 91; the death drive and, 106–7, 122, 123, 128, 145; domination and, 112, 124–25, 127; the Enlightenment and, 90; *Eros and Civilization* and, 25; Freud on, 95–96, 110, 145–46; hope and, 149; as imperative, 186; Marcuse on, 123, 125; the performance principle and, 127; pessimism about, 111–12; psychoanalysis and, 25, 105–11; racism and, 111; the reality principle and, 127; reparation and, 145, 149

projection: intersubjectivity and, 53; phantasy and, 45–46; primary narcissism and, 46

propaganda, 66

psyche, the: development of the subject and, 96; the ego and, 140; the infant and, 113; metapsychology and, 16; primary narcissism and, 93, 94; reality and, 93; soma and, 36

psychic development, 29, 50, 51

psychoanalysis: Adorno and, 1, 151–52, 180; aims of, 73, 77, 81, 146, 147, 159, 163, 166, 178; constellations and, 178; criteria of success of, 182; critical theory and, 152–53, 159–60, 169, 175; critique and, 17, 154–55, 171, 233n19; the death drive and, 136; development and, 10; enlightenment and, 194–195; Foucault and, 172, 237n102; the Frankfurt School and, 1, 151; Habermas and, 2, 22–23, 151, 152–53; Marxism and, 123; negative dialectics and, 151–52; philosophical anthropology and, 3; philosophy and, 177; political relevance of, 189; progress and, 25, 121–22; racism and, 99, 206n64; rationalist interpretation of, 161–62; subjectivity and, 172; theory and praxis and, 187; transference and, 153; in the United States, 122; utopia and, 19

psychoanalytic method, 161–68

psychology, 68–69

psychopathology, 52

psycho-sexual development, 29

racism, 90, 98, 111, 186, 206n64, 223–24n105

rational insight, 23, 153, 161, 168, 175–76. *See also* insight

rationalism, 12, 110

rationality, 157

rationalization, 178

real, the: Adorno on, 177; fractal nature of, 179–80; the infant and, 47; normalization and, 21; omnipotence and, 92; phantasy and, 47, 51–52, 72; politics and, 195; the psyche and, 93

reality principle, the: civilization and, 107; the depressive position and, 213n98; the father and, 92; Klein on, 72; pleasure principle and, 91–92, 106, 125; progress and, 127; regression and, 130

reason: dictatorship of, 93; Freud and, 104; individuation and, 129; phantasy and, 131

recapitulation thesis, 90, 99, 112

recognition, 5, 6, 27

reconciliation, 129, 138, 156, 228n57

redemption, 20

reflexivity, 23

reformism, 18–19

refusal, 129–130

regression, 127, 130

reification, 178

reified consciousness, 180–81

religion, 101–2, 104

"Remembering, Repeating, and Working Through" (Freud), 162

Rensmann, Lars, 65–66

renunciation, 61
reparation: ambivalence and, 86, 120; colonialism and, 118–20; creativity and, 199; the death drive and, 132, 135; defined, 138; the depressive position and, 33, 135; genuine form of, 80, 135, 137; guilt and, 133; love and, 118, 132–33; manic form of, 80, 87, 134; Marcuse on, 25; omnipotence and, 135; primary aggression and, 78, 137; progress and, 145, 149; reconciliation and, 138, 196
reparative reason, 87
repression: individuation and, 129; Marcuse on, 18, 124; the nonconceptual and, 152; rationalization and, 178; revisionist psychoanalysis and, 70; sublimation and, 138–40
repressive desublimation, 127–28, 139–40, 190, 229n84
repressive principle, the, 62
Republican Party, the, 188
resignation, 142, 145, 199
responsibility, 77, 120
ressentiment, 194
revisionist psychoanalysis: Adorno on, 68–74; 217n58; the death drive and, 68, 226n5; drive theory and, 2, 68; Marcuse on, 2
Romanticism, 89
Rose, Jacqueline, 117
Roudinesco, Élisabeth, 221n40, 222n65
Rustin, Michael, 208n9
Ruti, Mari, 20, 22, 167

Saar, Martin, 178, 238n129
sacrifice, 61
"savages," 100
schizophrenia, 64
science, 95, 101–2, 104
secondary process, 91–92
second nature, 180
Sedgwick, Eve, 209n25
Segal, Hanna: on aesthetics, 86; on the ego, 29–30, 140; on Kleinian aesthetics, 144; on phantasy and reality, 52; on position, 31; on reality, 47; on technique, 166
self, the, 16

self-reflexivity, 160–61
self-transparency, 168
self-understanding, 153, 154, 160–61
sensation, 45
Seth, Sanjay, 12, 205n47
sexuality. See Eros
social change, 155
social evolution, 10–11, 11
sociality, 53
socialization, 9, 10, 186
social theory, 99, 124–25
social transformation, 23, 24
society, 68
sociology, 68–69
soma, 36
Sovereign Good, the, 147
speech, 170–71
Stern, Daniel, 3, 4–5, 203n18
strong ego, the, 195
Struggle for Recognition, The (Honneth), 4
Studies on Hysteria, The (Freud), 146
subject, the, 82, 83, 91, 148, 171
subject formation, 79
subjectivity, 53, 54, 64, 114, 172
sublimation, 138–140, 144, 145, 219n127
superego, the: aggression and, 136; analyst's representation of, 51; civilization and, 108; the death drive and, 136; ethics and, 136; formation of, 230n93; Klein on, 50; in postliberal societies, 66; repressive desublimation and, 190
surplus repression, 18, 125

taboo, 101, 107
talking cure, the, 162
technique, 166
Thanatos, 108. See also death drive, the
totality, 179
Totem and Taboo (Freud), 100, 103
totemism, 102, 103
"Traditional and Critical Theory" (Horkheimer), 182
transference: ambivalence of, 73–74; the analysand and, 162, 165, 170, 178; in analysis, 147, 153, 162; the analyst and, 51, 170; countertransference and, 174, 236n79;

critical theory and, 23, 153; critique and, 169–75; Foucault and, 172, 173; Freud on, 169; Habermas on, 154; importance of, 168; Klein on, 51, 165, 166, 170; Lacan on, 166, 170, 174; Lear on, 154, 169; of love, 119; love and, 166–67, 236n79; method and, 25; primary caregiver and, 163; rational insight and, 153, 176; speech and, 170–71
Trump, Donald, 188, 192
trust, 78
truth, 151–52
truth and reconciliation commissions, 137–38, 196

unconscious, the: aims of analysis and, 163–64; the analysand and, 164; the ego and, 57; Habermas and, 15; the nonconceptual and, 152; phantasy and, 43; utopia and, 17
unhappy consciousness, 64
United States, the, 122
utopia: Adorno on, 19–20; Lacan on, 20, 21 Marcuse on, 149; post-Habermasian critical theory and, 19; psychoanalysis and, 19; the unconscious and, 17

validity claims, 10–11
violence, 61

"What Is Enlightenment?" (Foucault), 171
Whitebook, Joel: on Adorno, 62–63, 83; on *Ananke*, 130; on the archaic mother, 220n19; on countertransference, 173; on the ego, 62–63; on Freud, 89–98, 105, 111–12, 214n10; on Habermas, 18, 205n59, 205n60; Habermas and, 221n34; Honneth and, 203n24; on integration, 219n127; on Lacan, 13; on *Moses and Monotheism*, 220n4; on mourning and creativity, 142; on primary fusion, 5, 113; racism and, 90; on socialization, 9; on utopia, 17–18; on utopianism, 146
whole objects, 55, 76
"'Wild' Psychoanalysis" (Freud), 162
Winnicott, D. W.: Benjamin, J. and, 207n2; Honneth and, 3, 4, 27, 202n16; Klein and, 52
working-through, 165
work of art, the, 82, 86. *See also* art

Žižek, Slavoj, 22
Zuider Zee, 93, 95
Zurn, Christopher, 203–4n29

New Directions in Critical Theory

Narrating Evil: A Postmetaphysical Theory of Reflective Judgment, María Pía Lara

The Politics of Our Selves: Power, Autonomy and Gender in Contemporary Critical Theory, Amy Allen

Democracy and the Political Unconscious, Noëlle McAfee

The Force of the Example: Explorations in the Paradigm of Judgment, Alessandro Ferrara

Horrorism: Naming Contemporary Violence, Adriana Cavarero

Scales of Justice: Reimagining Political Space in a Globalizing World, Nancy Fraser

Pathologies of Reason: On the Legacy of Critical Theory, Axel Honneth

States Without Nations: Citizenship for Mortals, Jacqueline Stevens

The Racial Discourses of Life Philosophy: Négritude, Vitalism, and Modernity, Donna V. Jones

Democracy in What State?, Giorgio Agamben, Alain Badiou, Daniel Bensaïd, Wendy Brown, Jean-Luc Nancy, Jacques Rancière, Kristin Ross, Slavoj Žižek

Politics of Culture and the Spirit of Critique Dialogues, edited by Gabriel Rockhill and Alfredo Gomez-Muller

Mute Speech: Literature, Critical Theory, and Politics, Jacques Rancière

The Right to Justification: Elements of Constructivist Theory of Justice, Rainer Forst

The Scandal of Reason: A Critical Theory of Political Judgment, Albena Azmanova

The Wrath of Capital: Neoliberalism and Climate Change Politics, Adrian Parr

Media of Reason: A Theory of Rationality, Matthias Vogel

Social Acceleration: A New Theory of Modernity, Hartmut Rosa

The Disclosure of Politics: Struggles Over the Semantics of Secularization, María Pía Lara

Radical Cosmopolitics: The Ethics and Politics of Democratic Universalism, James Ingram

Freedom's Right: The Social Foundations of Democratic Life, Axel Honneth

Imaginal Politics: Images Beyond Imagination and the Imaginary, Chiara Bottici

Alienation, Rahel Jaeggi

The Power of Tolerance: A Debate, Wendy Brown and Rainer Forst, edited by Luca Di Blasi and Christoph F. E. Holzhey

Radical History and the Politics of Art, Gabriel Rockhill

Starve and Immolate: The Politics of Human Weapons, Banu Bargu

The Highway of Despair: Critical Theory After Hegel, Robyn Marasco

A Political Economy of the Senses: Neoliberalism, Reification, Critique, Anita Chari

The End of Progress: Decolonizing the Normative Foundations of Critical Theory, Amy Allen

Recognition or Disagreement: A Critical Encounter on the Politics of Freedom, Equality, and Identity, Axel Honneth and Jacques Rancière, edited by Katia Genel and Jean-Philippe Deranty

What Is a People?, Alain Badiou, Pierre Bourdieu, Judith Butler, Georges Didi-Huberman, Sadri Khiari, and Jacques Rancière

Death and Mastery: Psychoanalytic Drive Theory and the Subject of Late Capitalism, Benjamin Y. Fong

Left-Wing Melancholia: Marxism, History, and Memory, Enzo Traverso

Foucault/Derrida Fifty Years Later: The Futures of Genealogy, Deconstruction, and Politics, edited by Olivia Custer, Penelope Deutscher, and Samir Haddad

The Habermas Handbook, edited by Hauke Brunkhorst, Regina Kreide, and Cristina Lafont

Birth of a New Earth: The Radical Politics of Environmentalism, Adrian Parr

Genealogies of Terrorism: Revolution, State Violence, Empire, Verena Erlenbusch-Anderson

The Practice of Political Theory: Rorty and Continental Thought, Clayton Chin

Queer Terror: Life, Death, and Desire in the Settler Colony, C. Heike Schotten

Naming Violence: A Critical Theory of Genocide, Torture, and Terrorism, Mathias Thaler

Avicenna and the Aristotelian Left, Ernst Bloch

The Experience of Injustice: A Theory of Recognition, Emmanuel Renault

Fear of Breakdown: Politics and the Work of Psychoanalysis, Noëlle McAfee

Transitional Subjects: Critical Theory and Object Relations, edited by Amy Allen and Brian O'Connor

Capitalism on Edge: How Fighting Precarity Can Achieve Radical Change Without Crisis or Utopia, Albena Azmanova

GPSR Authorized Representative: Easy Access System Europe, Mustamäe tee 50, 10621 Tallinn, Estonia, gpsr.requests@easproject.com

www.ingramcontent.com/pod-product-compliance
Lightning Source LLC
Chambersburg PA
CBHW021938290426
44108CB00012B/886